LANCASHIRE FOLK-LORE

LANCASHIRE FOLK-LORE

COMPILED AND EDITED
BY
JOHN HARLAND, F.S.A.
AND
T. T. WILKINSON, F.R.A.S.

with a new foreword by
A. E. GREEN
Institute of Dialect and Folk Life Studies,
University of Leeds

Republished S.R. Publishers Ltd., 1972
First published John Heywood,
Manchester and London, 1882

© 1972 S.R. Publishers Limited,
East Ardsley, Wakefield,
Yorkshire, England

ISBN 0 85409 722 8

Please address all enquiries to S.R. Publishers Ltd.
(address as above)

Reprinted by Scolar Press Ltd.,
Menston, Yorkshire, U.K.

FOREWORD

In 1830, John Harland, a twenty-four year old Hull-born printer and part-time freelance journalist, published a report of a sermon, based on notes taken in his own refined version of the short-hand then in use. The accuracy and vivacity of his account, it seems, so impressed J. E. Taylor, the editor of the *Manchester Guardian*, that Harland was hired as a full-time member of the newspaper's reporting staff; on his retirement through ill-health, thirty years later, he had risen to the position of chief-reporter. The *Guardian's* obituary (April 25th, 1868) is perhaps partial — if generous — in claiming that Harland had placed it "at the head of the provincial press in the department of reporting"; but there is no reason to doubt its description of the energy and conscientiousness with which its late chief-reporter had done his job —

> "Harland . . . exhibited remarkable endurance in the pursuit of his profession, undertaking long journeys, and writing out the notes of the day in the stage-coach."

It was during his exhaustive news-coverage of the region that Harland — stimulated no doubt by the comparisons that must have struck him with "his earliest remembrances with the Folk-Lore of East Yorkshire", and with the material available to him through his reading of the growing list of publications on folk-lore and mythology, in English and German — began to record the tales and ballads, customs and beliefs of his adopted county. His job, however, while it gave him ample opportunity for field-work, left little time for the publication of his findings. Nevertheless, 1850 saw the first of a series of publications in the field of local history — a subject which he had begun to investigate for features in the *Guardian* — when the Historic Society of Lancashire and Cheshire printed a paper "On a Charter of Feoffment of Gorton"[1]. For the next decade, until his retirement from journalism, he concentrated on this field in his spare-time writing, presenting papers to the

[1] *Proceedings and Papers*, Session II, 1849/50, 19ff.

Historic Society[2], which had elected him a member in 1849, and editing documents for the Chetham Society[3]. Although his first small article on folk-lore appeared in 1852[4], and he contributed during the 'fifties occasional brief pieces to *Notes and Queries,* it was not until he retired that he was able to work systematically towards the publication of his collection of local traditions.

In the meantime, however, his membership of the Historic Society had brought him into contact with a fellow-member, Thomas Turner Wilkinson, whose interests coincided in part with his own. Wilkinson, born near Blackburn, where he lived for most of his life, becoming for a period an alderman of the town, was a man of even broader interests than Harland. Early in the 'fifties he began to contribute to *Notes and Queries* on the subject of Lancashire folk-lore, and produced a number of pamphlets on mathematics. After his election to membership of the Historic Society in 1854, he contributed regularly to the *Proceedings* of the society on subjects as diverse as geometry and the work of the auto-didact artisan-geometers of Lancashire, broadside ballads, folk-lore, the site of the battle of Brunanburh, archaeology and coal-mining[5], as well as producing, in 1856, a *History of the Parochial Church at Burnley.* From the point of view of his later collaboration with Harland, his most important work was undoubtedly a series of three papers 'On the Popular Customs and Superstitions of Lancashire'[6], in which he presented the results of his own observations, over a long period, of the traditions of an area "within a circle of some forty miles in

[2] e.g. "Account of the Grant of Free Warren, by Henry III, to Thomas Gresley" *Proceedings and Papers,* Session IV, 1851/52, 44ff.

[3] e.g. "The House and Farm Accounts of the Shuttleworths of Gawthorpe Hall", Chetham Society, *Remains,* vols. 35, 41, 43 and 46, Manchester 1856/58.

[4] "A Lancashire Charm, in Cypher, against Witchcraft and Evil Spirits", *Proceedings and Papers,* Session IV, 1851/52, 44ff.

[5] See *Proceedings and Papers,* vols. VII/XV, 1854/63.

[6] Vols. XI/XIII, 1858/61.

diameter, taking Blackburn as a centre." These three papers were to form the basis of the introduction to *Lancashire Folk-Lore*.

From 1860 onwards, until his death, Harland devoted himself exclusively to scholarship. His editorial and critical work for the Chetham Society increased[7]; he revised Edward Baines' celebrated *History of the County Palatine and Duchy of Lancaster*[8]; wrote an *Account of Seats and Pews in old Parish Churches of the County Palatine of Lancaster*[9]; prepared *A Glossary of Words used in Swaledale*, not published until after his death[10]; and produced a series of works on Lancashire traditions.

The first to appear, in 1865, was *Ballads and Songs of Lancashire, chiefly older than the Nineteenth Century*, followed the next year by its companion volume, *Lancashire Lyrics, modern songs and ballads of the County Palatine*. The collaboration with Wilkinson was now under way, and in 1867 appeared its first fruits, *Lancashire Folk-Lore*. Sadly, the first fruits were also, as far as Harland was concerned, the last, for he died the following year. The collaboration, however, was not entirely at an end; for, before his death in 1875, Wilkinson had completed the manuscript of their *Lancashire Legends, Traditions, Pageants, Sports*, published in 1873, and produced a revised and enlarged edition of the *Ballads and Songs*, which appeared in the year of his death.

The importance of the work of Harland and Wilkinson, and of *Lancashire Folk-Lore* — the best of their books — in particular, is manifest. Thomas Sternberg's *Dialect and Folk-Lore of Northamptonshire*, published in 1850, heralded a new way of studying folk-lore, that is, on a regional basis. Sternberg's lead was followed in 1866 by William Henderson's *Notes on the Folk-Lore of the Northern Counties of England and the Borders*; and over the next seven years Harland and Wilkinson showed triumphantly, in their four volumes, what could be achieved by intensive recording of all the non-

[7] See *Remains*, 53, 56, 57, 58, 64, 68, 72, 74; *Miscellanies*, 3.
[8] 2 vols., 1868/70.
[9] Manchester 1863.
[10] English Dialect Society Publications, 3, London 1873.

material aspects of traditional culture in a small region. They, together with Henderson, were an important influence when the Folk-Lore Society planned its important series of county volumes.

Even if, in the nineteenth century way, Harland and Wilkinson set little store by the placing of their collections in the context of a total way of life, including material culture, and preferred to speculate on origins and to draw sometimes far-fetched parallels between modern and Roman Britain, and even between nineteenth century Lancashire and Old Testament Israel, their work is of immense value and interest as an extremely comprehensive record of the beliefs and customs of their region in their day. Their observations on divination and fortune-telling are of particular interest, both for their great detail, and because of the pains they take to show the importance of printed as well as orally-transmitted material in this field. It is important to know that *The Royal Dream Book* and *Napoleon's Book of Fate* sold extensively among working-people, and fascinating to have such a detailed account of the activities, stock-in-trade and reference library of the artisan fortune-teller "Owd Rollison".

Lancashire Folk-Lore has been out of print since its second impression (reprinted here) appeared in 1882. Everyone interested in the traditions of the British Isles will welcome this re-issue.

A. E. GREEN
Institute of Dialect and Folk Life Studies,
University of Leeds

LANCASHIRE

FOLK-LORE:

ILLUSTRATIVE OF THE

SUPERSTITIOUS BELIEFS AND PRACTICES,

LOCAL CUSTOMS AND USAGES

OF

THE PEOPLE OF THE COUNTY PALATINE.

COMPILED AND EDITED BY

JOHN HARLAND, F.S.A.

AND

T. T. WILKINSON, F.R.A.S.

JOHN HEYWOOD,
DEANSGATE AND RIDGEFIELD, MANCHESTER;
AND 11, PATERNOSTER BUILDINGS,
LONDON.
1882.

JOHN HEYWOOD,
EXCELSIOR STEAM PRINTING AND BOOKBINDING WORKS
HULME HALL ROAD. MANCHESTER.

PREFACE.

"Folk-lore," though a term that will not be found in our standard dictionaries, from Johnson down to Webster, is nevertheless simply a modern combination of two genuine old English words—*Folc,* the folk, the people, "the common people;" and *Lár, Laer, Lora,* learning, doctrine, precept, law. In the earlier days of our English tongue, folk-land, folk-gemote, folk-right, &c., were terms in common use, and amongst this class of compound words our fore-elders had *folc-lare,* by which they denoted plain, simple teaching suited for the people, what we should now call "popular instruction," and hence *folk-lare* also meant a sermon. *Folk-Lore,* in its present signification—and for its general acceptance we are largely indebted to the Editor of that valuable periodical *Notes and Queries,*— means the notions of the folk or people, from childhood upwards, especially their superstitious beliefs and practices, as these have been handed down from generation to generation, in popular tradition and tale, rhyme, proverb, or saying, and it is well termed Folk-Lore in contradistinction to book-lore or scholastic learning. It is the unlearned people's inheritance of tradition from their ancestors, the modern reflection of ancient faith and usage. This Folk-Lore has not been wholly without record in our literature. Hone in his delightful *Every-Day Book, Year Book,* and *Table Book,* has preserved many a choice bit of England's Folk-Lore; and his example has been ably followed in

Chambers's *Book of Days*. Brand's *Popular Antiquities,*
Aubrey's *Miscellanies,* Allies' *Antiquities and Folk-Lore of
Worcestershire,* and other like works, have noted down for
the information and amusement of future generations the
prevalent superstitions, and popular customs and usages of
the people in particular districts, during a past age, and at
the present time. But the greatest and best depository and
record of the Folk-Lore of various nations is that excellent
periodical *Notes and Queries,* from which a charming little
volume entitled " *Choice Notes from Notes and Queries,—
Folk-Lore,*" was compiled and published in 1859.

But Lancashire has hitherto been without adequate record, at least in a collected form, of its Folk-Lore. This
has not been because of any lack of such lore. The
North of England generally, and Lancashire in particular,
is remarkably rich in this respect. Possessed and peopled
in succession by the Celts of ancient Britain, by the
Angles and other Teutonic peoples, by the Scandinavian
races, and by Norman and other foreign settlers at early
periods,—the result of the respective contributions of these
various peoples is necessarily a large mass of traditionary
lore. To bring this together and present it in a collected
form is the object of this little volume. Its editors have
been long engaged, apart,—distinctly, and indepen-
dently of each other,—in collecting particulars of the
superstitions in belief and practice, and of the peculiar
customs and usages of the people of Lancashire. One of
them, born in one of its rural districts, still rich in these
respects, is thus enabled to remember and to preserve many
of those customs and usages of his childhood and youth,
now rapidly passing into decay, if not oblivion. The other,
conversant from his earliest remembrances with the Folk-
Lore of East Yorkshire, and with that of Lancashire for
the last thirty-five years, is thus enabled to compare the

customs and usages of both, and to recognise the same essential superstition under slightly different forms. Similarity of pursuit having led to personal communication, the Editors agreed to combine their respective collections; and hence the present volume. They do not pretend herein to have exhausted the whole range of Lancashire Folk-Lore; but simply to have seized on the more salient features of its superstitious side, and those of popular custom and usage. Part I. comprises notices of a great number of superstitious beliefs and practices. Part II. treats of various local customs and usages, at particular seasons of the year; during the great festivals of the church; those connected with birth and baptism; betrothal and wedding; dying, death-bed, and funeral customs; as well as manorial and feudal tenures, services, and usages.

Should the present volume find favour and acceptance, its Editors may venture hereafter to offer another, embracing the fertile and interesting subjects of popular pageants, maskings and mummings, rushbearings, wakes and fairs, out-door sports and games; punishments, legal and popular; legends and traditions; proverbs, popular sayings and similes; folk-rhymes, &c. &c.

September, 1866.

But for unavoidable delay, consequent on the preparation of a large-paper edition, this volume would have been published prior to "Notes on the Folk-Lore of the Northern Counties of England and the Borders," by Wm. Henderson. As that work has appeared, it may be as well to state that, notwithstanding similarity of subject, the two books do not clash. Mr. Henderson's work relates chiefly to the three north-eastern counties,—Northumberland, Durham, and Yorkshire,—with large notices not only of the Scottish borders, but of Scotland generally, and many details as to Devonshire folk-lore. Its notices of Cumberland and Westmoreland are fewer than of the three counties first named ; and Lancashire is only two or three times incidentally mentioned. The field of this county palatine is therefore left free for the present volume.

January, 1867.

CONTENTS.

PART I.

SUPERSTITIOUS BELIEFS AND PRACTICES.

DIVINATION.

MISCELLANEOUS FOLK-LORE.

MIRACLES.

OMENS AND PREDICATIONS.

SUPERSTITIONS, GENERAL AND MISCELLANEOUS.

WITCHES AND WITCHCRAFT.

PART II.

LOCAL CUSTOMS AND USAGES AT VARIOUS SEASONS.

DYING, DEATH-BED, AND FUNERAL CUSTOMS.

CUSTOMS OF MANORS.

LANCASHIRE FOLK-LORE.

PART I.

SUPERSTITIOUS BELIEFS AND PRACTICES.

INTRODUCTION.

> " 'Tis a history
> Handed from ages down; a nurse's tale
> Which children open-eyed and mouth'd devour,
> And thus, as garrulous ignorance relates,
> We learn it and believe."

In this large section of the Folk-lore of Lancashire we propose to treat of all the notions and practices of the people which appear to recognise a supernatural power or powers, especially as aids to impart to man a knowledge of the future. An alphabetical arrangement has been adopted, which is to some extent also chronological. Beginning with the pretended sciences or arts of Alchemy and Astrology, the succeeding articles treat of Bells, Beltane fires, Boggarts, Charms, Demons, Divination, &c.

Many of these superstitions are important in an ethnological point of view, and immediately place us *en rapport* with those nations whose inhabitants have either colonized or conquered this portion of our country. In treasuring up these records of the olden times, tradition has, in general, been faithful to her vocation. She has occasionally grafted portions of one traditional custom, ceremony, or superstition, upon another; but in the majority of cases enough has been left to enable us to determine with considerable certainty the probable origin of each. So far as regards the greater portion of our local Folk-lore, we may safely assert that it is rapidly becoming obsolete, and many of the most curious relics must be sought in the undisturbed nooks and corners of the county. It is there where popular opinions are cherished and preserved, long after an improved education has driven them from more intelligent communities; and it is a remarkable fact that many of these, although composed of such flimsy materials, and dependent upon the fancies of the multitude for their very existence, have nevertheless survived shocks by which kingdoms have been overthrown, and have preserved their characteristic traits from the earliest times down to the present.

As what are called the Indo-European, or Aryan, nations—viz., the Celts, Greeks, Latins, Germans (Teuton and Scandinavian), Letts, and Sclaves—as is now generally acknowledged, have a common ancestry in the race which once dwelt together in the regions of the Upper Oxus, in Asia; so their mythologies, however diverse in their later European developments, may be regarded as naving a common origin. Space will not allow us to enlarge on this great subject, which has been ably treated by Jacob Grimm, Dr. Adalbert Kuhn, and many other German writers, and of which an excellent *résumé* is given in Kelly's *Curiosities of Indo-European Tradition and Folk-lore.*

When we refer to the ancient Egyptians, and to the oldest history extant, we find some striking resemblances between their customs and our own. The rod of the magician was then as necessary to the practice of the art as it still is to the " Wizard of the North." The glory of the art of magic may be said to have departed, but *the use of the rod* by the modern conjuror remains as a connecting link between the harmless deceptions of the present, and that powerful instrument of the priesthood in times remote. The divining rod, too, which indicates the existence of a hidden spring, or treasure, or even a murdered corpse, is another relic of the wand of the Oriental Magi. The divining cup, as noticed in the case of Joseph and his brethren, supplies a third instance of this close connexion. Both our wise men and maidens still whirl the tea-cup, in order that the disposition of the floating leaves may give them an intimation of their future destiny, or point out the direction in which an offending party must be sought. We have yet "wizards that do peep and mutter," and who profess to foretell future events by looking "through a glass darkly." The practice of "causing children to pass through the fire to Moloch," so strongly reprobated by the prophet of old, may be cited as an instance in which Christianity has not yet been able to efface all traces of one of the oldest forms of heathen worship. Sir W. Betham has observed, in his *Gael and Cymbri,* pp. 222–4, that "we see at this day fires lighted up in Ireland, on the eve of the summer solstice and the equinoxes, to the Phœnician god Baal; and they are called *Baal-tane,* or Baal's fire, though the *object* of veneration be forgotten." Such fires are still lighted in Lancashire, on Hallowe'en, under the names of Beltains or Teanlas; and even such *cakes* as the Jews are said to have made in honour of the Queen of Heaven, are yet to be found at this season amongst the inhabitants of the banks of the Ribble. These circumstances may appear the less strange when we reflect that this river is almost certainly the Belisama of the Romans; that it was especially dedicated to the Queen of Heaven, under the designation of Minerva Belisamæ; and that her worship was long prevalent amongst the inhabitants of Coccium, Rigodunum, and other Roman stations in the north of Lancashire. Both the fires and the cakes, however, are now connected with superstitious notions respecting Purgatory, &c., but their origin and perpetuation will scarcely admit of doubt.

A belief in astrology and in sacred numbers prevails to a considerable extent amongst all classes of our society. With many the stars still " fight in their courses," and our modern fortune-tellers are yet ready to " rule the planets," and predict good or ill fortune, on payment of the customary fee. That there is " luck in *odd* numbers" was known for a fact in Lancashire long before Mr. Lover immortalized the tradition. Our housewives always take care that their hens shall sit upon an *odd* number of eggs; we always bathe *three* times in the sea at Blackpool, Southport, and elsewhere; and our names are called over *three* times when our services are required in courts of law. *Three* times *three* is the orthodox number of cheers; and we still hold that the *seventh* son of a *seventh* son is destined to form an infallible physician. We inherit all such popular notions as these in common with the German and Scandinavian nations; but more especially with those of the Saxons and the Danes. Triads of leaders, or ships, constantly occur in their annals; and punishments of *three* and *seven* years' duration form the burden of many of the Anglo-Saxon and Danish laws.

A full proportion of the popular stories which are perpetuated in our nurseries most probably date their existence amongst us from some amalgamation of races; or, it may be, from the intercourse attendant upon trade and commerce. The Phœnicians, no doubt, would impart a portion of their Oriental Folk-lore to the southern Britons; the Roman legions would leave traces of their prolific mythology amongst the Brigantes and the Sistuntii; and the Saxons and the Danes would add their rugged north-ern modifications to the common stock. The " History of the Hunchback" is common to both England and Arabia; the " man in the moon" has found his way into the popular literature of almost every nation with which we are acquainted; " Cinderella and her slipper" is " The little golden shoe" of the ancient Scandinavians, and was equally familiar to the Greeks and Romans; " Jack and the bean-stalk" is told in Sweden and Norway as of " The boy who stole the giant's treasure;" whilst our renowned " Jack the giant-killer" figures in Norway, Lapland, Persia, and India, as the amusing story of " The herd boy and the giant." The labours of Tom Hickathrift are evidently a distorted version of those of Hercules; and these again agree in the main with the journey of Thor to Utgard, and the more classical travels of Ulysses. In Greece the clash of the elements during a thunderstorm was attributed to the chariot wheels of Jove; the Scandinavians ascribed the sounds to the ponderous wagon of the mighty Thor; our Lancashire nurses *Christianize* the phenomenon by assuring their young companions, poetically enough, that thunder " is the noise which God makes when passing across the heavens." The notion that the gods were wont to communicate knowledge of future events to certain favoured individuals appears to have had a wide range in ancient times; and this curiosity regarding futurity has exerted a powerful influence over the minds of men in every stage of civilization. Hence arose the consulting of oracles and the practice of divination amongst the ancients, and to the same principles we must attribute the credulity

which at present exists with respect to the "*wise men*"
who are to be found in almost every town and village in
Lancashire. The means adopted by some of the oracles
when responses were required, strangely remind us of the
modern feats of ventriloquism; others can be well illus-
trated by what we now know of mesmerism and its
kindred agencies; whilst these and clairvoyance will
account for many of those where the agents are said by
Eustathius to have spoken out of their bellies, or breasts,
from oak trees, or been " cast into trances in which they
lay like men dead or asleep, deprived of all sense and
motion; but after some time returning to themselves,
gave strange relations of what they had seen and heard."

The ancient Greeks and Romans regarded dreams as so
many warnings; they prayed to Mercury to vouchsafe to
them a night of good dreams. In this county we still
hold the same opinions; but our country maidens, having
Christianized the subject, now invoke St. Agnes and a multitude of other saints to be similarly propitious. There are
many other points of resemblance between the Folk-lore
of Lancashire and that of the ancients. Long or short
life, health or disease, good luck or bad, are yet predicted
by burning a lock of human hair; and the fire is frequently
poked with much anxiety when testing the disposition of
an absent lover. Many persons may be found who never
put on the *left* shoe first; and the appearance of a
single magpie has disconcerted many a stout Lancashire
farmer when setting out on a journey of business or
pleasure. In the matter of sneezing we are just as superstitious as when the Romans left us. They exclaimed,
" May Jove protect you," when any one sneezed in their
presence, and an anxious " God bless you" is the common
ejaculation amongst our aged mothers. To the same
sources we may probably attribute the apprehensions

which many Lancashire people entertain with respect to spilling the salt; sudden silence, or fear; lucky and unlucky days; the presence of thirteen at dinner; raising ghosts; stopping blood by charms; spitting upon, or drawing blood from persons in order to avert danger; the evil eye; and a multitude of other minor superstitions. We possess much of all this in common with the Saxons and the Danes, but the original source of a great, if not the greater portion, is probably that of our earliest conquerors.

Divination by means of the works of Homer and Virgil was not uncommon amongst the ancients; the earlier Christians made use of the Psalter or New Testament for such purposes. In Lancashire the Bible and a key are resorted to, both for deciding doubts respecting a lover, and also to aid in detecting a thief. Divination by water affords another striking parallel. The ancients decided questions in dispute by means of a tumbler of water, into which they lowered a ring suspended by a thread, and having prayed to the gods to decide the question in dispute, the ring of its own accord would strike the tumbler a certain number of times. Our " Lancashire witches" adopt the same means, and follow the Christianized formula, with a wedding-ring suspended by a hair, whenever the time before marriage, the number of a family, or even the length of life, becomes a matter of anxiety.

Most nations, in all ages, have been accustomed to deck the graves of their dead with appropriate flowers, much as we do at present. The last words of the dying have, from the earliest times, been considered of prophetic import; and according to Theocritus, some one of those present endeavoured to receive into his mouth the last breath of a dying parent or friend, " as fancying the soul

to pass out with it and enter into their own bodies." Few
would expect to find this singular custom still existing in
Lancashire; and yet such is the fact. Witchcraft can
boast her votaries in this county even up to the present
date, and she numbers this practice amongst her rites and
ceremonies.

A very large portion of the Lancashire Folk-lore is
identical in many respects with that which prevailed
amongst the sturdy warriors who founded the Heptarchy,
or ruled Northumbria. During the Saxon and Danish
periods their heathendom had a real existence. Its practices were maintained by an array of priests and altars,
with a prescribed ritual and ceremonies; public worship
was performed and oblations offered with all the pomp
and power of a church establishment. The remnants of
this ancient creed are now presented to us in the form of
popular superstitions, in legends and nursery tales, which
have survived all attempts to eradicate them from the
minds of the people. Christ, his apostles, and the saints,
have supplanted the old mythological conceptions; but
many popular stories and impious incantations which now
involve these sacred names were formerly told of some
northern hero, or perhaps invoked the power of Satan
himself. The great festival in honour of Eostre may be
instanced as having been transferred to the Christian celebration of the resurrection of our Lord; whilst the lighting of fires on St. John's eve, and the bringing in of the
boar's head at Christmas, serve to remind us that the
worship of Freja is not extinct. When Christianity
became the national religion, the rooted prejudices of the
people were evidently respected by our early missionaries,
and hence the curious admixture of the sacred and the
profane, which everywhere presents itself in our local
popular forms of expression for the pretended cure of

various diseases. The powers and attributes of Woden and Freja are attributed to Jesus, Peter, or Mary; but in all other respects the spells and incantations remain the same.

Our forefathers appear to have possessed a full proportion of those stern characteristics which have ever marked the Northumbrian population. Whatever opinions they had acquired, they were prepared to hold them firmly; nor did they give up their most heathenish practices without a struggle. Both the " law and the testimony" had to be called into requisition as occasion required; and even the terrors of these did not at once suffice. In one of the Anglo-Saxon *Penitentiaries,* quoted by Mr. Wright in his *Essays,* we find a penalty imposed upon those women who use "any witchcraft to their children, or who draw them through the earth at the meeting of roads, because that is great heathenishness." A Saxon *Homily,* preserved in the public library at Cambridge, states that divinations were used, " through the devil's teaching," in taking a wife, in going a journey, in brewing, when beginning any undertaking, when any person or animal is born, and when children begin to pine away or to be unhealthy. The same *Homily* also speaks of divination by fowls, by sneezing, by horses, by dogs howling, and concludes by declaring that " he is no Christian who does these things." In a Latin *Penitentialia* now in the British Museum, we find allusions to incantations for taking away stores of milk, honey, or other things belonging to another, and converting them to our own use. He who rides with Diana and obeys her commands, he who prepares *three* knives in company in order to predestine happiness to those born there, he who makes inquiry into the future on the first day of January, or begins a work on that day in order to secure prosperity during the whole of the year, is pointed out for reprobation; whilst hiding charms in grass, or on a tree, or in a path, for the preservation of cattle, placing children in a furnace, or on the roof of a house, and using characters for curing disease, or charms for collecting medicinal herbs, are enumerated, for the purpose of pointing out the penances to be undergone by those found guilty of "such heinous sins." Nearly all these instances may be said to belong to the transition state of our Folk-lore, and relate at once both to the ancient and the modern portions of our subject. We have seen that much the same practices were used by the Greeks and Romans; and it is a curious fact that many of the more important are still in vogue amongst the peasantry of Lancashire. Many persons will still shudder with apprehension if a dog howl during the sickness of a friend: dragging a child across the earth at " four lane ends" is yet practised for the cure of whooping-cough : fern seed is still said to be gathered on the Holy Bible, and is then believed to be able to render those invisible who will dare to take it. We still have prejudices respecting the first day of the new year; black-haired visitors are most welcome on the morning of that day; charms for the protection of families and cattle are yet to be found; and herbs for the use of man and beast are still collected when their "proper planets are ruling" in the heavens. More copies of Culpepper's *Herbal* and Sibley's *Astrology* are sold in Lancashire than all other works on the same subjects put together, and this principally on account of the planetary influence with which each disease and its antidote are connected. Old Moore's *Almanac*, however, is now sadly at a discount, because it lacks the table of the Moon's signs; the farmers are consequently at a loss to know which will be healthy cattle, and hence they prefer a spurious edition which supplies the grave omission.

Several lucky stones for the protection of cattle have, within a few years past, been procured by the writer from the "shippons" of those who, in other respects, are not counted behind the age; and it would have been easy to collect an ample stock of horse-shoes and rusty sickles from the same sources. However, during the last forty years the inhabitants of Lancashire have made rapid progress both in numbers and intelligence. They have had the "schoolmaster abroad" amongst them, and have consequently divested themselves of many of the grosser superstitions which formed a portion of the popular faith of their immediate predecessors; but there is yet a dense substratum of popular opinions existing in those localities which have escaped the renovating influences of the spindle or the rail. As time progresses many of these will become further modified, or perhaps totally disappear; and hence it may be desirable to secure a permanent record of the customs and superstitions of the county.

As to the most ancient forms of religious belief or cult, we may surely assume that the *simple* must of necessity precede the *complex*, and consequently the idea of *one* supernatural Being must be anterior in point of time to that of *two* or more. Under this view, the good and the evil principles would form the second stage of development —a necessary consequence of increased observation—and, accordingly, we find the Great Spirit and his Adversary among the prevailing notions of some of the least civilized communities. A gradual progression from one to many gods appears to have been the natural process by which all known mythologies have been formed. The tendency of observation to multiply causes, real or ideal, and to personify ideas, may be ranked as one of the tendencies of unassisted human nature; and the operation of this natural force must have been equally efficient at all times and in all countries. In the early stages of social improvement, man would be very forcibly affected by natural phenomena. The regular succession of day and night—the order of the seasons—the heat of summer—the cold of winter— storms and tempests on sea and land—the sensations of pleasure and pain, hope and fear—would each impress him with ideas of effects for which he could assign no adequate causes; but having become susceptible of supernatural influences, the addition of imaginary beings to his mytho- logy would keep pace with his experience, until every por- tion of the heavens, the earth, and the sea, was peopled with, and presided over, by its respective deity or demi- god. Thus it was that the rolling thunder and the " lightning's vivid flash " suggested the idea of a Jupiter grasping his destructive bolts, or of a Thor wielding his ponderous hammer. The " raging tempest " and the " boiling surge " gave birth to a Neptune or Njörd, each endowed with attributes suited to the aspects of the locality where the observations were made, and specially adapted to the intellectual condition of the community which first deified the conception. As society progressed in civilization, so did the study of philosophy and religion. The poets and the priests, however, did not entrust their speculations to the judgment of the people; they were too sensible of the power which secrecy conferred upon their occult pursuits, and hence they allegorized their conceptions of supernatural agencies, and also their ideas of the ordinary operations of nature and art. The elements were spoken of as persons, and the changes which these underwent were regarded as the actions of individuals; and these in the lapse of ages, by losing their esoteric meaning, came to be considered as realities, and so passed into the popular belief. This is eminently the case with the northern mythology, respecting which we are at present more particularly concerned; for by far the greater portion of these highly poetical, though rugged myths, admit of a very plausible and rational explanation on astronomical and physical principles.* Whether this was equally the case with the Greek and Roman mythologies is now, perhaps, more difficult to determine. Enough, however, remains in the etymology of the names to prove that both these and the northern systems had much in common. The fundamental conceptions of each possess the same leading characteristics; and both are probably due to the conquering tribes who migrated into Europe from the fertile plains of Central Asia.†

During these early ages, war was considered to be the most honourable occupation. Valour constituted the highest virtue; and in the absence of all written records, tradition, in course of time, would add considerably to the prowess of any daring chieftain. A mighty conqueror would be considered by his followers as something more than human. The fear of his enemies would clothe him with attributes peculiar to their conceptions of inferior deities; and this, together with the almost universal "longing after immortality" which seems to pervade society in all its stages, sufficiently accounts for the origin of the heroes and heroines—the demi-gods and goddesses of every mythology. Hence Hercules—the younger Odin —and a numerous train of minor worthies to whom divine honours were decreed in the rituals of Italy and of the north.

On the introduction of Christianity, a powerful reactionary force was brought into the popular belief, and many of its grosser portions were speedily eliminated. The

* See Thorpe's *Northern Mythology*, vol. i. pp. 118-231.
† See Mallet's *Northern Antiquities*, Keightley's *Mythology of Greece and Rome*, and Kelly's *Indo-European Tradition and Folk-lore.*

whole of the mythological creations were divided into
two distinct classes, according to the attributes for which
they were more particularly distinguished. Those whose
tendencies inclined towards the benefit of mankind were
translated to heavenly mansions, with God as supreme;
whilst the wickedly disposed were consigned to the infernal regions, under the dominion of the Devil. The festivals of the gods were transformed into Christian seasons
for rejoicing, their temples became churches, and the
names of Christ, his apostles, the Virgin Mary, and the
saints, took the places of those of Jupiter, Mercury, Thor,
Freja, and Woden. All the inferior deities that presided over
the woods, the mountains, the seas, and the rivers, were degraded into demons, and were classed amongst those fallen
spirits who are employed by the evil one to harass and de-
ceive mankind. Our early missionaries, however, had studied
human nature too well to attempt too violent a change.
They contented themselves, for the most part, with divert-
ing the current of thought into different channels; they
gave *new* names to *old* conceptions, and then left their
more rational and more powerful faith to produce its known
effects upon the superstitions of the masses. But the
habits and opinions of a people who have long been under
the influence of any mythological system, have become too
deeply rooted to admit of easy eradication; and hence, in
our own country, as in others, the transition from heathen-
ism to Christianity was effected by almost imperceptible
steps.

There are, however, many points of resemblance
between the early Scandinavian and the Roman mythologies. Both had probably a common origin, but each became modified by increased civilization and the character
of the localities occupied by each succeeding wave of a
migratory population. " Every country in Europe," says

the learned editor of Warton's *History of Poetry*, "has invested its popular belief with the same common marvels : all acknowledge the agency of the lifeless productions of nature; the intervention of the same supernatural machinery; the existence of elves, fairies, dwarfs, giants, witches, wizards, and enchanters; the use of spells, charms, and amulets." The explosions and rumbling sounds occasionally heard in the interior of Etna and Stromboli were attributed, in ancient times, to the rage of Typhon, or the labours of Vulcan : at this day, the popular belief connects them with the suffering souls of men in the infernal regions. "The marks which natural causes have impressed upon the unyielding granite were produced, according to the common creed, by the powerful hero, the saint or the god, and large masses of stone, resembling domestic implements in form, were the toys or the tools of the demi-gods and giants of old. The repetition of the voice among the hills of Scandinavia is ascribed by the vulgar to the dwarfs mocking the human speaker; in England the fairies are said to perform the same exploits; while the more elegant fancy of Greece gave birth to Echo, a nymph who pined for love, and who still fondly repeats the accents that she hears. The magic scenery occasionally presented on the waters of the Straits of Messina is ascribed by popular opinion to the power of the Fata Morgana; the gossamer threads which float through the haze of an autumnal morning are [in Lancashire also] supposed to be woven by the ingenious dwarfs; the verdant circlets in the dewy mead are traced beneath the light steps of the dancing elves; and St. Cuthbert is said to forge and fashion the beads that bear his name, and lie scattered along the shores of Lindisfarne."* If we draw

* Keightley's *Fairy Mythology*, pp. 2, 3.

our parallels a little closer, we shall find, as has been well observed, that " the Nereids of antiquity are evidently the same with the Mermaids of the British and northern shores : the inhabitants of both are placed in crystal caves, or coral palaces, beneath the waters of the ocean ; they are alike distinguished for their partialities to the human race, and their prophetic powers in disclosing the events of futurity. The Naiades differ only in name from the Nixens of Germany, the Nisses of Scandinavia, or the Water-elves of the British Isles. The Brownies are of the same kindred as the Lares of Latium [and these agree exactly with the Portuni mentioned by Gervase of Tilbury in his *Otia Imperialis*]. The English Puck [the Lancashire Boggart], the Scotch Bogle, the French Goblin, the Gobelinus of the Middle Ages, and the German Kobold, are probably only varied names for the Grecian Khobalus, whose sole delight consisted in perplexing the human race, and evoking those harmless terrors that constantly hover round the minds of the timid. So, also, the German Spuck, and the Danish Spogel, correspond with the more northern Spog ; whilst the German Hudkin, and the Icelandic Puki, exactly answer to the character of the English Robin Goodfellow."* Our modern devil, with his horns and hoof, is derived from the Celtic Ourisk and the Roman Pan.

Some of our elves and satyrs are arrayed in the costumes of Greece and Rome ; and the Fairy Queen, with her attendants, have at times too many points of resemblance to escape being identified as Diana and her nymphs. The Roman Jupiter, by an easy transformation, becomes identical with the Scandinavian Thor—the thunderbolt and chariot of the former corresponding to the hammer and wagon of the latter. Odin takes the place of Mercury.

* Roby's *Traditions of Lancashire,* p. xiv.

Loki is the same as Lucifer, for, like him, he was expelled
from heaven for disobedience and rebellion. Hother en-
countered Thor, as Diomede did Mars. " The Grendels
of the north answer to the Titans of the south ; they were
the gods of nature to our forefathers—the spirits of the wood
and wave." Jupiter's eagle, the war-sign of the Romans,
is similar in character to Odin's raven among the Danes;
both nations considered that if the bird appeared to flutter
its wings on the banners, conquest was certain ; but if they
hung helplessly down, defeat would surely follow. Warcock Hill, on the borders of Lancashire and Yorkshire, has
probably derived its name from the unfurling of this terrible ensign during the conflicts between the Saxons and
*he Danes for the possession of Northumbria ;—the local
nomenclature of the district attests the presence of colo-
nists from both nations, and extensive traces of their forti-
fications still remain as evidence that our slopes and hill-
tops formed at once the battle-fields and the strongholds of
the country.

The power of the Devil, his personal appearance and
the possibility of bartering the soul for temporary gain,
must still be numbered among the articles of our popular
faith. Repeating the Lord's Prayer backwards is said to
be the most effectual plan for causing him to rise from
beneath ; but when the terms of the bargain are not satisfactory, his exit can only be secured by making the sign of
the cross and calling on the name of Christ.*

When we come to examine the miscellaneous customs
and superstitions of the county, we find many remarkable

* It may be stated that this introductory essay is abridged from two
papers read before the Historical Society of Lancashire and Cheshire, in
1859 and 1860, which were written long before the writer saw any of
the almost identical general deductions and conclusions in Dr. Dasent's
introduction to his *Popular Tales from the Norse.*

traces of a former belief. Tradition has again been true to her vocation ; and in several instances has been most careful to preserve the *minutiæ* of the mode of operation and supposed effects of each minor spell and incantation. The principal difficulty now lies in the selection; for the materials are so plentiful that none but the most striking can be noticed. Among these we observe that, a ringing in the ears ; shooting of the eyes ; throwing down, or spilling the salt ; putting on the left shoe first; lucky and unlucky days ; pouring melted lead into water ; stopping blood by means of charms ; the use of waxen images; enchanted girdles ; and lovers' knots, are all observed and explained almost exactly as amongst the Greeks and Romans. The details in many have been preserved to the very letter, whilst the supposed effects are exactly the same both in the ancient and modern times. Our marriageable maidens never receive knives, or any pointed implements, from their suitors, for the very same reason that such presents were rejected by their Scandinavian ancestors—they portend a "breaking off" in the matrimonial arrangements, and are notorious for "severing love."

> "If you love me as I love you,
> No knife shall cut our love in two."

We never return thanks for a loan of pins. A "winding sheet" on the candle forebodes death ; and dogs howling indicate a similar calamity.* Almost every one is aware that cuttings of human hair ought always to be burnt ; that if *thirteen* sit down to dinner one of them will die before the end of the year; that it is unlucky to meet a woman the first thing in the morning ; and that a horseshoe nailed or let into the step of the door will prevent the

---

* This popular opinion appears to be very ancient and widespread; for it has been noticed by Moses as prevailing in Egypt.— *Exodus* xi. 5-7.

entrance of any evil-disposed person. We have probably
derived nearly the whole of these notions from the Scandinavian settlers in the North of England. They considered it quite possible too to raise the Devil by the same
means now practised by our " wise men;" and after their
conversion to Christianity they are known to have marked
their dough with a cross in order to ensure its rising—a
practice which many of our country matrons still retain.
Sodden bread is always considered to be bewitched, provided the yeast be good, and hence the necessity for the
protection of the cross.

We always get out of bed either on the right side, or
with the right foot first; we take care not to cross two
knives on the table; mothers never allow a child to be
weighed soon after its birth; our children still blow their
ages at marriage from the tops of the dandelion; and all these
for similar reasons, and with similar objects, to those of the
peasantry of Northumbria during the period of Danish
rule. They supposed that the dead followed their usual
occupations in the spirit-world, and hence, probably, the
weapons of war and the implements of domestic life which
we find amongst the ashes of their dead. They were also
of opinion that buried treasure caused the ghosts of the
owners to haunt the places of concealment; and many of
our country population retain the same opinions without
the slightest modification.

The Folk-lore of dreams is an extensive subject, and
would require a series of essays for its full elucidation.
The *Royal Dream Book,* and *Napoleon's Book of Fate,*
command an extensive sale amongst our operatives,
and may be consulted for additional information. Our
country maidens are well aware that *triple* leaves plucked
at hazard from the common ash, are worn in the breast
for the purpose of causing prophetic dreams respecting a

dilatory lover. The leaves of the yellow trefoil are supposed to possess similar virtues; and the Bible is not unfrequently put under their pillows with a crooked sixpence
placed on the 16th and 17th verses of the first chapter of
Ruth, in order that they may both dream of, and see, their
future husbands. "Opening the Bible for direction" is
still practised after any troublesome dream, or when about
to undertake any doubtful matter. To dream of the teeth
falling out betokens death, or the loss of a lawsuit. Other
signs of death are dreaming of seeing the Devil; or hearing a sound like the stroke of a wand on any piece of furniture. The proverb that "lawyers and asses always die
in their shoes," is invariably quoted when any sudden
calamity befalls one of the profession.

Like the ancients, the folk of Lancashire have various
superstitious observances and practices connected with the
moon, especially with the new moon. Christmas thorns
are said to blossom only on *Old* Christmas Day; and persons will go considerable distances at midnight in order to
witness the blossoming. Oxen, too, are supposed to
acknowledge the importance of the Nativity of Christ,
by going down on their knees at the same hour; and
this is often quoted as a proof that our legislators were
wrong in depriving our forefathers of their "eleven
days" when the new style was enforced by Act of
Parliament.*

Some of our farmers are superstitious enough to hang
in the chimney a portion of the flesh of any animal which
has died of distemper, as a protection from similar afflictions; they also preserve with great care the membrane

* The use of the old style in effect, is not yet extinct in Lancashire.
The writer knows an old man, R. H., of Habergham, about 77 years of
age, who always reckons the changes of the seasons in this manner. He
alleges the practice of his grandfather and father in support of his
method; and states with much confidence that—"Perliment didn't
change t' seeasuns wen thay changd't' day o't' munth."

which sometimes envelopes a newly born foal, in the hope
that it will ensure them good luck for the future. Sailors
do not like to set sail on a Friday. Servant girls will
rarely enter upon a new service either on a Friday, or on
a Saturday : should they do so, they have an opinion that
they will disagree with their mistresses and " not stay long
in place." Most females entertain strong objections
against giving evidence, or taking oaths, before the magistrates, when *enceinte*. At Burnley, not long ago, a witness
in a case of felony was threatened with imprisonment
before she would comply with the necessary forms. All
children that are born in the twilight of certain days are in
consequence supposed to be endowed with the faculty of
seeing spirits ; and some of our " wise men" take advantage
of this, and persuade their dupes that they were so circum-
stanced at birth.

Such instances might be multiplied to an almost indefi-
nite extent, did space permit ; but the preceding will
suffice to prove both the probable origin and prevalence
of many of our popular superstitions. To a greater or
less extent their influence pervades all classes of society ;
and he who would elevate the intellectual condition of the
people must not neglect this thick stratum of *common
notions* which underlies the deepest deposits of mental
culture. As a recent writer in the *Quarterly Review*
reports of Cornwall, so we may state of Lancashire :—
" Pages might be filled, not with mere legends wrought up
for literary purposes, but with serious accounts of the wild
delusions which seem to have lived on from the very birth
of Pagan antiquity, and still to hold their influence among
the earnest and Christian people of this portion of England. . . . . . Superstition lives on, with little abatement
of vitality, in the human heart. In the lower classes it
wears its old fashions, with very slow alterations—in the

higher, it changes with the rapidity of modes in fashionable circles. We read with a smile of amusement and
pity, the account of some provincial conjuror, who follows,
with slight changes, the trade of the Witch of Endor; and
we then compose our features to a grave expression of interest—for so society requires—to listen to some enlight-
ened person's description of the latest novelties in table-
turning or spirit-rapping ; or to some fair patient's
account of her last conversation with her last quack-
doctor."

The labours of Croker, Keightley, Thorpe, and Kemble,
following in the wake of the Brothers Grimm, have added
considerably to our knowledge of the Folk-lore of the
North of Europe; but much yet remains to be collected
before the subject can be examined in all its bearings.

It is hoped that in the following pages the facts collected
will suffice to prove that the superstitious beliefs, observances, and usages of Lancashire are by no means unworthy of the attention of the antiquary, the ethnologist,
or the historian.

LANCASHIRE ALCHEMISTS.

Alchemy (from *al*, Arab. the, and χημεία, chemistry), the pretended art of transmuting the inferior metals into gold or silver, by means of what was called the Philosopher's Stone, or the powder of projection, a red powder possessing a peculiar smell, is supposed to have originated among the Arabians; Geber, an Arabian physician of the seventh century, being one of the earliest alchemists whose works are extant; but written so obscurely as to have led to the suggestion that his name was the origin of our modern term *gibberish*, for unintelligible jargon. A subsequent object of alchemy was the discovery of a universal medicine, the *Elixir Vitæ*, which was to give perpetual life, health, and youth. The Egyptians are said to have practised alchemy; and Paulus Diaconus, a writer of the eighth century, asserts that Dioclesian burned the library of Alexandria, in order to prevent the Egyptians from becoming learned in the art of producing at will those precious metals which might be employed as " the sinews of war" against himself.* The earliest English writer on alchemy was probably St. Dunstan, Archbishop of Canterbury, in the tenth century. " He who shall have the happiness to meet with St. Dunstan's work, 'De Occulta Philosophia' [that on the 'Philosopher's stone' is in the Ashmole Museum], may therein read such stories as will make him amazed to think what stupendous and immense things are to be performed by virtue of the Philosopher's Mercury."† A John Garland is also said to have written on alchemy and mineralogy prior to the Conquest.‡

* *Conybeare*, p. 242.
† Charnock's *Breviary of Natural Philsophy* in Ashmole's *Theatrum Chemicum*, p. 297.
‡ *Companion to Almanac* for 1837, p. 22.

Alchemy was much studied in conventual establishments*
and by the most learned doctors and schoolmen, and the
highest Church dignitaries—nay, even by kings and popes.
Albertus Magnus, a German, born in 1282, wrote seven
treatises on alchemy; and Thomas Aquinas "the angelic
doctor" (said to have been a pupil of Albert), wrote three
works on this subject. Roger Bacon ("Friar Bacon"),
born at Ilchester in 1214, though he wrote against the
folly of believing in magic, necromancy, and charms,
nevertheless had faith in alchemy; and his chemical and
alchemical writings number eighteen. Of his *Myrrour of
Alchemy*, Mr. J. J. Conybeare observes, "Of all the
alchemical works into which I have been occasionally led
to search, this appears the best calculated to afford the
curious reader an insight into the history of the art, and of
the arguments by which it was usually attacked and de-
fended. It has the additional merit of being more intelli-
gible and more entertaining than most books of the same
class."†

Raymond Lully, born at Majorca in 1235, is said to
have been a scholar of Roger Bacon, and to have written
nineteen works on alchemy. Arnoldus de Villa Nova,
born in 1235, amongst a number of works on this subject,
wrote *The Rosarium*, a compendium of the alchemy of his
time. He died in 1313, on his way to visit Pope
Clement V. at Avignon. Another pope, John XXII.,
professed and described the art of transmuting metals, and
boasts in the beginning of his book that he had made two
hundred ingots of gold, each weighing one hundred pounds.
Among English alchemists of the fourteenth century may
be mentioned Cremer, abbot of Westminster (the disciple
and friend of Lully), John Daustein, and Richard, who

* Maier's *Symbola Ameæ Mensæ.*
† Thomson's *Annals of Philosophy*, n. s., vol. vi. p. 241.

both practised and wrote upon the " hermetic philosophy,"
as it was termed. In the fifteenth century was born
George Ripley, a canon registrar of Bridlington, who
wrote the *Medulla Alchymiæ* (translated by Dr. Salmon
in his *Clavis*), and another work in rhyme, called "The
Compound of Alchemie," which was dedicated to
Edward IV. Dr. John Dee (born 1527), the warden of
Manchester College, and his assistant, or "seer," Edward
Kelly (born 1555), were both avowed alchemists. Dee
wrote a *Treatise of the Rosie Crucian Secrets, their excellent methods of making Medicines and Metals,* &c. Ashmole says of him, that "some time he bestowed in vulgar
chemistry, and was therein master of divers secrets :
amongst others, he revealed to one Roger Cooke 'the
great secret of the elixir' (as he called it) 'of the salt of
metals, the projection whereof was one upon a hundred.' "*

" 'Tis generally reported that Dr. Dee and Sir Edward
Kelly were so strangely fortunate as to find a very large
quantity of the elixir in some parts of the ruins of Glas-
tonbury Abbey. It had remained here, perhaps, ever
since the time of the highly gifted St. Dunstan, in the
tenth century.† The great Lord Bacon relates the following story in his *Apothegms :*—

" Sir Edward Dyer, a grave and wise gentleman, did
much believe in Kelly, the alchemist, that he did indeed

---

* Ben Jonson, in his play of the *Alchemist,* has the following
lines :—
> " But when you see th' effects of the Great Medium,
> Of which one part projected on a hundred
> Of Mercury, or Venus, or the Moon,
> Shall turn it to as many of the Sun ;
> Nay to a thousand, so ad infinitum,
> You will believe me."

† Godwin's *Lives of Necromancers,* Art. Dee. Dr. Dee's *Diary*
(Camden Soc.) contains many references to his alchemical pursuits.—See
pp. 7, 22, 25, 27, 28, 37, and 63.

the work, and made gold; insomuch that he went into Germany, where Kelly then was, to inform himself fully thereof. After his return he dined with my Lord of Canterbury, where at that time was at the table Dr. Brown, the physician. They fell in talk of Kelly. Sir Edward Dyer, turning to the archbishop, said—'I do assure your Grace that that I shall tell you is truth : I am an eye-witness thereof; and if I had not seen it, I should not have believed it. I saw Master Kelly put of the base metal into the crucible; and after it was set a little upon the fire, and a very small quantity of the medicine put in, and stirred with a stick of wood, it came forth, in great proportion, perfect gold, to the touch, to the hammer, and to the test.' My Lord Archbishop said, ' You had need take heed what you say, Sir Edward Dyer, for here is an infidel at the board.' Sir Edward Dyer said again pleasantly, ' I would have looked for an infidel sooner in any place than at your Grace's table.' ' What say you, Dr. Brown ?' said the archbishop. Dr. Brown answered, after his blunt and huddling manner, ' The gentleman hath spoken enough for me.' ' Why,' saith the archbishop, ' what hath he said ?' ' Marry,' saith Dr. Brown, ' he said he would not have believed it except he had seen it; and no more will I.' "

Professor De Morgan observes that " Alchemy was more than a popular credulity : Newton and Boyle were amongst the earnest inquirers into it." Bishop Berkeley was of opinion that M. Homberg made gold by introducing light into the pores of mercury. Amongst the works of the Hon. Robert Boyle (vol. iv. 13–19), is *An Historical Account of a Degradation of Gold, made by an anti-Elixir : a Strange Chemical Narrative,* in which he says— " To make it more credible that other metals are capable of being graduated or exalted into gold, by way of pro-

jection, I will relate to you, that by the like way, gold has
been degraded or imbased . . . . . Our experiment plainly
shows that gold, though confessedly the most homogene-
ous and the least mutable of metals, may be in a very
short time (perhaps not amounting to many minutes), exceedingly changed, both as to malleableness, colour,
homogeneity, and (which is more) specific gravity; and
all this by so very inconsiderable a portion of injected
powder," &c.

"When Locke, as one of the executors of Boyle, was
about to publish some of his works, Newton wished him
to insert the second and third part of Boyle's recipes (the
first part of which was to obtain 'a mercury that would
grow hot with gold'), and which Boyle had communicated to him on condition that they should be published
after his death."* "Mangetus relates a story of a stranger
calling on Boyle, and leaving with him a powder, which
he projected into the crucible, and instantly went out.
After the fire had gone out, Boyle found in the crucible a
yellow-coloured metal, possessing all the properties of
pure gold, and only a little lighter than the weight of the
materials originally put in the crucible."†

From these proofs of the credulity of great men, let us
turn to the encouragements vouchsafed to alchemy and
its adepts by the Kings and Parliaments of England.
Raymond Lully visited England on the invitation of
Edward I.; and he affirms in one of his works, that in
the secret chamber of St. Katherine, in the Tower of
London, he performed in the royal presence the experiment of transmuting some crystal into a mass of
diamond, or adamant, as he calls it; on which Edward,

---

* Brewster's *Life of Sir Isaac Newton*, vol. ii. p. 376.
† Preface to *Bibl. Chem. Curiosa*, quoted by Thomson, p. 18. For
a list of Boyle's works connected with alchemy, see the *Philosophical
Epitaphs*, by W. C.

he says, caused some little pillars to be made for the
tabernacle of God. It was popularly believed, indeed, at
the time, that the English king had been furnished by
Lully with a great quantity of gold for defraying the
expense of an expedition which he intended to make to
the Holy Land. Edward III. was not less credulous on
this subject than his grandfather, as appears by an order
which he issued in 1329, in the following terms:—
"Know all men that we have been assured that John of
Rous, and Master William of Dalby, know how to make
silver by the art of alchemy; that they have made it in
former times, and still continue to make it; and considering that these men, by their art, and by making
the precious metal, may be profitable to us and to our
kingdom, we have commanded our well-beloved Thomas
Cary to apprehend the aforesaid John and William
wherever they can be found, within liberties or without, and bring them to us, together with all the instruments of their art, under safe and sure custody." The
first considerable coinage of gold in England was begun
by Edward III. in 1343: and "The alchemists did affirm,
as an unwritten verity, that the rose nobles, which were
coined soon after, were made by projection or multiplication alchemical, by Raymond Lully, in the Tower of
London." But Lully died in 1315; and the story only
shows the strength of the popular faith in alchemy.
That this pretended science was much cultivated in the
fourteenth century, and with the usual evil results, may
be inferred from an Act passed 5 Hen. IV. cap. 4 (1404),
to make it felony " to multiply gold or silver, or to use
the craft of multiplication," &c. It is probable, however,
that this statute was enacted from some apprehension that
the operations of the multipliers might possibly affect the
value of the king's coin. Henry VI., a very pious, yet

very weak and credulous prince, was as great a patron of
the alchemists as Edward III. had been before him.
These impostors practised with admirable success upon
his weakness and credulity, repeatedly inducing him to
advance them money wherewith to prosecute the operations, as well as procuring from him protections (which he
sometimes prevailed upon the Parliament to confirm) from
the penalties of the statute just mentioned.* In 1438, the
king commissioned three philosophers to make the precious
metals ; but, as might be expected, he received no returns
from them in gold or silver.† His credulity, however,
seems to have been unshaken by disappointment, and we
next find him issuing one of these protections, which is too
long to print entire, granted to the "three famous men,"
John Fauceby, John Kirkeby, and John Ragny, which
was confirmed by Parliament May 31, 1456. In this
document the object of the researches of these "philosophers" is described to be "a certain most precious
medicine, called by some philosophers 'the mother and
empress of medicines;' by some, 'the inestimable glory;'
by others, 'the quintessence;' by others, 'the philosopher's stone;' by others, 'the elixir of life;' which
cures all curable diseases with ease ; prolongs human life
in perfect vigour of faculty to its utmost natural term ;
heals all healable wounds; is a most sovereign antidote
against all poisons ; and is capable of preserving to us and
our kingdom other great advantages, such as the transmutation of other metals into the most real and finest gold and
silver."‡ Fauceby, here mentioned, is elsewhere designated the king's physician.§ We have not traced the
position of the other two adepts named. Fauceby, how-

* *Pictorial History of England,* vol. ii. p. 207.
† Baines's *Lancashire.*
‡ *Fœdera,* vol. ix. p. 379.　　　§ *Rot. Parl.,* vol. v. p. 314a.

ever, notwithstanding his power of gold-making, did not refuse to accept a grant from the king, in 1456, of a pension of 100*l.* a year for life.*

We come now to the two most distinguished of Lancashire alchemists, both knights, and at the head of the principal families of the county. They seem to have been actively engaged together in the delusive pursuit of the transmutation of metals; and, self-deceived, to have deluded the weak king with promises of wealth which never could be realised. These Lancashire adepts were Sir Edmund de Trafford, Knight, and Sir Thomas Ashton [of Ashton], Knight. The former was the younger of two sons of Henry de Trafford, Esq., and Elizabeth his wife, daughter of Sir Ralph Radcliffe, Knight. The elder son, Henry, dying at the early age of twenty-six years, this Edmund succeeded as his heir about King Henry V. (1414), and he was knighted by Henry VI. at the Whitsuntide of 1426. He married Dame Alice Venables, eldest daughter and co-heir to Sir William Venables, of Bollyn, Knight. Their only son, Sir John Trafford, knighted about 1444, in his father's life-time, married Elizabeth, daughter of Sir Thomas Ashton, of Ashton-under-Lyne, Knight; whilst Sir Edmund's youngest daughter, Dulcia, or Douce, married Sir John Ashton, a son of Sir Thomas, in 1438; so that the two families were connected by this double alliance. Sir Thomas Ashton, the alchemist, was the eldest son of Sir John de Ashton (Knight of the Bath at the coronation of Henry IV. in 1399, Knight of the Shire in 1413, and Constable of Coutances in 1417), and of his first wife, Jane, daughter of John Savile, of Tankersley, county York. Sir Thomas married Elizabeth, daughter of Sir John Byron. The date of his death is

* *Rot. Parl.,* vol. v. p. 314*a.*

not known. Sir Edmund Trafford died in 1457. Their
supposed power of transmuting the baser metals into
gold had great attractions for a weak king, whose
treasury was low, and who was encumbered with debt.
They were not mere adventurers, but men descended
from ancient families, opulent, and of high estimation in
their native county. Fuller found in the Tower of
London, and copied,* a patent granted to these two knights
by Henry VI., in the twenty-fourth year of his reign
(1446), of which he gives the following translation:—
"The King to all unto whom, &c., greeting—Know ye,
that whereas our beloved and loyal Edmund de Trafford,
Knight, and Thomas Ashton, Knight, have, by a certain
petition shown unto us, set forth that although they were
willing by the art or science of philosophy to work upon
certain metals, to translate [transmute] imperfect metals
from their own kind, and then to transubstantiate them
by their said art or science, as they say, into perfect gold or
silver, unto all manner of proofs and trials, to be expected
and endured as any gold or silver growing in any mine;
notwithstanding certain persons ill-willing and maligning
them, conceiving them to work by unlawful art, and so may
hinder and disturb them in the trial of the said art and
science: WE, considering the premises, and willing
to know the conclusion of the said work or science,
of our special grace have granted and given leave to the
same Edmund and Thomas, and to their servants, that
they may work and try the aforesaid art and science
lawfully and freely, without any hindrance of ours, or of
our officers, whatsoever; any statute, act, ordinance, or
provision made, ordained, or provided to the contrary notwithstanding. In witness whereof, &c., the King at

* *Worthies,* &c., p. 122.

Westminster, the 7th day of April" [1446.]* Fuller
leaves this curious document, which might fitly have been
dated the *first* instead of the 7th April, without a word
of comment. The two knightly alchemists, doubtlessly
imposing on themselves no less than on their royal patron,
kept the king's expectation wound up to the highest
pitch; and in the following year he actually informed his
people that the happy hour was approaching when by
means of " the stone" he " should be able to pay off his
debts !"† It is scarcely necessary to add that the stone
failed, and the king's debts must have remained unpaid,
if his majesty had not pawned the revenue of his Duchy
of Lancaster, to satisfy the demands of his clamorous
creditors. Henry VI. was deposed by Edward IV. in
March, 1461, and though he was nominally restored to
the throne in October, 1470, he lost both crown and
life in May, 1471, being found dead (most probably murdered) in the Tower on the evening or the
morrow of the day on which Edward IV. entered London
after his victory at Barnet. Such are some of the most
notable facts in the practice of alchemy as connected with
Lancashire. It will naturally be asked if alchemy is still
practised in this county ? We can only say, that if it be
it is in very rare instances, and with the greatest secresy.
The more chemistry is known—and the extent to which
it has been developed within the last twenty years is truly
marvellous—the more completely it takes the ground from
under the feet of a believer in alchemy. It is not like
astrology, which accepts the facts of the true science of
astronomy, and only draws false conclusions from true
premisses. Alchemy could only have sprung up at a
period when all the operations of the chemist's laboratory

* For a copy of this patent in the original Latin, see Baines's *Lancashire,* vol. i. p. 406.

† Pennant's *London.*

were of the most rude, imperfect, and blundering character; when the true bases of earths and minerals and metals were unknown; when what was called chemistry was without analysis, either quantitative or qualitative; before the law of definite proportions had been discovered; when, in short, chemistry was a groping in the dark without the help of any accurate weight or measure, or other knowledge of the countless substances which are now so extensively investigated, and so accurately described in the briefest formulas. A man, to become an alchemist in the nineteenth century, must study only the hermetical writings of past ages, shutting both eyes and ears to all the facts of modern chemistry. It is scarcely possible at this day to find such a combination of exploded learning and scientific ignorance. Hence we conclude that alchemy is in all probability, from the very nature of things, an obsolete and forgotten lore.

LANCASHIRE ASTROLOGERS.

Astrology (literally the Science of the Stars), is now understood to signify the mode of discovering future events by means of the position of the heavenly bodies, which has been termed judicial astronomy. This quasi science found universal belief among all the nations of antiquity except the Greeks. Among the Romans it was eagerly cultivated from the time of the conquest of Egypt. In the second century the whole world was astrological. All the followers of Mohammed have ever been, and still are, believers in it. The Church of Rome has repeatedly condemned the art, but popes and cardinals rank amongst its votaries. Cardinal d'Ailly (about 1400), calculated the horoscope of Jesus Christ; and in the fifteenth century

Pope Calixtus III. directed prayers and anathemas against
a comet which had either assisted in or predicted the
success of the Turks against the Christians. The establishment of the Copernican system was the death of
astrology. The last of the astrologers was Morin, best
known as the opponent of Gassendi. The latter in youth
had studied and believed in the art, but afterwards re-
nounced and written against it. Morin, who worked
thirty years at a book on astrology, and who disbelieved
in the motion of the earth, repeatedly predicted the death
of Gassendi, but was always wrong, as he was in foretelling the death of Louis XIII. Since his death, in 1656,
the pseudo-science has gradually sunk, and has not since,
it is believed, been adopted by any real astronomer.
Roger Bacon and other early English philosophers were
believers in astrology, no less than in alchemy. In Lancashire the most remarkable practisers of the art were Dr.
John Dee, warden of Manchester College, his friend and
"seer," Sir Edward Kelly, and John Booker, of Manchester. Dee was the son of a wealthy vintner, and was
born in London in 1527. At the age of fifteen he was
entered at St. John's College, Cambridge, where he seems
to have devoted himself to the study of mathematics,
astronomy, and chemistry; displaying great assiduity and
industry. At twenty he made a year's tour on the Continent, chiefly in Holland, and on his return was made
one of the fellows of Trinity College on its foundation by
Henry' VIII., in 1543. In 1548 he was strongly suspected of being addicted to "the black art," probably
from his astrological pursuits; and having taken his degree
of A.M., he again went abroad to the university of Lou-
vaine and to Rheims, and elsewhere in France; returning
to England in 1551, when he was presented by Cecil to
King Edward VI., who assigned him a pension of one

hundred crowns, which he subsequently relinquished for the rectory of Upton-on-Severn. Shortly after the accession of Mary, he was accused of "practising against the queen's life by *enchantment;*" the charge being founded on some correspondence between him and " the servants of the Lady Elizabeth." He was long imprisoned and frequently examined, but as nothing could be established against him he was set at liberty by an order of the church in 1555. On the accession of Elizabeth, Dee was consulted by Lord Robert Dudley respecting "a propitious day" for the coronation. He says, " I wrote at large and delivered it for her Majesty's use, by the commandment of the Lord Robert (afterwards Earl of Leicester), what in my judgment the ancient astrologers would determine on the election day of such a time as was appointed for her Majesty to be crowned in." He was presented to the queen, who made him great promises (not always fulfilled); amongst others, that where her brother Edward " had given him a crown, she would give him a noble" [onethird more—viz., from 5s. to 6s. 8d.]. Nothing can better mark the belief in astrology than the fact that Queen Elizabeth's nativity was cast, in order to ascertain whether she could marry with advantage to the nation. Lilly, some eighty years later, declares* that he received twenty pieces of gold, in order that he might ascertain where Charles I. might be most safe from his enemies, and what hour would be most favourable for his escape from Carisbrooke Castle.

In 1564 Dee again visited the Continent, and was presented to the Emperor Maximilian, probably on some secret mission; for Lilly says, " he was the Queen's intelligencer, and had a salary for his maintenance from the

* *History of his Life and Times*

D 2

Secretaries of State. He was a ready-witted man, quick
of apprehension, and of great judgment in the Latin and
Greek tongues. He was a very great investigator of the
more secret hermetical learning (alchemy), a perfect
astronomer, a curious astrologer, a serious geometrician;
to speak truth, he was excellent in all kinds of learning."*
Dee was repeatedly and urgently sent for one morning
"to prevent the mischief which divers of her Majesty's
privy council suspected to be intended against her
Majesty, by means of a certain image of wax, with a
great pin stuck into it, about the breast of it, found in
Lincoln's Inn Fields." For some years Dee led a life of
privacy and study at Mortlake in Surrey, collecting books
and MSS., beryls and magic crystals, talismans, &c. So
strong was the popular belief in his neighbourhood that he
had dealings with the devil, that in 1576 a mob assembled,
broke into his house, and destroyed nearly all his library
and collections; and it was with difficulty that he and his
family escaped the fury of the rabble. In October, 1578,
by the Queen's command, he had a conference with
Dr. Bayley, her Majesty's physician, "about her Majesty's
grievous pains, by reason of toothache and the rheum,"
&c.; and the same year he was sent a winter journey of
about 1500 miles by sea and land, "to consult with the
learned physicians and philosophers [*i.e.*, astrologers], for
her Majesty's health-recovering and preserving." Passing
over his more useful and valuable services to the State and
to the world, as we are only noting here his doings as an
astrologer, &c., we may remark that most of his proceedings
and writings in this pseudo-science or art were accomplished
after he had passed his fiftieth year. It was in 1581 that
he took into his service, as an assistant in his alchemical and

* Lilly's *Life and Times*, p. 224.

astrological labours, an apothecary of Worcester named Edward Kelly, born in 1555, and who was called " The Seer," because, looking into magic crystals or speculæ, it was said he saw many things which it was not permitted to Dee himself to behold. Kelly also acted as Dee's amanuensis, and together they held "conversations with spirits." They had a black speculum, it is said "a polished piece of cannel coal," in which the angels Gabriel and Raphael appeared at their invocation. Hence Butler says—

> " Kelly did all his feats upon
> The devil's looking-glass—a stone."

In 1583 a Polish noble, Albert Lasque, palatine of Siradia [? Sieradz]being in England, Dee and Kelly were introduced to him, and accompanied him to Poland. He persuaded them to pay a visit to Rodolph, king of Bohemia, who, though a weak and credulous man, is said to have become disgusted with their pretensions. They had no better success with the king of Poland, but were soon after invited by a rich Bohemian noble to his castle of Trebona, where they continued for some time in great affluence, owing, as they asserted, to their transmuting the baser metals into gold. Kelly is said to have been sordid and grasping, without honour or principle. Lilly asserts that the reason of many failures in the conferences with spirits was because Kelly was very vicious, " unto whom the angels were not obedient, or willingly did declare [answers to] the questions propounded." Dee and Kelly quarrelled and separated in Bohemia ; Dee returning to England, while Kelly remained at Prague. He died in 1595. In 1595 the Queen appointed Dee warden of Manchester College, he being then sixty-eight years of age. He resided at Manchester nine years, quitting it in 1604 for his old abode at Mortlake, where he died in 1608, aged eighty-one, in great poverty, and leaving a numerous family and a great many printed works and forty unpublished writings behind him. The catalogue of Dee's library at Mortlake shows that it was rich in the works of preceding astrologers and alchemists, especially those of Roger Bacon, Raymond Lully, Albertus Magnus, Arnold de Villa Nova, &c.

John Booker, a celebrated astrologer of the seventeenth century, was the son of John Bowker (commonly pronounced Booker), of Manchester, and was born 23rd March, 1601. He was educated at the Manchester Grammar School, where he acquired some acquaintance with Latin. From childhood he showed an inclination for astrology, and amused himself with studying almanacks and other books on that subject. After serving some time to a haberdasher in London, he practised as a writing-master at Hadley, Middlesex; and was subsequently clerk for some time to the aldermen at Guildhall. Becoming famous by his studies, he was appointed Licenser of Mathematical Publications, which then included all those relating to the " celestial sciences." Lilly tells us that he once thought him the greatest astrologer in the world; but he afterwards came to think himself a much greater man. George Wharton, who had been one of his astrological acquaintances, quarrelled with him, and in consequence published at Oxford in 1644, in answer to one of Booker's pamphlets, what he called " Mercurio-Cœlica-Mastyx; or an Anticaveat to all such as have heretofore had the misfortune to be cheated and deluded by the great and treacherous impostor, John Booker; in an answer to his frivolous pamphlet, entitled ' Mercurius-Cœlicus, or a Caveat to all the People of England.' " Booker died of dysentery in April, 1667, and was buried in St. James's Church, Duke's Place, London, where the following monument was erected to him by Ashmole, who was one of his greatest admirers:—"Ne oblivione conteretur Urna Johannis Bookeri, Astrologi, qui Fatis cessit 6 idus Aprilis, A.D. 1667. Hoc illi posuit amoris Monumentum, Elias Ashmole, Armiger." Lilly, in his *Life and Times*, gives the following character of Booker :—

"He was a great proficient in astrology, whose excellent verses upon the twelve months, framed according to the configurations of each month, being blest with success according to his predictions, procured him much reputation all over England. He was a very honest man ; abhorred any deceit in the art he studied; had a curious fancy in judging of thefts ; and was successful in resolving love questions. He was no mean proficient in astronomy; understood much of physic ; was a great admirer of the antimonial cup ; not unlearned in chemistry, which he loved, but did not practise; and since his decease I have seen a nativity of his performance, exactly directed, and judged with as much learning as from astrology can be expected. His library of books came short of the world's approbation, and were sold by his widow to Elias Ashmole, Esq., who most generously gave far more than they were worth."

Lilly and Booker were frequently consulted during the differences between the king and the parliamentary army, and were once invited by General Fairfax, and sent in a coach-and-four to head quarters at Windsor, to give their opinions on [*i.e.*, their predictions as to] the prosecution of the war. Booker became famous for a prediction on the solar eclipse of 1613, in which year both the king of Bohemia and Gustavus, king of Sweden, died. Booker's works (chiefly tracts or pamphlets) were about fifteen or sixteen in number. The only work now worth notice is his *Bloody Irish Almanack* (London, 1646, quarto), which contains some memorable particulars relative to the war in Ireland.*

Another Lancashire astrologer was Charles Leadbetter, who was born at Cronton, near Prescot, and was the author of a *Treatise on Eclipses of the Sun and Moon, commencing* A.D. 1715, *and ending* A.D. 1749; in which he gives the horoscope of every eclipse of importance; and, from the aspects of the stars, predicts the principal occurrences that may be expected within limited periods. He failed, however, to predict the Rebellion of 1715, or that of 1745; and though under the years 1720 and 1721 he predicated " Sea Fights and Death of Fish," no hint of the " South Sea Bubble," the great event of those years, can be found amongst his prophecies. He entertained no doubt of an " eclipse of the moon, moving subjects to seduction [? sedition], servants to disobedience, and wives to a disorder against their husbands." Yet Leadbetter's Works on Astronomy, &c., were held in able repute, and he taught the " Arts and Sciences Mathematical" with much success, " at the Hand and Pen, Cock Lane, near Shore Ditch, London."

If we close here our notices of Lancashire Astrologers, it is not because we suppose the class to be wholly extinct. But those to whom we have so far referred, were well acquainted with astronomy, and erred only in superadding the delusions of astrology to the truths of that real science. The class still remaining in Lancashire, chiefly in country districts, are (with very few exceptions) greatly inferior in knowledge, and, mixing up the arts of the so-called sorcerer or conjuror with the deductions of the so-called " astral science" (of which they are blundering smatterers, often ignorant of the very elements of astro-

* Whatton's *Memoir* in Baines's *Lancashire,* vol. ii. p. 367.

nomy), they do not merit the name of astrologers, but should be classed with the numerous " wise men," " cunning women," and other varieties of fortune-tellers, who have not even the negative merit of being self-deluded by the phenomena of a supposed science; but are in their way mere charlatans and cheats, knowingly cozening their credulous dupes of as much money as they can extort. Some notices of this class will be found in later pages.

BELLS.

It is not with Bells generally, but only with Church Bells, and not with all their uses, but only such of them as are superstitious, that we are called upon to deal here. The large church bells are said to have been invented by Paulinus, Bishop of Nola, in Campania (whence the low Latin name of Campana), about A.D. 400. Two hundred years afterwards they appear to have been in great use in churches. Pope John XIII., in A.D. 968, consecrated a very large newly-cast bell in the Lateran Church at Rome, giving it the name of John. This is the first instance known of what has since been called " the baptising of bells," a Roman Catholic superstition of which vestiges remain in England in the names of great bells, as " Tom of Lincoln," " Great Tom of Oxford," &c. The priests anciently rung them themselves. Amongst their superstitious uses, were to drive away lightning and thunder; to chase evil spirits from persons and places; to expedite childbirth, when women were in labour; and the original use of the soul-bell or passing-bell was to drive away any demon that might seek to take possession of the soul of the deceased. Grose says that the passing-bell was anciently rung for two purposes : one, to bespeak the prayers of all good Christians for a soul just departing; the other, to drive away the evil spirits who stood at the bed's foot and about the house, ready to seize their prey, or at least to molest and terrify the soul in its passage. By the ringing of the bell they were kept aloof, and the soul, like a hunted hare, gained the start, or had what sportsmen call "law." Hence the high charge for tolling the great bell of the church, which, being louder, the evil spirits must go further off to be clear of its sound, by which the poor soul got so much the more start of them; besides, being heard further off, it would likewise procure the dying man a greater number of prayers. Till about 1830, it was customary at Roman Catholic funerals in many parts of Lancashire, to ring a merry peal on the bells, as soon as the interment was over. Doubtless the greater the clang of the bells, the further the flight of the fiends waiting to seize the soul of the departed. There are some monkish rhymes in Latin on the uses of church bells, some of which are retained in the following doggerel :—

Men's deaths I tell	By doleful knell;
Lightning and thunder	I break asunder;
On Sabbath all	To church I call;
The sleepy head	I raise from bed;
The winds so fierce	I do disperse;
Men's cruel rage	I do assuage.

The following verses (the spelling modernized) further illustrate the subject :*—

" If that the thunder chance to roar, and stormy tempest shake,
A wonder is it for to see the wretches how they quake;
How that no faith at all they have, nor trust in any thing,
The clerk doth all the bells forthwith at once in steeple ring;
With wondrous sound and deeper far than he was wont before,
Till in the lofty heavens dark the thunders bray no more.
For in these christen'd bells they think doth lie much pow'r and might
As able is the tempest great and storm to vanquish quite.

* From Barnaby Googe's Translation of the *Regnum Papisticum* (or Popish Kingdom) of Naogeorgus, fol. 41 *b.*

I saw myself at Nurnberg once, a town in Toring coast,
A bell that with this title bold herself did proudly boast:
By name I " Mary" callèd am, with sound I put to flight
The thunder-cracks and hurtful storms, and every wicked sprite.
Such things when as these bells can do, no wonder certainly
It is, if that the papists to their tolling always fly,
When hail, or any raging storm, or tempest comes in sight,
Or thunderbolts, or lightning fierce, that every place doth smite."

Wynkin de Worde* tells us that bells are rung during thunder-storms, to the end that the fiends and wicked spirits should be abashed, and flee, and cease the moving of the tempest.† Bells appear to have had an inherent power against evil spirits, but this power was held to be greatly increased by the bells being christened. There is a custom in some Lancashire parishes, in ringing the passing-bell, to conclude its tolling with nine knells or strokes of the clapper, for a man, six for a woman, and three for a child ; the vestiges of an ancient Roman Catholic injunction.‡ In an Old English Homily for Trinity Sunday,§ it is stated that " the form of the Trinity was found in man ; that was, Adam our forefather, on earth, one person, and Eve of Adam, the second person ; and of them both was the third person. At the death of a man three bells should be rung, as his knell, in worship of the Trinity, and for a woman, who was the second person of the Trinity, two bells should be rung." Two couplets on the passing-bell may be inserted here:—

" When the bell begins to toll,
   Lord have mercy on the soul!

When thou dost hear a toll or knell
Then think upon *thy* passing-bell."‖

The great bell which used to be rung on Shrove-Tues-

---

* *Golden Legend.*　　　† Hone's *Every-Day Book*, p. 141.
　　　‡ See Durand's *Rationale.*
　　§ Strutt's *Manners and Customs*, vol. iii. p. 176.
　　‖ Ray's *Collection of Old English Proverbs.*

day to call the people together for the purpose of confessing their sins, or to be "shriven," was called the "Pancake Bell," and some have regarded it simply as a signal for the people to begin frying their pancakes. This custom prevails still in some parts of Lancashire, and in many country places throughout the North of England. Another bell, rung in some places as the congregation quits the church on Sunday, is popularly known among country people as the "pudding-bell," they supposing that its use is to warn those at home to get the dinner ready, as, in homely phrase, "pudding-time has come." A Lancashire clergyman* states that this bell is still rung in some of the old Lancashire parish churches; but he does not suggest any more probable reason for tolling this bell. The Curfew Bell [*couvre feu*, cover-fire] is commonly believed to be of Norman origin; a law having been made by William the Conqueror that all people should put out their fires and lights at the eight o'clock (evening) bell, and go to bed. In one place the sexton of a parish was required to lie in the church steeple, and at eight o'clock every night to ring the curfew for a quarter of an hour. The curfew-bell is still rung at Burnley, Colne, Blackburn, Padiham, and indeed in most of the older towns and many of the villages of Lancashire. It has nearly lost its ancient name, and is a remarkable instance of the persistence of an old custom or usage, long after all its significance or value has ceased. It is now merely called "the eight o'clock bell." A morning bell, rung anciently at four, now more commonly at six o'clock, is also to be heard in Burnley and other places, and is called "the six o'clock bell." Of what may be called "the vocal ghosts of bells" many stories might be told. Opposite the Cross-slack, on the sands near Blackpool, out

* "P. P." in *Notes and Queries*, vol. ix. p. 569.

at sea, once stood the church and cemetery of Kilgrimol, long since submerged. Many tales are told of benighted wanderers near this spot being terrified with the sound of bells pealing dismal chimes o'er the murmuring sea.*

BEAL-TINE OR BELTANE FIRES; RELICS OF BAAL WORSHIP.

Among the dim traces of an extinct worship of Bel, or Baal, the ancient sun-god, perceptible still among Celtic peoples, especially in Ireland and Scotland, are the three festival periods when fires are kindled on eminences in honour of the sun. The *Bel,* or *Belus,* the chief deity of the Babylonians and the Assyrians, seems to have been identical with the *Baal* of the Phœnicians and Cartha-ginians. The Chaldee *Bel* and the Hebrew *Baal* alike mean " Lord;" and under these names worship was paid by the old Asiatics to the sun, whose light and heat-giving properties were typified by fires kindled on the tops of high hills. In parts of Lancashire, especially in the Fylde, these traces of a heathen cult still linger. " From the great heaps of stones on eminences, called Cairns, from the Toot-hills (*i.e.,* the hills dedicated to the worship of the Celtic god, Tot, or Teut, or Teutates, the same with the Egyptian Thoth), and the Belenian eminences, whereon was worshipped Bel, or Belus, or Belenus, the sun-god; from these three kinds of heights the grand sacred fires of the *Bel-Tine* flamed thrice a year, at three of the great festivals of the Druids, in honour of Beal, or the Sun— viz., on the eve of May-day, on Midsummer Eve, and on the eve of the 1st November. Two such fires were kindled by one another on May-day Eve in every village

---

* Thornber's *History of Blackpool,* p. 342.

of the nation, as well throughout all Gaul as in Britain,
Ireland, and the outlying lesser islands, between which
fires the men and the beasts to be sacrificed were to pass;
from whence came the proverb, 'Between Bel's two
fires,' meaning one in a great strait, not knowing how to
extricate himself. One of the fires was on the cairn, and
the other on the ground. On the eve of the 1st of November
all the people, out of a religious persuasion instilled into
them by the Druids, extinguished their fires. Then every
master of a family was religiously obliged to take home a
portion of the consecrated fire, and to kindle the fire
anew in his house, which for the ensuing year was to be
lucky and prosperous. Any man who had not paid all
his last year's dues to the Druids was neither to have a
spark of this holy fire from the cairns, nor dared any of his
neighbours let him take the benefit of theirs, under pain
of excommunication; which, as managed by the Druids,
was worse than death. If, therefore, he would live the
winter out, he must pay the Druids' dues by the last day
of October. The Midsummer fires and sacrifices were to
obtain a blessing on the fruits of the earth, now becoming
ready for gathering; as those on the 1st of May, that they
might prosperously grow; and those on the last of
October were a thanksgiving for finishing their harvest.
But in all of them regard was had to the several degrees
of increase and decrease in the heat of the sun. At the
cairn fires it was customary for the lord of the place, or
his son, or some other person of distinction, to take the
entrails of the sacrificed animal into his hands, and walking bare-foot over the coals thrice, after the flames had
ceased, to carry them to the Druid, who waited in a whole
skin at the altar. If the fire-treader escaped harmless, it
was reckoned a good omen, and welcomed with loud
acclamations; but if he received any hurt, it was deemed

unlucky both to the community and to himself."* In
Ireland, May-day is called *la na Beal tina,* and its eve,
neen na Beal tina—*i.e.,* the day and eve of Beal's fire,
from its having been in heathen times consecrated to the
god Beal, or Belus. The ceremony practised on May-
day Eve, of making the cows leap over lighted straw or
faggots, has been generally traced to the worship of this
deity.†

The Irish have ever been worshippers of fire and of Baal,
and are so to this day. The chief festival in honour of the sun
and fire is upon the 21st [24th] June, when the sun arrives at
the summer solstice, or rather begins its retrograde motion.
" At the house where I was entertained, in the summer of
1782, it was told me that we should see at midnight
the most singular sight in Ireland, which was *the lighting
of fires in honour of the sun.* Accordingly, exactly at midnight, the fires began to appear ; and, going up to the leads
of the house, which had a widely-extended view, I saw,
on a radius of thirty miles all around, the fires burning on
every eminence. I learned from undoubted authority that
the people danced round the fires, and at the close went
through these fires, and made their sons and daughters,
together with their cattle, pass the fire ; and the whole was
conducted with religious solemnity."‡　　Bonfires are still
made on Midsummer Eve in the northern parts of England and in Wales. The 1st of November was considered
among the ancient Welsh as the conclusion of summer,
and was celebrated with bonfires, accompanied with ceremonies suitable to these events, and some parts of Wales
still retain these customs. Dr. Jamieson, in his *Dictionary
of the Scottish Language,* mentions a festival called *Beltane*

　　* Toland's *History of the Druids.*
　　† Hone's *Every-Day Book,* vol. i. p. 594.
　　‡ *Gentleman's Magazine.* February, 1795.

or *Beltein,* annually held in Scotland on Old May Day (May 13th). A town in Perthshire is called *Tillee Beltein* —*i.e.,* the eminence or high place of the fire of Baal. Near it are two Druidical Temples of upright stones, with a well adjacent to one of them, still held in great veneration for its sanctity. The doctor describes the drawing of bits of a cake, one part of which is made perfectly black with charcoal, and he who draws the black bit is considered as " devoted to Baal, and is obliged to leap three times through the flame." Pennant, in his *Tour in Scotland,* gives a like account, with other ceremonies. The custom existed in the Isle of Man on the eve of the 1st of May, of lighting *two* fires on a hill-top, in honour of the pagan god Baal, and of driving cattle between those fires, as an antidote against murrain or any pestilent distemper for the year following. It was also customary to light these fires on St. John's Eve (June 23rd), and up to the present time a stranger is surprised to see on this day, as evening approaches, fires springing up in all directions around him, accompanied with the blowing of horns and other rejoicings.* Macpherson notices the *Beltein* ceremonies in Ireland, and adds, "Beltein is also observed in Lancashire." On Horwich Moor are two heaps of stones, or cairns, which are called by the country people "The Wilder Lads." It is believed that on May Day Eve the Druids made prodigious fires on cairns, situated as these are, on lofty eminences, which being every one in sight of some other like fire, symbolized a universal celebration. These fires were in honour of *Beal,* or *Bealan,* latinized into *Belenus,* by which name the Gauls and their colonies denoted the sun ; and to this time the first day of May is by the Irish called *La Bealtine,* or the Day of Belen's Fire.

---

* Mr. William Harrison's notes on Waldron's *Description of the Isle of Man,* p. 125.

It bears a like name among the Highlanders of Scotland, and in the Isle of Man.*

The last evening in October was called the "Teanlay Night," or "The Fast of All Souls." At the close of that day, till of late years, the hills which encircle the Fylde, shone brightly with many a bonfire; the mosses of Marton, &c., rivalling them with their fires, kindled for the avowed object of succouring their friends, whose souls were supposed to be detained in purgatory. A field near Poulton in which the mummery of the "Teanlay" was once celebrated (a circle of men standing with bundles of straw, raised on high with forks), is named "Purgatory" by the old inhabitants. Formerly this custom was not confined to one village or town of the Fylde district, but was generally practised as a sacred ceremony.†

BOGGARTS, GHOSTS, AND HAUNTED PLACES.

What is a Boggart? A sort of ghost or sprite. But what is the meaning of the word Boggart? Brand says that "in the northern parts of England, ghost is pronounced *gheist* and *guest*. Hence *bar-guest*, or *bar-gheist*. Many streets are haunted by a guest, who assumes many strange appearances, as a mastiff-dog, &c. It is a corruption of the Anglo-Saxon *gast*, spiritus, anima." Brand might have added that *bar* is a term for gate in the north, and that all the gates of York are named "bars," so that a *bar-gheist* is literally a gate-ghost; and many are the tales of strange appearances suddenly seen perched on the top of a gate or fence, whence they sometimes leaped upon the shoulders of the scared passenger. Drake, in his

---

* Hampson's *Medii Ævi Kalendarium*, vol. i. p. 252.
† Rev. W. Thornber's *History of Blackpool.*

E

Eboracum, says (Appendix, p. 7), " I have been so frightened with stories of the *barguest* when I was a child, that
I cannot help throwing away an etymology upon it. I
suppose it comes from Anglo-Saxon *burh,* a town, and
gast, a ghost, and so signifies a town sprite. N.B.—*Guest*
is in the Belgic and Teutonic softened into *gheist* and
geyst." The "Boggart Hole" therefore means the hollow haunted by the bar-gheist or gate-ghost.

BOGGART HOLE CLOUGH.

" Not far from the little snug, smoky village of Blakeley
or Blackley, there lies one of the most romantic of dells,
rejoicing in a state of singular seclusion, and in the
oddest of Lancashire names, to wit, the 'Boggart Hole.'
[In the present generation, by pleonasm, the place is
named "Boggart Hole Clough."] Rich in every requisite for
picturesque beauty and poetical association, it is impossible
for me (who am neither a painter nor a poet) to describe
this dell as it should be described ; and I will, therefore,
only beg of thee, gentle reader, who, peradventure, mayst
not have lingered in this classical neighbourhood, to fancy
a deep, deep, dell, its steep sides fringed down with hazel,
and beech, and fern, and thick undergrowth, and clothed
at the bottom with the richest and greenest sward in the
world. You descend, clinging to the trees, and scrambling
as best you may, and now you stand on haunted ground !
Tread softly, for this is the Boggart's Clough, and see, in
yonder dark corner, and beneath the projecting mossy
stone, where that dusky sullen cave yawns before us, like
a bit of Salvator's best, there lurks that strange elf, the
sly and mischievous Boggart. Bounce ! I see him coming;
oh no, it was only a hare bounding from her form ; there

it goes—there !"—Such is the introduction to a tale of a
boggart, told by Crofton Croker, in Roby's *Traditions of
Lancashire;* but which, if memory serve us faithfully,
is but a localized version of a story told of an Irish
sprite, and also of a Scotch brownie; for in all three tales
when the farmer and his family are " flitting " in order to
get away from the nocturnal disturbance, the sprite pops
up his head from the cart, exclaiming, " Ay, neighbour,
we're flitting !" Tradition, which has preserved the name
of the clough selected by the Lancashire boggart for his
dômicile, has failed to record any particular pranks of
this individual elf, and we can only notice this charming
little clough, as conveying by its popular name the only
remaining vestige of its lost traditions. Perhaps the best
story of this clough is that graphically told by Bamford*
of three friends seeking by a charm (consisting in gathering three grains of St. John's fernseed there), to win for
one of them the love of a damsel who was indifferent to
him.

BOGGARTS OR GHOSTS IN OLD HALLS.

There is scarcely an old house, or hall, of any antiquity
in Lancashire, that cannot boast of that proud distinction
over the houses of yesterday, a ghost or boggart. *Radcliffe
Tower* was haunted by a black dog; perhaps in commemoration of the Fair Ellen of Radcliffe, who, by order of her
stepmother, was murdered by the master cook, and cut
up small, and of her flesh a venison pasty made for her
father's dinner !

Smithells Hall, near Bolton, was formerly haunted by
the ghost of the martyr George Marsh, whose stamped
footstep indenting a flagstone, is still shown there.

* *Passages in the Life of a Radical,* vol. i. p. 130

Ince Hall stands about a mile from Wigan, on the left-hand of the high road to Bolton. It is a very conspicuous object, its ancient and well-preserved front—one of those black and white half-timbered façades now almost confined to the two counties palatine of Lancashire and Cheshire—generally attracting the notice and inquiry of travellers. About a mile to the south-east stands another place of the same name, once belonging to the Gerards of Bryn. The manor is now the property of Charles Walmsley, Esq., of Westwood, near Wigan. The two mansions *Ince Hall* and *Ince Manor House*, are sometimes confounded together in topographical inquiries; and it is not now certain to which of them properly belongs a tradition about a forged will and a ghost, on which Mr. Roby has founded a very graphic story, in his *Traditions of Lancashire*. There are the Boggart of *Clegg Hall*, near Rochdale; the *Clayton Hall* Boggart, Droylsden; the *Clock House* Boggart, in the same neighbourhood; the *Thackergate* Boggart, near Alderdale; and many others : indeed they are too numerous for us to attempt a full enumeration. Mr. Higson observes* that few sombre or out-of-the-way places, retired nooks and corners, or sequestered by-paths, escaped the reputation of being haunted. Many domiciles had their presiding boggart, and *feeorin'* [fairies] swarmed at every turn of the dark old lanes, and arch-boggarts held revel at every " three-road-end." After dusk, each rustle of the leaves, or sigh of the night wind through the branches, to the timid wayfarer heralded the instant and unceremonious appearance of old wizards and witches, " Nut Nans," and "Clapcans," or the terrific exploits of headless trunks, alias " men beawt yeds," or other traditionary "sperrits," hobgoblins, and sprites,

* *History of Droylsden,* p. 67.

or the startling semblances of black dogs, phantoms, and other indescribable apparitions. Aqueous nymphs or *nixies,* yclept "Grindylow," and "Jenny Green Teeth," lurked at the bottom of pits, and with their long, sinewy arms dragged in and drowned children who ventured too near. On autumnal evenings, the flickering flame (carburetted hydrogen, spontaneously ignited) of the "Corpse Candle," "Will-o'-th'-Wisp," or "Jack" or "Peg-a-Lantern" (for the sex was not clearly ascertained), performed his or her fantastic and impossible jumps in the plashy meadows near Edge Lane, to the terror of many a simple-minded rustic. Fairies, also, were believed to commit many depredations; such as eating the children's porridge, nocturnally riding out the horses, loosing the cows in the shippon, or churning the milk whilst "calving," by the fireside, and stealing the butter; and hence, behind many a door, as yet observable in Clayton, both of dwelling and shippon, was carefully nailed a worn horse-shoe, believed to be a potent counter-charm or talisman against their freaks and fancies. There were certain localities in the township of Droylsden notorious as the rendezvous or favourite promenades of boggarts and feeorin', which after nightfall few persons could muster pluck sufficient to linger in, or even pass by, for—

> "Grey superstition's whisper dread,
> Debarr'd the spot to vulgar tread."

Manifestly pre-eminent was "th' owd Green Lone," which "Jem Hill, th' king o' Dreighlesdin," used to assert "swaarmt wi' fairees, witches, un' boggerts, un' which nob'dy could mester bur hissel'." The boggart located at Thackergate, near Alderdale, has well-nigh scared many a sober person out of his senses. Herds of four-footed boggarts used to issue from a pit at East End, in form re-

sembling " great big dhogs, wi' great glarin' een, as big
as tay-cups." The boggart at the croft-tenter's lodge
(South) Clock-house, as fancy dictated, stalked through
the chamber and stripped the bedclothes off the sleepers;
or, assuming gigantic proportions and snow-white vest-
ments, perched in the solemn yew-tree, a startling object
by contrast. At last, being exorcised by an array of
divines, it was *laid* for a time, beneath its favourite tree.
A field-path from Fairfield to Ashton Hill-lane was
nightly traversed by a being of another world, mostly representing a shadowy lady, draped according to whim,
either in a loose white robe, or in rustling black silk. For
a certain distance she glided in advance of the pedestrian,
and then, by suddenly vanishing, most likely left his hair
standing on end. At one of the Greenside farms a murder
was said to have been committed in the shippon; and the
exact spot was supposed to be indicated by the impossi-
bility of securely fastening a cow in one particular boose;
for, however carefully its occupant was chained overnight,
next morning she was sure to be found at large, and once
was actually discovered on the shippon balks. Thither, it
was believed, the cow had been carried by supernatural
agency; but, be that as it may, it was necessary to lower
her cautiously down, with the aid of ropes and blocks.
At a cottage adjoining, a boggart varied its amusements
by drumming on the old oaken chest, still preserved; or,
growing emboldened, shook the hangings of the bed, or
rustled amongst the clothes; the alarmed occupants sometimes in despair rolling up the coverlet, and unavailingly
whirling it at their invisible tormentor. At a neighbouring farm-house, amongst other vagaries, the boggart
would snatch up the infant, whilst asleep between its
parents, and, without awakening them, would harmlessly
deposit it on the hearthstone, downstairs. " Clayton

Ho' " [Hall] was of course honoured with a boggart,which at dead of night diversified its pranks by snatching the clothes from the beds, trailing heavy iron weights on the floors, or rattling ponderous chains through the crazy apartments. These pranks becoming insufferable, the help of a clergyman from the parish church was obtained; and fortunately, with the aid of counter-spells and incantations, he succeeded in *laying* the spirit for ever, declaring that,

> " Whilst ivy climbs and holly is green,
> Clayton Hall Boggart shall no more be seen."

Even yet one room in the mansion is named "the Bloody Chamber," from some supposed stains of human gore on the oaken floor planks; which, however, in reality are only natural red tinges of the wood, denoting the presence of iron. Even since the formation of the new road, J. W——, the last of the ancient race of boggart-seers in the township, used to combat with feeorin' between East End and Droylsden toll-gate; but as he died a few years ago without bequeathing his gift, he (happily) carried with him his mantle to the grave. At a period just within memory, oft, after sunset, has the weary and tardy pedestrian quickened his speed on approaching some lonely place, by remembering how its tutelar spirit or Boggart could assume at will the shape of a rabbit, dog, bear, or still more fearful form. On its appearance, of course, the wayfarer fled in affright, and from fear and unwonted exertion, often reached home utterly exhausted. Next day the story would be widely circulated through the thinly populated district, detailing at length (and of course gathering minuteness and improvement in its transmission), how "Owd Yethurt o' Grunsho," or "Lung Tum woife," " th' neet afore wur welly ta'en by a great black Boggart, wi' great lung hurms, un' a whiskin' tail, un' yure as black as soot, un' rowlin' e'en as big as saucers." The decadence of all these old superstitions is to be attributed to a variety of causes. Straight, well-paved roads; increased intellectual activity in useful channels, informing the minds of one locality with the ideas of another, the publication of scientific works; and lastly, according to one aged unbeliever, the introduction of " Owd Ned [the steam-engine], un' lung chimblies; fact'ry folk havin' summat else t'mind nur wanderin' ghosts un' rollickin' sperrits." The same authority archly declared as a clincher, " There's no Boggarts neaw, un' iv ther' were, folk han grown so wacken, they'd soon catch 'em." *

HOUSE BOGGARTS, OR LABOURING GOBLINS.

These humbler classes of boggarts are by turns both useful and troublesome to the farmers of the district where they choose to reside. Syke Lumb Farm, near Black-burn, is reputed to be still visited by one of these anoma-lous beings, and many of his mad pranks are still talked of and believed in the neighbourhood. When in a good humour, this noted goblin will milk the cows, pull the hay, fodder the cattle, harness the horses, load the carts, and stack the crops. When irritated by the utterance of some unguarded expression or mark of disrespect, either from the farmer or his servants, the cream-mugs are smashed to atoms; no butter can be obtained by churn-ing; the horses and other cattle are turned loose or driven into the woods; two cows will sometimes be found fas-tened in the same stall; no hay can be pulled from the mow ; and all the while the wicked imp sits grinning with delight upon one of the cross-beams in the barn. At

* Mr. John Higson's *Notices of Droylsden.*

other times the horses are unable to draw the empty carts across the farm-yard; if loaded, they are upset; whilst the cattle tremble with fear, not at any visible cause. Nor do the inmates of the house experience any better or gentler usage. During the night the clothes are said to be violently torn from off the beds of the offending parties, whilst invisible hands drag these individuals down the stone stairs by the legs, one step at a time, after a more uncomfortable manner than we need describe. Hothershall Hall, near Ribchester, was formerly the scene of similar exploits; but the goblin is understood to have been "laid" under the roots of a large laurel tree at the end of the house, and will not be able to molest the family so long as the tree exists. It is a common opinion in that part of the country that the roots have to be moistened with milk on certain occasions, in order to prolong its existence, and also to preserve the power of the spell under which the goblin is laid. None but the Roman Catholic priesthood are supposed to have the power of "laying an evil spirit," and hence they have always the honour to be cited in our local legends. Sometimes, too, they have the credit of outwitting the goblins; and many an old farm residence has the reputation of having thus been freed from these imps of darkness till they can spin a rope from the sands of the Ribble. The mansion at Towneley does not escape the imputation of having its "*Boggart*," although its visits are now limited to once in seven years, when its thirst for vengeance has to be satisfied by the untimely death of one of the residents at the Hall. A Sir John Towneley is supposed to have injured the poor of the district, nearly four hundred years ago, by "laying-in" a considerable portion of common to his park, and, as a punishment for this offence, his soul is said to haunt the scenes of his oppression. The peasantry still aver "that the old

knight's spirit, being unable to rest, wanders about the
mansion, and may be heard over the very parts taken in,
crying, in most piteous tones—

> "Be warned! Lay out! Be warned! Lay out!
> Around Hore-law and Hollin-hey clough:
> To her children give back the widow's cot,
> For you and yours there is still enough."*

The popular story of "The Boggart Flitting" is common to both Lancashire and Yorkshire; and indeed to
most of the nations in the North of Europe.

Of boggarts the Rev. William Thornber observes,† that
there were several different kinds, having their haunts in
that part of the Fylde near Blackpool; as, for instance,
the wandering ghost of the homicide or the suicide; that
of the steward of injustice, or that of the victim of a cruel
murder; again, the lubber-fiends, the horse-boggarts, and
the house-boggarts, or industrious, yet mischievous imps,
haunting dwellings. He names, "The headless Boggart
of White-gate Lane," as a sample of the first class. So
was "The Boggart of Staining Hall," near Blackpool,
said to be the wandering ghost of a Scotchman who was
murdered there near a tree, which has since marked the
deed by perfuming the soil around with a sweet odour of
thyme. Of another kind were those whose appearance
was the forerunner of death in some families. The
Walmsleys, of Poulton-le-Fylde, he adds, were haunted
by a boggart of this description, always making its appearance with alarming noises before the decease of one of the
family.

Of the lubber-fiends, house-boggarts, or brownies, so

---

* See *Pictorial History of Lancashire*, p. 189, and Whittaker's
History of Whalley, p. 342.
　　　　　† *History of Blackpool*, p. 332.

strikingly described by Milton,* Mr. Thornber mentions the ancient one of Rayscar and Inskip, which at times kindly housed the grain, collected the horses, and got them ready for the market; but at other times played the most mischievous pranks. The famous "Boggart of Hackensall Hall" had the appearance of a huge horse, which was very industrious if treated with kindness. Every night it was indulged with a fire, before which it was frequently seen reclining; and when deprived of this indulgence by neglect, it expressed its anger by fearful outcries.

HORNBY PARK MISTRESS AND MARGARET BRACKIN.

The following story is told and believed by some persons in Hornby. The Park Mistress may be supposed to be the ghost of Lady Harrington, who committed murder three hundred years ago. Margaret Brackin was born in 1745, and died in 1795. The dialect is that of the locality:—

> "In days that oud folks tell on still,
>   Meg Brackin went up Windy Bank;
> Shou lated kinlin' on the hill,
>   Till owr t' Lake Mountains t' sun it sank.

---

* In his *L'Allegro*, where he

> "Tells how the drudging goblin sweat
> To earn the cream-bowl duly set,
> When, in one night, ere glimpse of morn,
> His shad'wy flail had thresh'd the corn,
> That ten day-labours could not end;
> Then lies him down the *lubber-fiend*,
> And stretch'd out all the chimney's length,
> Basks at the fire his hairy strength,
> And, cropful, out of doors he flings,
> Ere the first cock his matin rings.'

Nat lang at efter t' sun was set,
    And shou hed fill'd her brat wi' sticks.
Shou sid aside at t' Park wood yett,
    A woman stan'in mang the wicks.

T' leaves on t' trees, they owm'ered t' land,
    And fadin' was the summer light,
When Marget sid that woman stand
    Donn'd like a ghoost o' oor iᵃ white.

Marget was fear'd, but spak and ex'd,
    'Hey Missis! let me gang wi' ye,
I hope as that ye'll nut be vext,
    But it is gitten dark and dree.'

T' Park Mistress e'en shin'd o' wi' leet;
    Shou whyatly cam te Marget's side;
T' gerss didn't bend underneath her feet;
    Shou seem'd in t' air te float and glide.

As soon's shou cam whare Marget stood,
    Shou gript a tight houd on her hand;
Shou led her first intul t' Park wood,
    Then back and forret o' owr t' land.

They kept na road, they kept na path,
    They went thro' brackins, scrogs, and briar,
Marget shou soon was out of breath,
    But t' lady didn't seem te tire.

They baath com down te Wenning's brink,
    And Marget's throat was dry wi' dread,
But shou dursn't ex te stop and drink,
    Saa forret still that woman led.

Owr shillar and rough staans they trod,
    Intu t' Wenning, then out fra t' stream;
Surlie their walkin' wasn't snod,
    T' way they travell'd was naan saa weam.

Marget lous'd t' strings of her brat,
    And trail'd it gerss and bushes through,
Till deg'd and damp and wet it gat;
    Then suck'd it out for t' cooling dew.

Fra Weaver's Ayr they went up t' wood,
    Now gaain' straight and then aslant,
They niver stopt, they niver stood,
    But raac'd up t' brow saa rough and brant.

Marget could niver gradely say
  Where nesht wi' t' ghoost shou went that neet;
On Windy Bank, when it was day,
  They fun' her liggin, spent wi' freet.

Marget hed been stout and throddy,
  But t' walk she tuk that summer neet,
Left lile fatness on her body;
  At efter shou was thin and leet."

———◆———

BOGGARTS IN THE NINETEENTH CENTURY.

Having fallen into conversation with a working man on
our road to Holme Chapel, we asked him if people in
those parts were now ever annoyed by beings of another
world. Affecting the *esprit fort*, he boldly answered,
"Noa! the country's too full o' folk;" while his whole
manner, and especially his countenance, as plainly said
"Yes!" A boy who stood near was more honest. " O,
yes !" he exclaimed, turning pale; "the Boggart has
driven William Clarke out of his house; he flitted last
Friday." "Why," I asked; "what did the Boggart do ?"
"O, he wouldn't let 'em sleep; he stripp'd off the
clothes." "Was that all ?" "I canna' say," answered
the lad, in a tone which showed he was afraid to repeat
all he had heard; "but they're gone, and the house is
empty. You can go and see for yoursel', if you loike.
Will's a plasterer, and the house is in Burnley Wood, on
Brown Hills."*

Edwin Waugh, in his story of " *The Grave of Grislehurst Boggart,*"† says, the most notable boggart of the hilly
district towards Blackstone Edge, was the Clegg Ho'
Boggart, still the theme of many a winter's tale among

* *Pictorial History of Lancashire.*
† *Sketches of Lancashire Life*, p. 192.

the people of the hills above Clegg Hall. The proverb,
"Aw 'm heere agen, like Clegg Ho' Boggart," is common there, and in all the surrounding villages. . . . Boggarts
appear, however, to have been more numerous than they
are now upon the country side, when working people wove
what was called "one lamb's wool" in a day; but when
it came to pass that they had to weave "three lambs'
wools" in a day, and the cotton trade arose, boggarts, and
fairies, and feeorin' of all kinds, began to flee away from
the clatter of shuttles. As to the Grislehurst Boggart,
here is part of the story as told to Waugh, or by him :—
"Whau it isn't aboon a fortnit sin' th' farmer's wife at the
end theer yerd seed summat i' th' dyhed time o' th' neet ;
an' hoo war welly thrut eawt o' bed, too, besides—so
then " . . "Th' pranks 'at it's played abeawt this plaze at
time an' time, 'ud flay ony wick soul to yer tell on
. . . . . . unyawkin' th' byes, an' turnin' carts an' things
o'er i' th' deep neet time ; an' shiftin' stuff up and deawn
th' heawse when folk are i' bed ; it's rayther flaysome yo
may depend."

———◆———

CHARMS AND SPELLS.

THESE may be placed in two classes — those directed
against evil beings, witchcraft, &c., and those which may
be termed in their object curative of "all the ills that
flesh is heir to." First as to

CHARMS AND SPELLS AGAINST EVIL BEINGS.

These are usually supplied for a consideration by
the fortune-tellers, astrologers, or "wise men" of a neighbourhood. The following is a correct copy of one of
these documents which was found over the door of a
house in the neighbourhood of Burnley. Its occupier had

experienced "ill luck," and he thus sought protection from
all evil-doers :—

"Sun, Moon, Mars, Mercury, Jupiter, Venus, Saturn,
Trine, Sextile, Dragon's Head, Dragon's Tail, I charge
you all to gard this hause from all evils spirits whatever,
and gard it from all Desorders, and from aney thing being
taken wrangasly, and give this famaly good Ealth &
Welth."

Another individual, well known to the writer, was so
far convinced that certain casualties that happened to his
cattle arose from the practice of witchcraft, that he un-
consciously resorted to Baal-worship, and consumed a live
calf in the fire, in order to counteract the influences of his
unknown enemies. At the same time, almost every door
about his house had its horse-shoe nailed to it as a charm,
to protect all within it from demons and witches.

A CHARM, WRITTEN IN CYPHER, AGAINST WITCHCRAFT AND EVIL SPIRITS.

Early in the nineteenth century, some men engaged in
pulling down a barn, or shippon, at West Bradford, about
two miles north of Clitheroe, were attracted by seeing a
small square piece of wood fall from one of the beams,
and from it dropped a paper, folded as a small letter, but
measuring, when opened, $7\frac{1}{4}$ by 6 inches. A sort of
superscription was in large and unknown characters, and
inside the paper was nearly covered with a species of
hieroglyphics, mixed with strange symbols; and in the
top left corner a table or square of thirty-six small squares,
filled with characters in red ink, the great bulk of the
writing being in black ink. The charm belongs to
Jeremiah Garnett, Esq., of Roefield, Clitheroe, and it was

first deciphered by his brother, the late Rev. Richard
Garnett, of the British Museum, in May, 1825. It is this
gentleman's explanation, with a very few additions and
corrections by the present writer, the substance of which
is now appended:—The table in the top corner is a sort
of magic square, called by astrologers "The Table of the
Sun." It consists of six rows of six small squares each,
and is so arranged that the sum of the figures in every
row of six squares, whether counted vertically, horizontally,
or diagonally, amounts to 111, and the sum total of the
table to 666—a favourite magical number, being that of
"the beast."* To mystify the thing as much as possible the numerals are expressed by letters, or rather by a
sort of cypher, chiefly formed from the Greek alphabet.
Thus 1 is represented by a; $2 = e$; $3 = i$; $4 = o$; $5 = u$;
$6 = l$; $7 = \acute{m}$; $8 = n$; $9 = r$; and $o = z$. In a tablet, or
space at the top of the paper, flanking this table, are five
mystical characters, or symbols, in red ink. The first consists of the symbols of the sun, and of the constellation
Leo, which, in astrology, is "the sun's own house," and
where, of course, he is supposed to have the greatest
power. A word in black-ink cyphers, under these
symbols, is *Machen,* the cabalistic name of "the third
[or fourth] heaven;" and the Archangel Michael being
supposed to preside over the sphere [and to be the "Angel
of the Lord's Day"], his seal, or cypher, is introduced
below these symbols—a series of joined lines and swirls,
like some long word written in one of the older English
shorthands. [This figure will be found under "The
Lord's Day," in the Heptameron of one Peter de Albano.]
In cyphers below, in black ink, is written his name,
"Michael." The next cabalistic character represents

---

* *Revelation,* xiii. 18.

" the *Intelligence* of the Sun," and over it, in cypher or Greek letters, is written " intelligence." Under this is another cabalistic symbol, denoting the " Spirit of the Sun," the word "spirit" being written within it. In astrology, every planet is supposed to have two beings, or spirits, attached to it, and called its Intelligence and its Spirit. The last figure (which contains in a sort of quartering the word *sigil,* seal) is " the seal of the Sun" himself, in astrological language. All these symbols show that the charm was meant to be put in operation on a Sunday, that being the day of the Archangel Michael, as well as of the sun. These symbols and table occupy the upper third of the paper, the remaining two-thirds being filled with the words of the charm itself, in fourteen lines, of a sort of cypher-writing, in which the five vowels are represented by a sort of arbitrary character, as are most of the consonants, g, l, m, n, and p, being written as Greek letters. The fourteen lines may be thus rendered in ordinary letters; and it may be supposed that whoever pronounces the incantation, makes the sign of the cross wherever it is indicated in the writing :—

Line 1. " apanton [or awanton] + hora + camab. + naadgrass + pynavet ayias + araptenas.

2 " + quo + signasque + payns [or pagns ? pagus] + sut gosikl + tetragrammaton +

3. " inverma + amo + θ [apparently an abbreviation for *Theos,* God] + dominus + deus + hora + [here a hole in the paper has destroyed a word] + fiat + fiat + fiat +

4. " ut dicitur decimo septimo cápitulo Sancti Matthæi a vigesimo carmine

5. " fide demoveatis montes, fiat secundum fidem, si sit, vel fuerit

6. " ut cunque fascinum vel dæmon habitat vel perturbat hanc

7. " personam, vel hunc locum, vel hanc bestiam, ad-
juro te, abìre

8. " Sine perturbatione, molestia, vel tumultu minime,
nomine

9. " Patris, et Filii, et Spiritus Sanctu.　Amen.　Pater
noster qui es

10. " in cœlis, sanctificetur nomen tuum, veniat regnum
tuum, fiat voluntas

11. " tuo, sicut in cœlo etiam in terra, panem nostrum
quotidianum da

12. " nobis in diem, et remitte nobis peccata nostra,
etenim ipsi

13. " remittimus omnibus qui nobis debent; et ne nos
inducas in tentat-

14. " -ionem, sed libera noṣ a malo.　Fiat."

It will be seen that the first three lines of this charm
are a sort of gibberish, with an admixture of Greek and
Latin words, constituting in itself a charm, supposed to be
efficacious in expelling or restraining evil spirits.　With
the fourth line, then, we begin our translation.

" As it is said in the seventeenth chapter of St. Matthew,
at the twentieth verse, ' By faith ye may remove mountains : be it according to [my] faith,'* if there is, or ever
shall be, witchcraft [or enchantment] or evil spirit, that
haunts or troubles this person, or this place, or this beast
[or these cattle], I adjure thee to depart, without disturbance, molestation, or trouble in the least, in the name
of the Father, and of the Son, and of the Holy Ghost.

* This is not a literal quotation.　The verse runs thus in the ordinary version : " If ye have faith as a grain of mustard-seed, ye shall
say to this mountain, Remove hence to yonder place, and it shall
remove; and nothing shall be impossible to you."

Amen." [Then follows the Lord's Prayer in Latin, end-ing with the word "Fiat" (be it done), instead of Amen.] These words are endorsed or written outside the paper in two lines :—

"Agla + On [or En] Tetragrammaton."

In a charm cited in the *Heptameron, or Mercurial Ele-ments* of Peter de Abano, these are called "the three secret names." The first two are names given to the Deity by the Jewish cabalists. The third (which is also the last word in the second line of the charm) is one also frequently in use amongst Talmudists and Jewish writers, meaning literally "four-lettered," as descriptive of the sacred and unpronounceable name ("Jehovah," written in Hebrew by four letters). The word is here endorsed, as if to authenticate the whole charm, and to show that it is the production of an artist who understood his business; for "tetragrammaton," and "fiat," are words of such potency, that a charm without them would be of no efficacy whatever. The Rev. Richard Garnett adds to his account of this charm (in May, 1825):—"I should think that the document is of no great antiquity, probably not more than thirty or forty years old. It was doubtless manufactured by some country 'wise man,' a regular dealer in such articles. There are, I believe, several persons within twenty miles of Blackburn, who still carry on a trade of this sort."

———

[In the *Heptameron*, already quoted, is "The Conjura-tion of the Lord's Day," which runs thus :—"I conjure and confirm upon you, ye strong and holy angels of God . . . . . [here follow various names of angels, including those 'who rule in the fourth heaven'], and by the name of his star, which is *Sol*, and by his sign, and by the im-

mense name of the living God, and by all the names aforesaid—I conjure thee, Michael, O! great angel, who art
chief ruler of the Lord's Day," &c.].

Amongst other charms against evil may be named that
of our ancestors, who, when eating eggs, were careful to
break the shells, lest the witches should use them to their
disadvantage. We do the same for a similar reason; it is
accounted unlucky to leave them whole. They avoided
cutting their nails on a Friday, because bad luck would
follow; but we have improved upon their practice, and
lay down the whole theory as follows:—

> " Cut your nails on a Monday, cut them for news;
> Cut them on Tuesday, a new pair of shoes;
> Cut them on Wednesday, cut them for health;
> Cut them on Thursday, cut them for wealth;
> Cut them on Friday, cut them for woe;
> Cut them on Saturday, a journey you'll go;
> Cut them on Sunday, you cut them for evil,
> For all the next week you'll be ruled by the Devil."

Most grandmothers will exclaim, " God bless you!"
when they hear a child sneeze, and they sum up the philosophy of the subject with the following lines, which used
to delight the writer in days of his childhood:—

> " Sneeze on a Monday, you sneeze for danger;
> Sneeze on a Tuesday, you kiss a stranger;
> Sneeze on a Wednesday, you sneeze for a letter;
> Sneeze on a Thursday, for something better;
> Sneeze on a Friday, you sneeze for sorrow;
> Sneeze on a Saturday, your sweetheart to-morrow;
> Sneeze on a Sunday, your safety seek,
> The Devil will have you the whole of the week."

These lines may be taken either as charms or spells to
produce the effect predicted; or as omens or warnings of
the results to follow. In most parts of Lancashire it is
customary for children to repeat the following invocation
every evening on retiring to bed, after saying the Lord's
Prayer and the Apostles' Creed:—

> " Matthew, Mark, Luke, and John,
> Bless the bed that I lie on;
> There are four corners to my bed,
> And four angels overspread,
> Two at the feet, two at the head.
>
> If any ill thing me betide,
> Beneath your wings my body hide.
> Matthew, Mark, Luke, and John,
> Bless the bed that I lie on.   Amen."*

The influence of the *" evil eye"* is felt as strongly in this county as in any other part of the world, and various means are resorted to in order to prevent its effects.   " Drawing blood above the mouth" of the person suspected is the favourite antidote in the neighbourhood of Burnley ; and in the district of Craven, a few miles within the borders of Yorkshire, a person who was well disposed towards his neighbours is believed to have slain a pear-tree which grew opposite his house by directing towards it " the first morning glances" of his evil eye.†   Spitting three times in the person's face; turning a live coal on the fire; and exclaiming, " The Lord be with us," are other means of averting its influence.

In Lancashire our boys spit over their fingers in order

---

* This is noticed by the Rev. W. Thornber in his *History of Blackpool*, p. 99; also in the *Oxford Essays*, 1858, p. 127; and the late Rev. James Dugan, M.A., T.C.D., informed the writer that the Irish midwives in Ulster use a very similar formula when visiting their patients.   They first mark each corner of the house, on the outside, with a cross, and previously to entering repeat the following words :—

> "There are four corners to her bed,
> Four angels at her head :
> Matthew, Mark, Luke, and John,
> God bless the bed that she lies on.
> New Moon, new Moon, God bless me,
> God bless this house and family."

† See Carr's *Craven Glossary*, vol. i. p. 137.—" Look, sir," said Mr. Carr's informant, " at that pear-tree, it wor some years back, sir, a maast flourishin' tree.   Ivvry mornin, as soon as he first oppans the door, that he may not cast his ee on onny yan passin' by, he fixes his een o' that pear-tree, and ye plainly see how it's deed away."

to screw up their courage to the fighting point, or to give them luck in the battle. Sometimes they do this as a sort of asseveration, to attest their innocence of some petty crime laid to their charge. Travellers and recruits still spit upon a stone and then throw it away, in order to insure a prosperous journey. Hucksters, market-people, &c., always spit upon the first money they receive in the morning, in order to insure ready sale and " good luck" during the day. " Hansell (they say) is always lucky when well wet."

The ancients performed certain rites and ceremonies at the changes of the moon ; and hence that luminary has added some curious items to the popular creed. *Old Mother Bunch's Garland* is an authority on these matters, and amongst many other things it teaches expectant females who desire to pry into futurity, to cross their hands on the appearance of the new moon, and exclaim—

> " All hail ! new Moon ; all hail to thee !
> I pray thee, good Moon, declare to me
> This night who my true love shall be."

We have noticed, in the introductory chapter, various other minor charms and spells to avert evil, or " bad luck," and to secure " good luck" or fortune for a coming period, usually a year.

THE CROW CHARM AND THE LADY-BIRD CHARM.

The following charms are repeated by children throughout Lancashire and Yorkshire :—

Crow Charm.

> " Crow, crow, get out of my sight,
> Or else I'll eat thy liver and lights."

Lady-Bird Charm.

> " Lady-bird, lady-bird, eigh [hie] thy way home,
> Thy house is on fire, thy children all roam ;
> Except little Nan, who sits in her pan,
> Weaving gold laces as fast as she can."

I remember as a child sitting out of doors on an evening of a warm summer or autumn day, and repeating the crow charm to flights of rooks, as they winged home to their rookery. The charm was chanted so long as a crow remained in sight, their final disappearing being to my mind strong proof of the efficacy of the charm. The lady-bird charm is repeated to the insect (the *Coccinella septem-punctata* of Linnæus), the common Seven-spotted Lady-bird, to be found in every field and garden during summer. The lady-bird is placed upon the child's open hand, and the charm is repeated until the insect takes to flight. The warmth and moisture of the hand no doubt facilitate this, although the child fully believes in the moving power of the charm. The lady-bird is also known as *lady-cow, cow-lady,* and is sometimes addressed as " *Cusha-cow-lady.*"*

One of the present editors has often joined in the lady-bird charm, in the East Riding of Yorkshire, where it ran—

> " Cusha-coo-lady, fly away home,
> Thy house is a-fire and all thy bairns gone," &c.

PIMPERNEL.

According to a MS. on Magic, preserved in Chetham's Library, Manchester, " the herb pimpernel is good to prevent witchcraft, as Mother Bumby doth affirm;" and the following lines must be used when it is gathered :—

> " Herb pimpernel I have thee found
> Growing upon Christ Jesus' ground;
> The same gift the Lord Jesus gave unto thee,
> When He shed his blood upon the tree.
> Arise up, pimpernel, and go with me,
> And God bless me,
> And all that shall wear thee. Amen."

---

* Mr. Robert Rawlinson in *Notes and Queries*, vol. iv. p. 55.

Say this fifteen days together, twice a day; morning early
fasting, and in the evening full.—(*MS. Ibid.*)

THE MOUNTAIN ASH, OR WICKEN OR WIGGEN TREE.

The anti-witching properties of this tree are held in very
high esteem in the northern counties of England. No
witch will come near it; and it is believed that its smallest
twig crossing the path of a witch, will effectually stop her
career. To prevent the churn being bewitched, so that
the butter will not come, the churn-staff must be made of
the wiggen-tree. So cattle must be protected from
witchery by sprigs of wiggen over or in the shippons. All
honest people wishing to have sound sleep must keep the
witches from their beds by having a branch of wiggen at
their bed-heads.*

The charms against the malevolence of witches and of
evil beings were very numerous. A horse-shoe nailed to
the door protected the family domicile; a *hag*-stone,
penetrated with a hole, and attached to the key of the
stable, preserved the horse within from being ridden by
the witch; and when hung up at the bed-head, was a
safeguard to the master himself. A hot heater, put into
the churn, kept witches and evil beings from spoiling the
cream or retarding the butter. The baking of dough was
protected by a cross, and so was the kneading-trough
barred against fiendly visitation. Another class of charms
was of those used by and amongst the witches themselves.

In the " Confession of James Device, prisoner at Lancaster," charged with being a witch and practising witchcraft, before " William Sands. James Anderton, and

---

* See Hone's *Table Book*, vol. i. p. 674.

Thomas Cowell, Esqrs.," we have the following " charm"
to get *" drink* within one hour after saying the said
prayer :"—

> " Upon Good Friday I will fast while I may,
> Untill I heare them knell
> Our Lord's own bell.
> Lord in his messe
> With his twelve Apostles good;—
> What hath he in his hand?
> Ligh in leath wand :
> What hath he in his other hand?
> Heaven's doore keys.
> Steck, Steck Hell door,
> Let Chrizun child
> Goe to its mother mild.
> What is yonder that casts a light so farrandly?
> Mine own dear Sonne that's naild to the tree.
> He is naild'sore by the head and hand;
> And Holy harne Panne.
> Well is that man
> That Friday spell can,
> His child to learne :—
> A cross of Blue and another of Red,
> As Good Lord was to the Roode.
> Gabriel laid him down to sleep
> Upon the ground of Holy weepe :—
> Good Lord came walking by,
> Sleepest thou, wakest thou, Gabriel?
> No, Lord, I am sted with stick and stake,
> That I can neither sleepe nor wake.
> Rise up, Gabriel, and go with me,
> The stick nor the stake shall never deere thee.
> Sweet Jesus. Our Lord. Amen."

But James Device's charm was not the only one
brought to light in this memorable trial;—the witches
themselves were liable to be bewitched by others of
superior power, nor were their domestic preparations altogether free from the malevolent effects of an envious
practitioner. In these cases *counter charms* were of frequent necessity, and none of these seem to be of greater
efficacy than the following one from the " Examination of
Anne Whittle, *alias* Chattox [a celebrated Lancashire

witch], before Roger Nowell, Esq., of Read, April 2nd,
1612." "A charm to help *drink* that is forespoken or
bewitched."

> " Three biters hast thou bitten.
> The Heart, ill Eye, ill Tongue.
> Three bitter shall be thy Boote,
> Father, Sonne, and Holy Ghost:—at God's name.
> Five Paternosters, five Avies and a Creede,
> In worship of five woundes of our Lorde."

The Scotch appear to have held similar notions on
these subjects with ourselves, for in Sinclair's "*Satan's
Invisible World Discovered*" we find the following charm,
"To preserve the house and those in it from danger at
night:"—

> " Who sains the house the night?
> They that sains it ilk a night,
> Saint Bryde and her brate;
> Saint Colme and his hat;
> Saint Michael and his spear;
> Keep this house from the weir—
> From running thiefe—
> And burning thiefe—
> And from and ill Rea:—
> That be the gate can gae :—
> And from an ill wight:—
> That be the gate can light.
> Nine reeds about the house;
> Keep it all the night.
> What is that what I see,
> So red, so bright, beyond the sea?
> 'Tis he was pierced through the hands,
> Through the feet, through the throat,
> Through the tongue,
> Through the liver and the lung.
> Well is them that well may
> Fast on Good Friday."

CHARMS TO CURE SICKNESS, WOUNDS, CATTLE DISTEMPER, ETC.

Many are the charms and spells which operate against
disease or sickness in two ways—they either ward it off, if

it threaten; or if too late for that, they dispel its virulence, and effect a marvellous cure. No medical man, we are told, will rub ointment on a wound with the forefinger of his right hand, because it is popularly accounted venomous. A dead man's hand is said to have the power of curing wens and other excrescences of the neck. Three spiders, worn about the neck, will prevent the ague. A string with *nine* knots tied upon it, placed about the neck of a child, is reported to be an infallible remedy for the whooping-cough. The same effect also follows from passing the child *nine* times round the neck of a she-ass, according to the popular creed of the county. Formerly silver rings, made from the hinges of coffins, were worn as charms for the cure of fits, or for the prevention of cramp, or even of rheumatism. The superstition continues, though the metal is of necessity changed, few coffins having now hinges of silver. The stranger in Lancashire can be nowhere, in town or country, amongst any considerable number of the humbler classes, without seeing on the fingers of women chiefly, but occasionally of men, what are called galvanized rings, made of two hoops, one of zinc, the other of copper, soldered together. Many wear a belt to charm away rheumatism; brimstone carried about the person is regarded as a sure remedy against cramp; so also is placing the shoes under the bed, the toes peeping outwards. These are the modern charms or cure-alls against disease. Fried mice are yet given to children in some parts of Lancashire, to cure non-retention of urine during sleep.

CHARMS FOR THE TOOTHACHE.

"The following," says the Rev. W. Thornber, of Blackpool, "is a foolish charm, yet much accredited amongst us [in the Fylde] for the toothache:"—

> " Peter sat weeping on a marble stone.
>   Jesus came near and said, ' What aileth thee, O Peter ?'
>   He answer'd and said, ' My Lord and my God !'
>   He that can say this, and believeth it for my sake,
>   Never more shall have the tooth-ache."

Our " wise men" still sell the following charm for the
cure of continued toothache, but it must be worn inside
the vest or stays, and over the left breast :—

" Ass Sant Petter sat at the geats of Jerusalm our
Blessed Lord and Sevour Jesus Crist Pased by and Sead,
What Eleth thee hee sead Lord my Teeth ecketh hee sead
arise and folow mee and thy Teeth shall never Eake Eney
moor.   Fiat + Fiat + Fiat."*

VERVAIN, FOR WOUNDS, ETC.

A magical MS. in Chetham's Library, Manchester, of
the time of Queen Elizabeth, supplies the following metrical prayer, to be said in gathering this herb :—

> " All-hele, thou holy herb, Vervin,
>   Growing on the ground ;
>   In the Mount of Calvary
>   There wast thou found ;
>   Thou helpest many a grief,
>   And stanchest many a wound.
>   In the name of sweet Jesus
>   I take thee from the ground.
>   O Lord, effect the same
>   That I do now go about."

The following lines, according to the same authority,
were to be said when pulling it :—

> ' In the name of God, on Mount Olivet
>   First I thee found ;
>   In the name of Jesus
>   I pull thee from the ground."

---

* Carr's *Glossary*, vol. ii. p. 264.

CHARMS TO STOP BLEEDING.

In an ancient 8vo. MS. volume, described by Dr. Whitaker, in his *History of Whalley*, entitled *Liber Loci Benedicti de Whalley*, commencing with the translation of the convent from Stanlaw (in 1296) and ending about the year 1346, are the following monkish charms (in Latin) for stopping hæmorrhage :—

"*For staunching bleeding from the Nostrils, or from Wounds, an approved remedy.*—O God, be Thou merciful to this Thy servant N., nor allow to flow from his body more than one drop of blood. So may it please the Son of God. So his mother Mary. In the name of the Father, stop O blood! In the name of the Son, stop, O blood! In the name of the Holy Ghost, stop, O blood! In the name of the Holy Trinity.

"*To staunch Bleeding.*—A soldier of old thrust a lance into the side of the Saviour: immediately there flowed thence blood and water,—the blood of Redemption, and the water of Baptism. In the name of the Father + may the blood cease. In the name of the Son + may the blood remain. In the name of the Holy Ghost + may no more blood flow from the mouth, the vein, or the nose."

To particular persons was attached the virtue of stopping bleeding by a word ; and a woman of Marton, near Blackpool, whose maiden name was Bamber, was so celebrated for her success, that she was sought for to stop hæmorrhage throughout a district of twenty miles around.

TOUCHING FOR THE KING'S EVIL.

The records of the Corporation of Preston contain two votes of money, to enable persons to go from Preston to be touched for the evil   Both are in the reign of James II.

In 1682, the bailiffs were ordered to " pay unto James Harrison, bricklayer, 10s. towards the carrying of his son to London, in order to the procuring of his Majesty's touch." And in 1687, when James was at Chester, the council passed a vote that " the bailiffs pay unto the persons undermentioned each of them 5s. towards their charge in going to Chester to get his Majesty's touch : Anne, daughter of Abel Mope, ——— daughter of Richard Letmore."*

CURES FOR WARTS

Steal a piece of meat from a butcher's stall or his basket, and, after having well rubbed the parts affected with the stolen morsel, bury it under a gateway at four lane ends, or, in case of emergency, in any secluded place. All this must be done so secretly as to escape detection ; and as the portion of meat decays, the warts will disappear. This practice is very prevalent in Lancashire, and two of my female acquaintances having tried the remedy, stoutly maintain its efficacy.†

The following superstition prevails in the neighbourhood of Manchester : Take a piece of twine, making upon it as many knots as there are warts to be removed ; touch each wart with the corresponding knot; then bury the twine in a moist place, saying at the same time, " There is none to redeem it besides thee." As the process of decay goes on [in the twine] the warts gradually disappear.‡

A snail hung upon a thorn is another favourite spell against warts ; as the snail wastes away, so do the warts. Again, take a bag of stones, equal in number with the

---

* Wm. Dobson, in *Notes and Queries*, 2nd series, vol. iv. p. 287.
† T. T. W., ibid., vol. ii. p. 68.　　　　‡ H., ibid.

warts to be destroyed, and throw them over the left shoulder; the warts soon quit the thrower. But who-ever chances to pick up one or more of these stones, takes with them as many of the warts, which are thus trans-ferred from the loser to the finder of the stones.

CURE FOR HYDROCEPHALUS IN CATTLE.

Dr. Whitaker mentions what he designates as "one practical superstition" in the district about Pendle, and peculiar to that neighbourhood. "The hydrocephalus (he says) is a disease incident to adolescent animals, and is sup-posed by the shepherds and herdsmen to be contagious; but in order to arrest the progress of the disease, whenever a young beast had died of this complaint, it was usual, and it has, I believe, been practised by farmers yet alive, to cut off the head and convey it for interment into the nearest part of the adjoining county. Stiperden, a de-sert plain upon the border of Yorkshire, was the place of skulls." Whitaker thinks the practice may have origi-nated in some confused and fanciful analogy to the case of Azazel (Numbers xvi. 22), an analogy between the re-moval of sin and disease—that as the transgressions of the people were laid upon the head of the scape-goat, the dis-eases of the herd should be laid upon the head of the deceased animal.*

CATTLE DISORDERS.—THE SHREW TREE IN CARNFORTH.

On an elevation in the township of Carnforth, in the parish of Warton, called Moothaw [? Moot Hall], the ancient Saxon courts were held. Near this place stood

* *History of Whalley.*

the "Shrew Tree" mentioned by Lucas, which, according to rustic superstition, received so much virtue from plugging up a number of living shrews, or field-mice, in a cavity prepared for their reception in the tree, that a twig cut from it, when freely applied to the backs of disordered cattle, would cure them of their maladies.*

CHARMS FOR AGUE.

"Casting out the ague" was but another name for "casting out the devil," for it was his possession of the sufferer that caused the body to shiver and shake. One man, of somewhat better education than his neighbours, acquired a reputation for thus removing the ague by exorcism, and was much resorted to for many years for relief.

STINGING OF NETTLES.

This was at once removed by the saying aloud of some charm in doggerel verse.

JAUNDICE.

Persons in the Fylde district suffering from this disorder were some years ago cured at the rate of a shilling per head, by a person living at the Fold, who, by some charm or incantation, performed on the urine of the afflicted person, suspended in a bottle over the smoke of his fire, was believed to effect most wonderful cures.

TO PROCURE SLEEP BY CHANGING THE DIRECTION OF THE BED.

There are two superstitions respecting restlessness. One is that it is caused by the bed standing north and south.

* Baines's *Lancashire.*

and that it will be cured if the bedstead be so moved as to stand east and west. The other goes further, and says that to effect a perfect remedy, not only must the bedstead range east and west, but that the head must be towards the east. One informant stated that this was because the earth revolved from west to east, or in an easterly course.

THE DEVIL.

The power of the devil, his personal appearance, and the possibility of bartering the soul for temporary gain, must still be numbered among the articles of our popular faith. Repeating the Lord's Prayer backwards is said to be the most effectual plan for "raising the devil;" but when the terms of the bargain are not satisfactory, his exit can only be secured by making the sign of the cross and calling on the name of Christ. In the neighbourhood of Blackburn a story prevails that two threshers once succeeded in raising him through the barn floor; but on their becoming alarmed at their success, he was summarily dismissed by means of a vigorous thrashing on the head with the flails. His partiality for playing at cards has long been proverbial, both in Lancashire and elsewhere. A near relative of the writer firmly believed that the devil had once visited their company when they had prolonged their play into Sunday. How he joined them they never rightly knew, but (as in the Danish legend respecting a similar visit) his presence was first suspected in consequence of his extraordinary "run of good luck;" and a casual detection of his *cloven foot* completed the dispersion of the players. It is not always, however, that he obtains the advantage; for he has more than once been outwitted by a crafty woman or a cunning priest. In the Lancashire tradition we find the poor tailor of Chatburn stipulating for *three* wishes, and, on the advice of his wife, consulting the "holy father of Salley" in his extremity. When the fatal day arrived, he freed himself from the bond by expressing as his last wish, that his tormentor "were riding back to his quarters on a dun horse, never to plague him more." The devil, it is said, gave a yell which was heard to Colne, on finding that he had lost his man. Mr. Roby in his *Traditions*, and the author of the *Pictorial History of Lancashire*, give humorous engravings of this noted ride; and the sign of "The Dule upo' Dun," over the door of the wayside inn, attests the popular belief in the local tradition. From these and many other instances it is evident that we have derived many of these superstitions from the Saxon and Danish settlers in Northumbria. The essential parts of each are identical, and as regards these particular bargains, it may be added as a curious circumstance, that in no case is the bond held to be binding unless it be signed with the blood of the person contracting.*

Offering fowls to evil spirits appears to have been an ancient and wide-spread practice. It was common to sacrifice a cock to the devil. Burns, in his "Address to the Deil," says—"Some cock or cat your rage must stop." Music and dancing are also associated in our popular superstitions with witches, evil spirits, and the devil. The devils, it is said, love music, but dread bells, and have a very delicate sense of smells. In the *True and Faithful Relation of what passed between Dr. Dee and some Spirits*, we learn that the devil appeared to the doctor "as an angel in a white robe, holding a bloody cross in his right hand, the same hand being also bloody," and in this guise he prayed,

* See *Transactions of Historical Society of Lancashire and Cheshire.*

and "anabaptistically bewailed the wickedness of the world."*

RAISING THE DEVIL.

The boys at the Burnley Grammar-school are said to have succeeded on one occasion in raising the devil. They repeated the Lord's Prayer backwards, and performed some incantations by which, as it is said, Satan was induced to make his appearance through a stone flag on the floor of the school-house. After he had got his head and shoulders well out, the boys became alarmed, and began to hammer him down with the poker and tongs. With much ado they drove him back; but the *black mark* he had left on the flag was shown in proof of his appearance until the schoolhouse was repaired, a few years ago, when the floor was boarded over, and the flagstone disappeared.

THE DEVIL & THE SCHOOLMASTER AT COCKERHAM.

It is said that the arch Spirit of Evil once took up his abode in Cockerham, and so scared and disturbed the inhabitants of that quiet place, that at length in public meeting, to consider how to free themselves from this fiendish persecution, they appointed the schoolmaster, as the wisest and cleverest man in the place, to do his best to drive the devil away. Using the prescribed incantation at midnight, the pedagogue succeeded in raising Satan; but when he saw his large horns and tail, saucer eyes, and long claws, he became almost speechless. According to the recognised procedure in such cases, the devil granted him the privilege of setting three tasks, which if he

* Casaubon, extracted from Dee's MSS., P. I., p. 22, fol. 1659.

(Satan) accomplished, the schoolmaster became his prey; if he failed, it would compel the flight of the demon from Cockerham. The first task, to count the number of dewdrops on certain hedges, was soon accomplished; and so was the second, to count the number of stalks in a field of grain. The third task was then proposed in the following words, according to a doggerel version of the tradition :—

> " Now make me, dear sir, a rope of yon sand,
> Which will bear washing in Cocker, and not lose a strand."

Speedily the rope was twisted of fine sand, but it would not stand washing; so the devil was foiled, and at one stride he stepped over the bridge over Broadfleet, at Pilling Moss. The metrical version of the legend is scarcely worth printing.

———◆———

OLD NICK.

According to Scandinavian mythology, the supreme god Odin assumes the name of Nick, Neck, Nikkar, Nikur, or Hnikar, when he acts as the evil or destructive principle. In the character of Nikur, or Hnikudur, a Protean water-sprite, he inhabits the lakes and rivers of Scandinavia, where he raises sudden storms and tempests, and leads mankind into destruction. Nick, or Nickar, being an object of dread to the Scandinavians, propitiatory worship was offered to him; and hence it has been imagined that the Scandinavian spirit of the waters became, in the middle ages, St. Nicholas, the patron of sailors, who invoke his aid in storms and tempests. This supposition (which has a degree of probability almost amounting to certainty) receives countenance from the great devotion still felt by the Gothic nations towards St. Nicholas, to whom many churches on the sea-shore are dedicated. The church of

St. Nicholas, in this situation at Liverpool, was consecrated in 1361; and, says Mr. Baines,* "in the vicinity there formerly stood a statue of St. Nicholas; and when the faith in the intercession of saints was more operative than at present, the mariners were wont to present a peace-offering for a prosperous voyage on their going out to sea, and a wave-offering on their return; but the saint, having lost his votaries, has long since disappeared." The Danish Vikings called the Scandinavian sea-god *Hold Nickar*, which in time degenerated into the ludicrous expression, "Old Nick."†

Another writer on this subject says:—We derive the familiar epithet of "*Old Nick*" from the Norwegian Nök, the Norse Nikr, or the Swedish Neck; and no further proof of their identity is required than a comparison between the attributes possessed in common by all these supernatural beings. The *Nök* is said to require a human sacrifice once a year, and some one is therefore annually missing in the vicinity of the pond or river where this sprite has taken up its abode. The males are said to be very partial to young maidens, whom they seize and drag under the water; whilst those of the opposite sex are quite as attractive and dangerous to the young fishermen who frequent the rivers. The German *Nixes* possess the same attributes. Both sexes have large green teeth; and the male wears a green hat, which is frequently mistaken by his victims for a tuft of beautiful vegetation. He is said to kill without mercy whenever he drags a person down; and a fountain of blood, which shoots up from the surface of the water, announces the completion of the deed. A perfect identification of this with our own popular belief is now easy. Nothing is more common at

* *History of Lancashire*, vol. iv. p. 63.
† Hampson's *Medii Ævi Kal.*, vol. i. p. 74.

present than for children who reside in the country to be cautioned against venturing too near the water's brink, lest " *Green Teeth*" or " *Bloody Bones*" should pull them in. " *Old Nick*" is said to lurk under the shady willows which overhang the deep water; and the bubbles of gas which may be observed escaping from the bottoms of quiet pools are attributed to the movements of the water-sprites which lurk beneath.

DEMONOLOGY.

A recent writer in *Blackwood's Magazine* asks if Demonology " was not a vague spirit-worship, the ancient religion of the bulk of mankind?" " This Demonology " (he continues) " may be said to have been imported into Christianity in its early days. It was the universal belief of the Pagan world, and not easily to be eradicated; as the early Church accepted things pretty much as it found them, and turned them to account; teaching that these objects of heathen awe and reverence were fallen angels, whose power for evil had been permitted to exist uncontrolled till the advent of our Saviour. The early Roman Church elaborately imitated, if it did not exceed, the Greeks and Romans in their demonology. Every class of men had their guardians, who practically represented the *Dii minores* or *minorum gentium;* the hills and dales and woods had their patrons, the successors of the Orcades, Napææ, and the Dryades; every kind of disease, from the toothache to the gout, had its special healer, and even birds and beasts their spiritual protectors." No one who has paid the most passing attention to the folk-lore of this country can have failed to note amongst us, even yet, the remnants of this curious superstition. In 1531, John Cousell, of Cambridge, and John Clarke, of Oxford, two

learned clerks, applied for and obtained from Henry VIII.
a formal license to practise sorcery, and to build churches,
a quaint combination of evil and antidote. They professed power to summon " the sprytes of the ayre," and to
make use of them generally, and particularly in the discovery of treasure and stolen property. Their seventh petition
is to build churches, bridges, and chapels, and to have cog-
nizance of all sciences. One of their petitions refers to a
certain "noyntment" to see the sprytes, and to speak
with them dayly. Strange that Henry VIII. should have
granted this license, seeing that a statute was passed in his
reign, making " witchcraft and sorcery felony, without
benefit of clergy."* Bishop Jewell, preaching before
Queen Anne, on the marvellous increase of witches and
sorcerers, after describing how the victims pined away,
even unto death, loyally concluded his sermon thus, " I
pray God they never practise further than upon the subject." The following charm or spell against St. Vitus's
Dance was, and very likely is still, in use in Devonshire.
It was written on parchment, and carried about by an old
woman so afflicted :—

> " Shake her, good Devil,
> Shake her once well ;
> Then shake her no more,
> Till you shake her in hell."

Some of our laws against sorcery remained unrepealed
a little more than forty years ago. The Irish law against
sorcery was only repealed in 1831. So late as August,
1863, an old man of eighty was flung into a mill-stream
in the parish of Little Hedingham, being what is called
" swimming for a wizard," and he died of his mal-treat-
ment. One curious book on Demonology is entitled " An
Account of Demoniacs, and the power of casting out

* 33 Henry VIII., cap. 8.

Demons, both in the New Testament, and the four first Centuries," by William Whiston, M.A. (London, 1737, 8vo). He observes that " The symptoms of these demoniacal distresses were very different from the symptoms of other diseases, and even included wild raving, irregular convulsions of the body, unnatural contortions ·of the limbs, or dismal malady of the mind, and came upon the unhappy patients by terrible fits of paroxysms, to the amazement of the spectators, and the horrible affection of the possessed, and included the sorest illness and madness in the world." The same symptoms revived in the extraordinary epidemic called the *hystero-demonopathy,* which visited Morzine, in Savoy, in 1857. The persons afflicted were violently and unnaturally convulsed; now rushed phrenetically into the woods, or to the river, now were subject to fits of coma; were insensible to pain; believed themselves to be haunted by evil spirits; were violent, but in their violence injured no one; and exhibited generally symptoms not observed in any known disorder.* The people of Morzine believed themselves possessed by spirits of dead persons, a peculiarity which appears to have occurred in many cases during the prevalence of the epidemic.

DEMON AND GOBLIN SUPERSTITIONS.

Among the more prominent of the demon superstitions prevalent in Lancashire, we may instance that of the *Spectre Huntsmar,* which occupies so conspicuous a place in the folk-lore of Germany and the North. This superstition is still extant in the Gorge of Cliviger, where he is believed to hunt a milk-white doe round the Eagle's Crag in the Vale of Todmorden, on All-Hallow's Eve.

* " The Devils of Morzine," in the *Cornhill Magazine,* April, 1865.

His hounds are said to fly yelping through the air on many
other occasions, and under the local name of " *Gabriel
Ratchets,*" are supposed to predict death or misfortune
to all who hear the sounds.*   The " *Lubber Fiend,*" or
stupid demon, still stretches his hairy length across the
hearth-stones of the farm-houses in the same district, and
the feats of the " *Goblin Builders* " form a portion of the
popular literature of almost every locality.   They are said
to have removed the foundations of Rochdale Church from
the banks of the river Roach, up to their present elevated
position.   Samlesbury Church, near Preston, possesses a
similar tradition.   The " *Demon Pig*" not only determined
the site of St. Oswald's Church, at Winwick, but gave a
name to the parish.   The parochial church at Burnley,
it is said, was originally intended to be built on the site
occupied by the old Saxon Cross in Godly Lane; but,
however much the masons might have built during the
day, both the stones and the scaffolding were invariably
found where the church now stands, on their coming to
work next morning.   The local legend states that on this
occasion, also, the goblins took the form of *pigs*, and a
rude sculpture of such an animal, on the south side of the
steeple, lends its aid to confirm and perpetuate the story.

Our peasantry retain the notion so prevalent in North
Germany, that the *Night-mare* is a demon, which sometimes takes the form of a cat or a dog, and they seek to
counteract its influence by placing their shoes under the
bed with the toes outwards, on retiring to rest.

The *Water Sprites*, believed in by our ancestors in the
north of England, still form a portion of the folk-lore of
Lancashire and Yorkshire.   There is scarcely a stream of
any magnitude in either county which does not possess a

---

* See Roby's *Traditions of Lancashire;* Homerton's *Isles of Loch
Awe* and *Choice Notes: Folk-Lore*, pp. 247-8.

presiding spirit in some part of its course. The stepping-stones at Bungerley, near Clitheroe, are said to be haunted by a malevolent sprite, who assumes almost as many shapes as Proteus of old. He is not known by any particular designation, nor are there any traditions to account for his first appearance; but at least *one* life in every *seven* years is required to appease the anger of the spirit of the Ribble at this place. It was at these stepping-stones that King Henry VI. was treacherously betrayed by a Talbot of Bashall and others; whence may have arisen a tradition of a malevolent spirit at that place.

Our local literature possesses Roby's traditions of " The *Mermaid* of Martin Mere," which has given permanence to the popular notions respecting mermen and mermaids. The *Schrat,* or *Schritel,* of the German nations, is identical with the more ancient *Skrat* of the Scandinavians. He is noted for making game of persons who are out late at night. Occasionally he places himself on a cart, or other vehicle, which then becomes so heavy that the horses are unable to move the load. They begin to tremble and perspire, as if sensible of the presence of something diabolical; but after a short time " *Old Scrat*" slips off behind, and disappears with a malicious laugh. In Lancashire we are no strangers to Old Scrat and his doings. With many the name is merely a synonyme for that of the devil; but our city carters are able to mark the distinction, and have besides a goodly store of anecdotes respecting the heavy loads which their horses have sometimes been compelled to draw, when nothing could be seen except the empty cart. One of them assured me that on such occasions his horses reared, and became almost frantic; their manes stood erect; and he himself could see the wicked imp actually dancing with delight between their ears. Another very respectable person affirms that, not many years ago, as a funeral was proceeding to church, the coffin became so heavy that it could not be carried. On this being made known to a clergyman, who was present, he offered up a short prayer, and commanded Old Scrat to take his own. This was no sooner done than the excessive weight was felt no more, and the corpse was carried forward to the place of interment. Similar superstitions prevail in the more northern cities with but slight variations; and hence sufficiently indicate their common origin. The *Barguest,* or *Barn-ghaist* of the Teutons, is also reported to be a frequent visitor in Lancashire. The appearance of this sprite is considered as a certain death-sign, and has obtained the local names of " *Trash*" and " *Skriker.*" He generally appears to one of the family from whom Death is about to select his victim, and is more or less visible, according to the distance of the event. I have met with persons to whom the barguest [bar-ghaist, *i.e.,* gate-ghost] has assumed the form of a white cow, or a horse; but on most occasions "Trash" is described as having the appearance of a very large dog, with very broad feet, shaggy hair, drooping ears, and eyes " as large as saucers." When walking, his feet make a loud splashing noise, like old shoes in a miry road, and hence the name of " Trash." The appellation " *Skriker*" has reference to the screams uttered by the sprite, which are frequently heard when the animal is invisible. When followed by any individual he begins to walk backwards with his eyes fixed full on his pursuer, and vanishes on the slightest momentary inattention. Occasionally he plunges into a pool of water, and at times he sinks at the feet of the persons to whom he appears with a loud splashing noise, as if a heavy stone were thrown into the miry road. Some are reported to have attempted to strike him with any weapon they had at hand, but there was no substance to receive the blows, although the Skriker kept his ground. He is said to frequent the neighbourhood of Burnley at present, and is mostly seen in Godly Lane, and about the parish church. But he by no means confines his visits to the churchyard, as similar sprites are said to do in other parts of England and Wales.*

DISPOSSESSING A DEMONIAC.

Richard Rothwell, a native of Bolton-le-Moors, born about 1563, a minister of the Gospel, ordained by Dr. Whitgift, Archbishop of Canterbury, who was called by his biographer, the Rev. Stanley Gower, minister of Dorchester—" *Orbis terrarum Anglicarum oculus*" (the eye of our English world), is said to have dispossessed one John Fox, near Nottingham, of a devil; with whom he had a discourse, by way of question and answer, a good while. Such dialogues are said to be frequent amongst the Popish exorcists, but being rare amongst Protestants, is the more to be observed, and not disbelieved, because vouched by so good a man. Mr. Rothwell died at Mansfield, Notts, in 1627, aged sixty-four.†

[There is a long account of this contest with the devil in Rothwell's *Life,* by Gower, pp. 178–183. After the devil had been driven out of him, John Fox was dumb for three years, but afterwards had speech restored to him, and wrote a book about the temptations the devil haunted him with.]

DEMONIACAL POSSESSION IN 1594.

Towards the close of the sixteenth century, seven persons in Lancashire were alleged to be " possessed by evil

* See *Transactions of Lancashire and Cheshire Historical Society.*
† *Magna Britannica,* by Rev. M. S. Cox, p. 1303.

spirits." According to the narrative of the Rev. John Darrell, himself a principal actor in the scene, there lived in 1594 at Cleworth (now called Clayworth), in the parish of Leigh, one Nicholas Starkie, who had only two children, John and Ann; the former ten and the latter nine years of age. These children, according to Mr. Darrell, became possessed with an evil spirit; and John Hartlay, a reputed conjuror, was applied to, at the end of from two to three months, to give them relief, which he effected by various charms, and the use of a magical circle with four crosses, drawn near Mr. Starkie's seat, at Huntroyd, in the parish of Whalley. Hartlay was conjuror enough to discover the difference between Mr. Starkie's table and his own, and he contrived to fix himself as a constant inmate in his benefactor's family for two or three years. Being considered so essential to their peace, he advanced in his demands, till Mr. Starkie demurred, and a separation took place; but not till five other persons, three of them the female wards of Mr. Starkie, and two other females, had become "possessed," through the agency of Hartlay, "and it was judged in the house that whomsoever he kissed, on them he breathed the devil." According to the narrative, all the seven demoniacs sent forth a strange and supernatural voice of loud shouting. In this extremity Dr. Dee, the Warden of Manchester College, was applied to, to exorcise the evil spirits; but he refused to interfere, advising that they should call in some godly preachers, with whom he would, if they thought proper, consult concerning a public or private fast; at the same time he sharply reproved Hartlay for his fraudulent practices. Some remission of violence followed, but the evil spirits soon returned, and Mr. Starkie's house became a perfect bedlam. John Starkie, the son, was "as fierce as a madman, or a mad dog;" his sister Anne was little better; Margaret

Hardman, a gay, sprightly girl, was also troubled, and aspired after all the splendid attire of fashionable life, calling for one gay thing after another, and repeatedly telling her "lad," as she called her unseen familiar, that she would be finer than him. Ellinor, her younger sister, and Ellen Holland, another of Mr. Starkie's wards, were also "troubled;" and Margaret Byrom, of Salford, a woman of thirty-three, who was on a visit at Cleworth, became giddy, and partook of the general malady. The young ladies fell down, as if dead, while they were dancing and singing, and " playing the minstrel," and talked at such a rate that nobody could be heard but themselves. The preachers being called in, according to the advice of Dr. Dee, they inquired how the demoniacs were handled. The "possessed" replied that an angel, like a dove, came from God, and said that they must follow him to heaven, which way soever he would lead them. Margaret Hardman then ran under a bed, and began to make a hole, as she said, that her "lad" (or familiar) might get through the wall to her; and, amongst other of her feats, she would have leaped out of the window. The others were equally extravagant in their proceedings, but when they had the use of their feet, the use of their tongues was taken away. The girls were so sagacious that they foretold when their fits would come on. When they were about any game or sport, they seemed quite happy; but any godly exercise was a trouble to them. Margaret Byrom was grievously troubled. She thought in her fits that something rolled in her inside like a calf, and lay ever on her left side; and when it rose up towards her heart, she thought the head and nose thereof had been full of nails, wherewith being pricked, she was compelled to shriek aloud with very pain and fear; sometimes she barked and howled, and at others she so much quaked that her teeth chattered in her head.

At the sight of Hartlay she fell down speechless, and saw a great black dog, with a monstrous tail and a long chain, running at her open-mouthed. Six times within six weeks the spirit would not suffer her to eat or drink, and afterwards her senses were taken away, and she was as stiff as iron.   Two nights before the day of her examination against Hartlay, who was committed to Lancaster Castle, the devil appeared to her in his likeness, and told her to speak the truth ! On the 16th of March, Maister George More, pastor of Cawlke, in Derbyshire, and Maister John Darrell, afterwards preacher at St. Mary's, in Nottingham, came to Cleworth, when they saw the girls grievously tormented. Jane Ashton, the servant of Mr. Starkie, howled in a supernatural manner—Hartlay had given her kisses, and promised her marriage. The ministers having got all the seven into one chamber, gave them spiritual advice ; but, on the Bible being brought up to them, three or four of them began to scoff, and called it—" Bib-le, Bab-le ; Bible, Bable." The next morning they were got into a large parlour, and laid on couches, when Maister More and Maister Dickens, a preacher (and their pastor), along with Maister Darrell and thirty other persons, spent the day with them in prayer and fasting, and hearing the word of God. All the parties afflicted remained in their fits the whole of the day.   Towards evening every one of them, with voice and hands lifted up, cried to God for mercy, and He was pleased to hear them, so that six of them were shortly dispossessed, and Jane Ashton in the course of the next day experienced the same deliverance.   At the moment of dispossession, some of them were miserably rent, and the blood gushed out both at the nose and mouth. Margaret Byrom said that she felt the spirit come up her throat, when it gave her "a sore lug" at the time of quitting her, and went out of the window with a flash

of fire, she only seeing it.   John Starkie said his spirit left
him, in appearance like a man with a hunch on his back,
very ill-favoured ; Ellinor Hardman's was like an urchin ;
Margaret Byrom's like an ugly black man, with shoulders
higher than his head.   Two or three days afterwards the
unclean spirits returned, and would have re-entered had
they not been resisted.   When they could not succeed
either by bribes or entreaties, they threw some of them
[the dispossessed] violently down, and deprived others of
the use of their legs and other members ; but the victory
was finally obtained by the preachers, and all the devils
banished from Mr. Starkie's household.   Meanwhile Hartlay the conjuror, who seems to have been a designing
knave, after undergoing an examination before two magistrates, was committed to Lancaster Castle, where, on the
evidence of Mr. Starkie and his family, he was convicted
of witchcraft, and sentenced to death, principally, as it is
stated, for drawing the magic circle, which seems to have
been the least part of his offence, though the most obnoxious to the law.   In this trial *spectral evidence* was
adduced against the prisoner, and the experiment was tried
of saying the Lord's Prayer.   When it no longer served
his purpose he endeavoured to divest himself of the character of a conjuror, and declared that he was not guilty
of the crime for which he was doomed to suffer ; the law,
however, was inexorable, and he was brought to execution.
On the scaffold he persisted in declaring his innocence,
but to no purpose ; the executioner did his duty, and the
criminal was suspended.   While hanging, the rope broke,
when Hartlay confessed his guilt ; being again tied up, he
died, the victim of his own craft, and of the infatuation
of the age in which he lived.   On the appearance of
Mr. Darrell's book, the *Narrative* of these remarkable
events, a long controversy arose on the doctrine of Demon-

ology, and it was charged upon him by the Rev. Samuel
Harsnet, afterwards Bishop of Chichester and Norwich,
and Archbishop of York, that he made a trade of casting
out devils, and that he instructed the " possessed" how to
conduct themselves, in order to aid him in carrying on the
imposition. Mr. Darrell was afterwards examined by the
Queen's Commissioners; and by the full agreement of the
whole court, he was condemned as a counterfeit, deposed
from the ministry, and committed to close confinement,
there to remain for further punishment. The clergy, in
order to prevent the scandal brought upon the Church by
false pretensions to the power of dispossessing demons,
soon afterwards introduced a new canon into the ecclesiastical law, in these terms:—" That no minister or ministers, without license and direction of the bishop, under his
hand and seal obtained, attempt, upon any pretence whatever, either of possession or obsession, by fasting and prayer,
to cast out any devil or devils, under pain of the imputation of imposture, or cozenage, and deposition from the
ministry." Some light is cast upon the case of Mr.
Starkie's household by " A Discourse Concerning the
Possession and Dispossession of Seven Persons in one
Family in Lancashire," written by George More, a puri-
tanical minister, who had engaged in exorcising devils.
This discourse agrees substantially with Darrell's narrative,
but adds some noteworthy facts : amongst others, that he
(Mr. More) was a prisoner in the Clinke for nearly two
years, for justifying and bearing witness to the facts stated
by Darrell. He also states that Mr. Nicholas Starkie
having married a gentlewoman that was an inheritrix [Ann,
widow of Thurstan Barton, Esq., of Smithells, and daughter
and sole heiress of John Parr, Esq., of Kempnough, and
Cleworth, Lancashire], and of whose kindred some were
Papists; these—partly for religion, and partly because the

estate descended but to heirs male—prayed for the perishing of her issue, and that four sons pined away in a strange manner; but that Mrs. Starkie, learning this circumstance, estated her lands on her husband, and *his* heirs, failing issue of her own body; after which a son and daughter were born, who prospered *well till* they became " possessed."*

DEMONIACAL POSSESSION IN 1689.

Richard Dugdale, called " The Surey Demoniac," was a youth just rising into manhood, a gardener, living with his parents at Surey, in the parish of Whalley, addicted to posture, and distinguished even at school as a posture-master and ventriloquist. During his " possession" he was attended by six Dissenting ministers—the Revs. Thomas Jolly, Charles Sagar, Nicholas Kershaw, Robert Waddington, Thomas Whalley, and John Carrington, who were occasionally assisted at the meetings held to exorcise the demon by the Rev. Messrs. Frankland, Pendlebury, and Oliver Heywood. According to the narrative, under their sanction, entitled *An Account of Satan's entering in and about the Body of Richard Dugdale, and of Satan's removal thence through the Lord's blessing of the within-mentioned Ministers and People*, when Dugdale was about nineteen years of age he was seized with an affliction early in 1689; and from the strange fits which violently seized him, he was supposed to be possessed by the devil. When the fit was upon him " he shewed great despite [says the narrative], against the ordinary of God, and raged as if he had been nothing but a devil in Richard's bodily shape; though when he was not in his fits he manifested great inclination to the word of God and

* Baines's *Lancashire.*

prayer; for the exercise of which in his behalf he desired that a day of fasting might be set apart, as the only means from which he could expect help, seeing that he had tried all other means, lawful and unlawful." Meetings were accordingly appointed of the ministers, to which the people crowded in vast numbers. These meetings began on the 8th May, 1689, and were continued about twice a month till the February following. At the first meeting the parents of the demoniac were examined by the ministers, and they represented that " at Whalley rush-bearing, on the James's tide, in July, 1688, there was a great dancing and drinking, when Richard offered himself to the devil, on condition that he would make him the best dancer in Lancashire." After becoming extremely drunk he went home, where several apparitions appeared to him, and presented to him all kinds of dainties and fine clothing, with gold and precious things, inviting him at the same time to "take his fill of pleasure." In the course of the day some compact, or bond, was entered into between him and the devil, after which his fits grew frequent and violent. While in these fits his body was often hurled about very desperately, and he abused the minister and blasphemed his Maker. Sometimes he would fall into dreadful fits; at others he would talk Greek and Latin, though untaught; sometimes his voice was small and shrill, at others hollow and hideous. Now he was as light as a bag of feathers, then as heavy as lead. At one time he upbraided the ministers for their neglect, at others he said they had saved him from hell. He was weather-wise and money-wise by turns; he could tell when there would be rain, and when he should receive presents. Sometimes he would vomit stones an inch and a half square, and in others of his trances there was a noise in his throat, as if he was singing psalms inwardly. But the

strongest mark of demoniacal possession consisted in a
lump, which rose from the thick of his leg, about the size
of a mole, and did work up like such a creature towards
the chest of his body, till it reached his breast, when it
was as big as a man's fist, and uttered strange voices. He
opened his mouth at the beginning of his fits so often, that
it was thought spirits went in and out of him. In agility
he was unequalled, " especially in dancing, wherein he
excelled all that the spectators had seen, and all that mere
mortals could perform. The demoniac would for six or
seven times together leap up, so as that part of his legs
might be seen shaking and quivering above the heads of
the people, from which heights he oft fell down on his
knees, which he long shivered and traversed on the ground,
at least as nimbly as other men can twinkle or sparkle their
fingers; thence springing up into his high leaps again, and
then falling on his feet, which seemed to reach the earth
but with the gentlest and scarce perceivable touches when
he made his highest leaps." And yet the divines by whom
he was attended most unjustly rallied the devil for the
want of skill in his pupil. The Rev. Mr. Carrington, addressing himself to the devil, says, " Cease dancing, Satan,
and begone from him. Canst thou dance no better,
Satan? Ransack the old record of all past times and
places in thy memory : canst thou not there find out some
other way of finer trampling? Pump thine invention
dry ! Cannot that universal seed-plot of subtle wiles and
stratagems spring up one new method of cutting capers ?
Is this the top of skill and pride, to shuffle feet and
brandish knees thus, and to trip like a doe, and skip like
a squirrel? And wherein differs thy leapings from the
hoppings of a frog, or bounces of a goat, or friskings of a
dog, or gesticulations of a monkey? And cannot a palsy
shake such a loose leg as that ? Dost thou not twirl like

a calf that has the turn, and twitch up thy houghs just
like a spring-hault [? spring-galled] tit?" In some of his
last fits he announced that he must be either killed or
cured before the 25th March. This, says the deposition
of his father and mother, and two of his sisters, proved
true; for on the 24th of that month he had his last fit,
the devil being no longer able to withstand the means used
with so much vigour and perseverance to expel him; one
of the most effectual of which was a medicine, prescribed,
in the way of his profession, by Dr. Chew, a medical
practitioner in the neighbourhood. Mr. Zachary Taylor
asserts that the preachers, disappointed and mortified at
their ill success in Dugdale's case, gave it out that some of
his connexions were witches, and in contract with the
devil, and that, they supposed, was the cause why they
had not been able to relieve him. Under this impression
they procured some of the family to be searched, that they
might see if they had not teats, or the devil's mark; and
they tried them by the test of saying the Lord's Prayer.
Some remains of the evil spirit, however, seem still to have
possessed Richard; for, though after this he had no fits,
yet once, when he had got too much drink, he was after
another manner than drunken persons usually are. In
confirmation of which feats, not only the eight ministers,
but twenty respectable inhabitants, affixed their attesta-
tions to a document prepared for the purpose; and three
of the magistrates of the district—Hugh, Lord Willoughby
[of Parham], Ralph Egerton, Esq., and Thos. Braddyll,
Esq.—received depositions from the attesting parties.
This monstrous mass of absurdity, superstition, and fraud
—for it was beyond doubt a compound of them all—was
exposed with success by the Rev. Zachary Taylor, the
Bishop of Chester's curate at Wigan, one of the King's
preachers in Lancashire; but the reverend divine mixed

with his censures too much party asperity, insisting that the whole was an artifice of the Nonconformist ministers, in imitation of the pretended miracles of the Roman Catholic priests, and likening it to the fictions of John Darrell, B.A., which had been practised a century before upon the family of Mr. Starkie, in the same county. Of the resemblance in many of its parts there can be no doubt; but the names of the venerable Oliver Heywood and Thomas Jolly form a sufficient guarantee against imposition on their part; and the probability is that the ministers were the dupes of a popular superstition in the hands of a dissolute and artful family.*

DIVINATION.

This word, derived from *divinare*, to foretell, denotes a mode of foretelling future events, and which, among the ancients, was divided into two kinds, natural and artificial. Natural divination was prophecy or prediction, the result of supposed inspiration or the divine afflatus; artificial divination was effected by certain rites, experiments, or observations, as by sacrifices, cakes, flour, wine, observation of entrails, flight of birds, lots, verses, omens, position of the stars, &c. In modern divination, two modes are in popular favour—thrusting a pin or a key between the leaves of a closed Bible, and taking the verse the pin or key touches as a direction or omen; and the divining-rod, a long forked branch or twig of hazel, which being held between the finger and thumb in a particular way, is said to turn of itself when held near the earth over any hidden treasure, precious metals, or over a spring of water. It has also been used to discover a buried body of one murdered.

* Baines's *Lancashire.*

DIVINATION AT MARRIAGES.

The following practices are very prevalent at marriages
in the districts around Burnley, and they are not noticed
in the last edition of Brand's *Popular Antiquities :*—
1. Put a wedding-ring into the *posset,* and after serving it
out, the unmarried person whose cup contains the ring
will be the first of the company to be married. 2. Make
a common flat cake of flour, water, currants, &c., and put
therein a wedding-ring and a sixpence. When the company are about to retire on the wedding-day the cake must
be broken, and distributed amongst the unmarried females.
She who gets the ring in her portion of the cake will
shortly be married, and the one who gets the sixpence
will die an old maid.*

DIVINATION BY BIBLE AND KEY.

When some choice specimen of the "Lancashire
Witches" thinks it necessary to decide upon selecting a
suitor from among the number of her admirers, she not
unfrequently calls in the aid of the Bible and a key to assist
in deciding her choice. Having opened the Bible at the
passage in Ruth : " Whither thou goest will I go," &c.,
and having carefully placed the wards of the key upon the
verses, she ties the book firmly with a piece of cord, and
having mentioned the name of an admirer, she very
solemnly repeats the passage in question, at the same time
holding the Bible suspended *by joining the ends of her
little fingers* inserted under the handle of the key. If the
key retain its position during the repetition the person whose
name has been mentioned is considered to be rejected ;
and so another name is tried, till the book turns round

* T. T. W., in *Notes and Queries,* vol. ii. p. 117.

and falls through the fingers, which is held to be a sure token the name just mentioned is that of an individual who will certainly marry her. I have a Bible in my possession which bears evidence of having seen much service of this description.*

ANOTHER LANCASHIRE FORM OF DIVINATION.

When a Lancashire damsel desires to know what sort of a husband she will have, on New Year's Eve she pours some melted lead into a glass of water, and observes what forms the drops assume. When they resemble scissors, she concludes that she must rest satisfied with a tailor; if they appear in the form of a hammer, he will be a smith or a carpenter, and so on of others. The writer has met with many instances of this class, in which the examples given did not admit of easy contradiction.

DIVINATION BY THE DYING.

Dying persons, especially if they have been distinguished for piety when in health, are considered to possess, for a short time, the spirit of prophecy. Hence many persons are then anxious to see them, in order that they may divine the *future* by means of their oracular words. They also *know* persons who have died before them. This is a curious remnant of the old Greek and Roman belief. Homer makes Hector foretell the death of Achilles, *Iliad,* v. 355. Virgil causes Orodes to foretell the death of Mezentius, *Æneid,* x. 739. Cicero also furnishes another instance, *De Divin.* lib. ii.

* T. T. W., in *Notes and Queries,* vol. ii. p. 5.

SECOND-SIGHT.

Though this faculty of seeing into the future has usually been regarded as limited to Scotland, and there chiefly possessed by natives of the Highlands, there have been individuals in Lancashire who have laid claim to the possession of this species of foresight. Amongst those in the Fylde district was a man named Cardwell, of Marton, near Blackpool, who foretold deaths and evil events from his vision of things to come. Men of superior ability were credulous enough to visit him, and to give implicit faith to his marvellous stories. The real form of second-sight is the seeing of the wraith, spirit, or ghost of one about to die; and in one notable instance Cardwell's second-sight failed him utterly. On seeing something in a vision, he concluded that his own child was about to die, and so strong was his own faith in this delusion that he carried sand to the churchyard to be ready for its grave. The death, however, did not happen: the child grew to maturity, and retaining robust health, lived for many years afterwards.

SPIRITS OF THE DYING AND DEAD.

1. Persons born during twilight are supposed to be able to *see* spirits, and to know who of their acquaintance will die next.

2. Some say that this property also belongs to those who happen to be born *exactly* at twelve o'clock at night.

3. The spirits of persons about to die, especially if the persons be in distant lands, are supposed to return to their friends, and thus predict the calamity. While the spirit is thus *away*, the person is supposed to be in a *swoon*, and unaware of what is passing. His *desire* to see his friends

is also necessary; he must have been *thinking* of them. I am not aware that these spirits ever *speak*.

4. If no one in a family can *see* a spirit, most can *hear* them, and hence strange noises are supposed to indicate death or misfortune to distant friends.

CASTING LOTS, ETC.

This is a species of divination or consulting of fate by omen. Great faith is placed by most in casting lots. Putting numbers in a box or bag is the common practice, and then drawing them out at random. Scripture was once quoted to the writer in proof that this mode of deciding doubtful matters was of God's appointment, and therefore could not fail. " The lot is cast into the bag, but the *disposal* thereof is the Lord's." (Prov. xvi. 33 ; 1. Sam. xiv. 41.) When boys do not wish to divide anything they decide " who must take all " by drawing " short-cuts." A number of straws, pieces of twine, &c., of different lengths, are held by one not interested; each boy draws one, and he who gets the *longest* is entitled to the whole.

DRUIDICAL ROCK BASINS.

Dr. Borlase, in his *Antiquities of Cornwall,* notices the existence of Druidical Rock Basins, which appear to have been scooped out of the granite rocks and boulders which lie on the tops of the hills in the county. Several such cavities in stones are found on Brimham Rocks, near Knaresborough, and they have also been found at Plumpton and Rigton, in Yorkshire,* and on Stanton Moor, in

------

* Allen's *History of Yorkshire,* vol. iii. pp. 421-425.

Derbyshire. The writer first drew attention to the fact of similar Druidical remains existing in Lancashire in a paper read before the Historical Society of Lancashire and Cheshire, in December, 1864. They are found in considerable numbers around Boulsworth, Gorple, Todmorden, and on the hills which separate Lancashire from Yorkshire between these places. Commencing the enumeration of the groups of boulders, &c., containing rock basins, with the slopes of Boulsworth, about seven miles from Burnley, we have first the Standing Stones, mostly single blocks of millstone grit, at short distances from each other on the north-western side of the hill. One is locally termed the Buttock Stone, and near it is a block which has a circular cavity scooped out on its flat upper surface. Not far from these are the Joiner Stones, the Abbot Stone, the Weather Stones, and the Law Lad Stones [? from *llad*, British, sacrifices]. Next come the Great and Little Saucer Stones, so named from the cavities scooped out upon them. The Little Chair Stones, the Fox Stones, and the Broad Head Stones lie at no great distance, each group containing numerous like cavities. Several of these groups are locally named from resemblance to animals or other objects, as the Grey Stones and the Steeple Stones on Barn Hill, and one spur of Boulsworth is called Wycoller Ark, as resembling a farmer's chest or ark. On Warcock Hill several groups of natural rocks and boulders are locally named Dave or Dew Stones. On the surface of one immense Dave Stone boulder is a perfect hemispherical cavity, ten inches in diameter. The surface of another contains an oblong basin of larger dimensions, with a long grooved channel leading from its curved contour towards the edge of the stone. On a third there are four circular cavities of varying dimensions, the largest in the centre, and three others surrounding it, but none of these is more than a few inches in diameter. At the Bride Stones, near Todmorden, thirteen cavities were counted on one block, and eleven on another. All the basins here and elsewhere are formed on the *flat* surfaces of the blocks; their upper surfaces being always parallel to the lamination of the stone. Along Widdop Moor we find the Grey Stones, the Fold Hole Stones, the Clattering Stones, and the Rigging Stones; the last named from occupying the rig or ridge of the hills in this locality. Amongst the Bride Stones is an immense mass of rock which might almost be classed among the rocking stones. It is about twenty-five feet in height, at least twelve feet across its broadest part, and rests on a base only about two feet in diameter. The Todmorden group contains the Hawk Stones, on Stansfield Moor, not far from Stiperden Cross, on the line of the Long Causeway (a Roman road); the Bride Stones, near Windy Harbour; the Chisley Stones, near Keelham; and Hoar Law, not far from Ashenhurst Royd and Todmorden. The rock basins on these boulders are very numerous, and of all sizes, from a few inches in diameter and depth to upwards of two feet. The elliptical axes of some of these basins did not appear to the writer to have been caused by the action of wind or water, or to follow any regular law. Lastly, taking for a centre, Gorple,* about five miles south-east of Burnley is another extensive group of naked rocks and boulders. Close to the solitary farm-house there are the Gorple Stones; and at a short distance the Hanging Stones form conspicuous objects in the sombre landscape. On Thistleden Dean are the Upper, Middle, and Lower Whinberry Stones, so named from the "whinberry" shrubs, with which this moor

* *Gort*, narrow; *gor*, upper, Brit.; *gór*, blood, A. S. *Gorple* may mean the bloody pile, or the upper pile.

abounds. The Higher and Lower Boggart Stones come next, and these are followed by the Wicken Clough, and other minor groups of stones. Above Gorple Bottom is another set of grey stones; and these are followed by the Upper, Middle, and Lower Hanging Stones, on Shuttle-worth Moor.* The rock basins here are very numerous, and mostly well defined. There are forty-three cavities in these Gorple, Gorple Gate, and Hanging Stones, ranging from four to forty inches in length, from four to twenty-five in breadth, and from two to thirteen inches in depth.

Dr. Borlase confidently asserts that the ancient Druids used these rock basins for baptismal and sacrificial pur-poses—a conjecture which the authors of the *Beauties of Derbyshire* admit to be probable; and so does Higgins in his elaborate work on the *Celtic Druids.* The supposition is supported by the fact of their occurring in such numbers mostly *on the tops of hills,* in so many counties, and in such different materials as the granite and the millstone-grit formations.† Whether they have been formed by natural or artificial means is still a matter of dispute. On the whole the writer's opinion is, that the rock basins of Scilly, Cornwall, Derbyshire, Yorkshire, and East Lan-cashire are partly natural, and partly artificial; the former being comparatively few, and easily distinguished by their

---

* From *Sceot-hull,* afterwards *Scout* or *Shoot-hill,* and *worth*—*i.e.,* the farm or hamlet of the projecting ledge or hill.

† Dr. Borlase's argument is cumulative. He observes that rock basins are always on the *top,* never on the *sides* of the stones; that the ancients sacrificed on rocks; that water was used by them for lustration and purification; that snow, rain, or dew, was preferred by them to running water; that it was not permitted to touch the earth; that the Druids practised similar rites, and held rain or snow-water to be holy; and they attributed a healing virtue to the gods inhabiting rocks; that their priests stood upon rocks to wash, sprinkle, and drink, &c. All these considerations, he conceives, favour his opinion that rock basins were *used,* if not *formed,* by the Druids.

varying depths and forms.*   Whether wholly or partially
natural or artificial, he thinks it safe to conclude that
they have been appropriated by the Druids to their religious worship, as furnishing the means by which they
could offer their sacrifices and perform their ablutions.
They would also suffice for baptism, and preserve the rain
or the dew from being polluted by touching the earth.
The Tolmen on the neighbouring hills† may be taken
as an additional reason for associating Druidical worship
with such remains.   These contain small basins on the
summits, which differ in no respect from those here
enumerated.   They have, therefore, most probably been
used for similar purposes.   Those above described form
a curious chapter in the oldest folk-lore of Lancashire.

ELVES AND FAIRIES.

"Like elves and fairies in a ring."—*Macbeth.*

England has ever been full of the favourite haunts of
those pleasantest of all the supernatural sprites of childhood
and superstition—elves and fairies.   Volumes might be
filled with the stories of their feats and pranks in all parts
of England; and our greatest poet has for ever embalmed
this superstition in the richest hues of poetic imagery and
fancy—especially in his *Midsummer Night's Dream.*   The
Fairies, or "Hill Folk," yet live amongst the rural people
of Lancashire.   Antique tobacco-pipes, "formerly belonging to the fairies," are still occasionally found in the
corners of newly-ploughed fields.   They themselves still
gambol on the grassy meads at dewy eve, and their revels

* See Watson's *History of Halifax,* pp. 27–36.
† Professor Hunt is of the same opinion.   See his recent work on
the *Drolls of Cornwall,* vol. i. pp. 186–228.

are yet believed to be witnessed at times by some privileged inhabitants of our " calm sequestered vales." It is generally stated that, in order to see one of these diminutive beings, the use of ointments, four-leaved clover, or other specific preparations, is necessary; but ,a near relative of the writer, not more imbued with super- stition than the majority, firmly believed that he once saw a real dwarf or fairy, without the use of any incanta- tion. He had been amusing himself one summer even- ing on the top of Mellor Moor, near Blackburn, close to the remains of the Roman encampment, when his atten- tion was arrested by the appearance of a dwarf-like man, attired in full hunting costume, with top-boots and spurs, a green jacket, red hairy cap, and a thick hunting whip in his hand. He ran briskly along the moor for a con- siderable distance, when, leaping over a low stone wall, he darted down a steep declivity, and was lost to sight. The popular opinion of the neighbourhood is, that an underground city exists at this place ; that an earthquake swallowed up the encampment, and that on certain days in the year the hill folk may be heard ringing their bells, and indulging in various festivities. Considerable quanti- ties of stone, which still remain around the ditches of this rectangular place, may have suggested the ideas of a city and an earthquake. On other occasions the fairies are supposed to exhibit themselves in military array on the mountain sides; their evolutions conforming in every respect to the movements of modern troops. Such appearances are believed to portend the approach of civil commotions, and are said to have been more than usually common about the time of the rebellion in 1745-6. This would suggest an explanation of a more rational character. [Doubtless the mirage, Fata Morgana, or Spectral appear- ances of the Hartz mountains.]

One Lancashire Fairy tale runs thus :—

Two men went poaching, and having placed nets, or rather sacks, over what they supposed to be rabbit holes, but which were in reality fairies' houses, the fairies rushed into the sacks, and the poachers (believing them to be rabbits), content with their prey, marched homewards again. One fairy missing another in the sack, called out (the story was told in the broad Lancashire dialect)— "Dick" (dignified name for a fairy), "where art thou ?" To which fairy Dick replied,—

> " In a sack,
> On a back,
> Riding up Barley Brow."

The story has a good moral ending ; for the men were so frightened that they never poached again.*

The Rev. William Thornber† characterizes the elves and fairies as kind, good-natured creatures, at times seeking the assistance of mortals, and in return, liberally reward-ing them. They have a favourite spot between Hardhorn and Staining, at a cold spring of water called "Fairies' Well" to this day. Most amusing stories of fairies are told around that district. A poor woman, when filling her pitcher at the well just named, in order to bathe the weak eyes of her infant child, was mildly accosted by a handsome man, who presented her with a box of ointment, and told her it would be a specific remedy. She was grateful for the gift, but love for her child made her somewhat mistrustful; so she first applied the ointment to one of her own eyes. Shortly afterwards, she saw her benefactor at Preston, stealing corn from the mouths of the sacks open for sale, and, much to his amazement, accosted him. On his

---

* T. G. C., in *Notes and Queries*, vol. vii. p. 177.
† In his *History of Blackpool*, pp. 333-4.

inquiry how she could recognise him, since he was invisible to all else around, she told him how she had used
his ointment, and pointed to the powerful eye; when he
immediately struck it out. A milkmaid, observing a jug
and a sixpence placed at her side by some invisible being,
filled the jug with milk, and took the money; this was
repeated for weeks, till, overjoyed with her good fortune,
she could not refrain from imparting it to her lover; but
the jug and sixpence never appeared again. A ploughman
when engaged in his daily labour, heard a plaintive cry,
" I have broken my *speet*."* Hastily turning round, the
ploughman beheld a lady, holding in her hand a broken
spittle, a hammer, and nails, and beckoning him to repair
it. He did so, and instantly received a handsome
reward; and then the lady vanished, apparently sinking
into the earth.

FOLK-LORE.

Under this general head we bring together a few
scattered notices not naturally falling under any precise
classification, but all showing the nature and character of
common and popular notions, beliefs, and superstitions.
Where, however, the subject will admit of it, many examples of this Folk-lore will be found in later pages, under
the general head of " Superstitions."

FOLK-LORE OF ECCLES AND THE NEIGHBOURHOOD.

A very curious book exhibits some of the usages of our
ancestors in this part of the county, early in the reign of
James I., entitled *The Way to the True Church* . . . . . .

* Speet, spit, or spittle, are names in Lancashire for a spade.

I

directed to all that seek for Resolution; and especially to all
his loving Countrymen of Lancashire, by John White,
Minister of God's Word at Eccles. [White was vicar of
Eccles only a few months—from May, 1609.] The fifth
edition or "impression" is a folio, printed at London,
1624; but the Preface is dated Oct. 29th, 1608. White
complains of " the prodigious ignorance" which he found
among his parishioners when he entered upon his minis-
trations, and he proceeds thus to tell his own tale:—" I
will only mention what I saw and learned, dwelling
among them, concerning the saying of their prayers; for
what man is he whose heart trembles not to simple people
so far seduced [or so ill-taught] that they know not how
to pronounce or say their daily prayers; or so to pray that
all that hear them shall be filled with laughter? And
while, superstitiously, they refuse to pray in their own
language with understanding, they speak that which their
leaders [Roman Catholic priests] may blush to hear.
These examples I have observed from the common people:

" ' *The Creed.*

" ' Creezum zuum patrum onitentem Creatorum ejus
anicum, Dominum nostrum qui sum sops, virgini Mariæ,
crixus fixus, Ponchi Pilati audubitiers, morti by Sonday,
father a fernes, scelerest unjudicarum, finis a mortibus.
Creezum spirituum sanctum, eccli Catholi, remissùrum pec-
caturum, communiorum obliviorum, bitam et turnam again.'

" ' *The Little Creed.*

" ' Little creed, can I need
     Kneele before our Ladies' knee;
     Candlelight, candles burne,
     Our Ladie pray'd to her dear Sonne
     That we all to heaven might come.
     Little creed, Amen.'

" This that followeth they call—

" ' *The White Paternoster.*

" ' White Paternoster, Saint Peter's brother,
    What hast i' th' t' one hand? White book leaves.
    What hast i' th' t'other hand? Heaven yate keys.
    Open heaven yates, and steyk [shut] hell yates :
    And let every crysome child creep to it own mother.
    White Paternoster, Amen.'

" ' *Another Prayer.*

" ' I bless me with God and the rood,
    With his sweet flesh and precious blood;
    With his cross and his creed,
    With his length and his breed,
    From my toe to my crown,
    And all my body up and down,
    From my back to my breast,
    My five wits be my rest ;
    God let never ill come at ill,
    But through Jesus' own will,
    Sweet Jesus, Lord, Amen.'

" Many also use to wear vervain against blasts; and, when they gather it for this purpose, first they cross the herb with their hand, and then they bless it thus :—

" ' Hallowed be thou, Vervain,
    As thou growest on the ground,
    For in the Mount of Calvary,
    There thou wast first found.
    Thou healedst our Saviour Jesus Christ,
    And staunchedst his bleeding wound;
    In the name of the Father, Son, and Holy Ghost,
    I take thee from the ground.'

" And so they pluck it up and wear it. Their prayers and traditions of this sort are infinite, and the ceremonies they use in their actions are nothing inferior to the Gentiles in number and strangeness. Which any man may easily observe that converseth with them."*

* L. B. in *Notes and Queries*, vol. viii. p. 613.—*Bibliographical Notice of the Works of the Learned and Rev. Divine, John White, D,D., &c.* London, 1624; in *Chet. Soc. Books*, vol. xxxviii. p. 52.

TREE BARNACLES; OR, GEESE HATCHED FROM SEA SHELLS.

The learned and venerable John Gerarde, author or translator of *A History of Plants, or Herball;* first published in folio in 1597, has the following marvellous story respecting barnacle-shells growing on trees, and giving birth to young geese ; not as a thing which some wonder-monger had related to him, but as what he had seen with his own eyes, and the truth of which he could, therefore, and does, most solemnly avouch.

" There are found in the north parts of Scotland, and the isles adjacent called Orcades, certain trees, whereon do grow certain shell-fishes, of a white colour, tending to russet ; wherein are contained little living creatures; which shells in time of maturity do open, and out of them grow those little living things ; which, falling into the water, do become fowls, whom we call barnacles, in the North of England brant geese, and in Lancashire tree geese; but the others that do fall upon the land perish and do come to nothing. Thus much by the writings of others, and also from the mouths of people of those parts, which may very well accord with truth. But *what our eyes have seen and hands have touched, we shall declare.* There is a small island in Lancashire called The Pile of Foulders [or Peel of Fouldrey] wherein are found the broken pieces of old and bruised ships, some whereof have been cast thither by shipwreck, and also the trunks or bodies, with the branches, of old rotten trees, cast up there likewise ; whereon is found a certain spume or froth, that in time breedeth unto certain shells, in shape like those of the mussel, but sharper pointed, and of a whitish colour; wherein is contained a thing in form like a lace of silk, finely woven as it were together, as of a whitish colour, one end whereof is fastened unto the inside of the shell, even as the fish of

oysters and mussels are. The other end is made fast unto
the belly of a rude masse or lump, which in time cometh
to the shape and form of a bird; when it is perfectly
formed the shell gapeth open, and the first thing that
appeareth is the foresaid lace or string; next comè
the legs of the bird hanging out; and as it groweth
greater it openeth the shell by degrees, till at length it is
all come forth and hangeth only by the bill. In short
space after it cometh to full maturity and falleth into the
sea, where it gathereth feathers and groweth to a fowl,
bigger than a mallard and lesser than a goose; and black
legs and bill, or beak, and feathers black and white,
spotted in such a manner as is our magpie (called in some
places a pie-annet), which [not the magpie, but the bar-
nacle-hatched fowl] the people of Lancashire call by no
other name than a tree goose; which place aforesaid, and
all those parts adjoining, do so much abound therewith,
that one of the best is bought for 3d.; For the truth
hereof, if any doubt, may it please them to repair to me,
and I shall satisfy them by the testimony of good witnesses (!) . . . They spawn as it were in March and April
the geese are formed in May and June, and come to fulness
of feathers in the month after." "There is another sort
hereof, the history of which is *true, and of mine own knowledge;* for travelling upon the shores of our English coast
between Dover and Romney, I found the trunk of an old
rotten tree, which (with some help that I procured by fishermen's wives, that were there attending their husbands' return from the sea) we drew out of the water upon dry
land. On this rotten tree I found growing many thousands of long crimson bladders, in shape like unto puddings newly filled, before they be sodden, which were
very clear and shining; at the nether end whereof did
grow a shell-fish, fashioned somewhat like a small mussel,

but much whiter, resembling a shell-fish that groweth upon the rocks about Guernsey and Jersey, called a limpet. Many of these shells I brought with me to London, which, after I had opened, I found in them living things, without form or shape; in others, which were nearer come to ripeness, I found living things that were very naked, in shape like a bird; in others, the birds covered with soft down, the shell half open, and the bird ready to fall out, which no doubt were the fowls called barnacles. . . . That which I have seen with my eyes and handled with my hands, I dare confidently avouch and boldly put down for verity. . . . We conclude and end our present volume with this wonder of God. For which God's name be ever honoured and praised." This author figures the *Britannica Conchæ Anatifera,* or the breed of barnacles; the woodcut representing a tree growing by the sea, with leaves like mussel shells, opening, and living creatures emerging; while others, swimming about in the sea beneath, are perfect goslings! Well may the old herbalist call this "one of the marvels of this land; we may say of the world." Dr. Charles Leigh, in his *Natural History of Lancashire,* gravely labours to refute the notion that barnacles grow into geese, as had been asserted by Speed and others.

Sir J. Emerson Tennent, writing in *Notes and Queries* (vol. viii. p. 223), referring to Porta's *Natural Magic* for the vulgar error that not only in Scotland, but in the river Thames, "there is a kind of shell-fish which get out of their shells and grow to be ducks, or such-like birds," observes that this tradition is very ancient, Porta, the author, having died in 1515. In *Hudibras* is an allusion to those—

> "Who from the most refin'd of saints,
>   As naturally grow miscreants,
>   As *barnacles* turn Soland geese,
>   In th' islands of the Orcades."

The story (says Sir James) has its origin in the peculiar formation of the little mollusc which inhabits the multivalve shell, the *Pentalasmi Anatifera,* which by a fleshy peduncle attaches itself by one end to the bottoms of ships or floating timber, whilst from the other there protrudes a bunch of curling and fringe-like cirrhi, by the agitation of which it attracts and collects its food. These cirrhi so much resemble feathers, as to have suggested the leading idea of a bird's tail; and hence the construction of the remainder of the fable, which is given with grave minuteness in *The Herball, or General Historie of Plants,* gathered by John Gerarde, Master in Chirurgie (London, 1597). After quoting the account, Sir James adds, that Gerarde, who is doubtless Butler's authority, says elsewhere, " that in the north parts of Scotland, and the islands called Orcades, there are certain trees whereon these tree geese and barnacles abound." The conversion of the fish into a bird, however fabulous, would be scarcely more astounding than the metamorphosis which it actually undergoes, the young of the little animal having no feature to identify it with its final development. In its early stage (see Carpenter's *Physiology,* i. 52) it has a form not unlike that of the crab, " possessing eyes and powers of free motion : but afterwards becoming fixed to one spot for the remainder of its life, it loses its eyes, and forms a shell, which, though composed of various pieces, has nothing in common with the jointed shell of the crab." Mr. T. J. Buckton (*Notes and Queries,* vol. viii. p. 224) says that Drayton (1613), in his *Polyolbion,* p. iii., in connexion with the river Dee, speaks of—

" Th' anatomised fish, and fowls from planchers sprung,"

to which a note is appended in Southey's edition (p. 609), that such fowls were " *barnacles,* a bird breeding upon old ships." In the *Entertaining Library,* " Habits of Birds,"

(pp. 363–379), the whole story of this extraordinary
ignorance of natural history is amply developed. The
barnacle-shells which I once saw in a sea-port attached to
a vessel just arrived from the Mediterranean had the
brilliant appearance at a distance of flowers in bloom.
(See *Penny Cyclopædia,* article " Cirripeda," vii. 206,
reversing the woodcut). The foot of the *Lepas Anatifera*
(Linn.), appeared to me like the stalk of a plant growing
from the ship's side. The shell had the semblance of a
calyx, and the flower consisted of the fingers (*tentacula*)
of the shell-fish, " of which twelve project in an elegant
curve, and are used by it for making prey of small fish."
The very ancient error was to mistake the foot of the
shell-fish for the neck of a goose, the shell for its head,
and the *tentacula* for a tuft of feathers. As to the body,
non est inventus. The Barnacle Goose is a well-known
bird ; and these shell-fish bearing, as seen out of the water,
resemblance to the goose's neck, were ignorantly, and
without investigation, confounded with geese themselves.
In France, the barnacle goose may be eaten on fast-days,
by virtue of this old belief in its fishy origin. From a passage in the *Memoirs of Lady Fanshaw,* it appears that Sir
Kenelm Digby, at the table of the Governor of Calais,
declared that barnacles, a bird in Jersey, was first a shell-
fish to appearance, and from that, sticking upon old wood,
became in time a goose ! An advertisement of June, 1807,
sets forth that the " Wonderful curiosity called the Goose
Tree, Barnacle Tree, or Tree bearing geese, taken up at
sea on the 12th January, 1807, by Captain Bytheway,
and was more than twenty men could raise out of the
water—may be seen at the Exhibition Rooms, Spring
Gardens, from ten o'clock in the morning till ten at night,
every day. The Barnacles which form the present exhibition possess a neck upwards of two feet in length, re-

sembling the windpipe of a chicken; each shell contains
five pieces, and notwithstanding the many thousands
which hang to eight inches of the tree, part of the fowl
may be seen from each shell. Sir Robert Moxay, in the
Wonders of Nature and Art, speaking of this singularly'
curious production, says, that in every shell he opened he
found a perfect sea-fowl [!], with a bill like that of a
goose, feet like those of water-fowl, and the feathers all
plainly formed." (*Ibid.*, p. 300.)

WARTS FROM WASHING IN EGG WATER.

It is commonly held that washing the hands in water in
which eggs have been boiled will produce a plentiful crop
of warts. Not long ago two young and intelligent ladies
stated that they had inadvertently washed their hands and
arms in egg water, and in each case this had been followed
by large numbers of warts. This sequence they affirmed
to be a consequence, and the warts were shown as an
ocular demonstration of the unpleasant results of such
lavation.

FORTUNE-TELLING.—WISE MEN AND CUNNING WOMEN, ETC.

There is scarcely a town of any magnitude in Lancashire, or in one or two adjacent counties, which does not
possess its local "fortune-teller" or pretender to a knowledge of astrology, and to a power of predicting the future
events of life, under the talismanic name of "fortune," to
a large and credulous number of applicants. The fortune-
teller of the nineteenth century professes to be able to
"cast nativities" and to "rule the planets." If, as is not
unfrequently the case, he be a medical botanist, he gathers

his herbs when the proper planet is "in the ascendant."
Some of these impostors also profess to "charge the
crystal" (*i.e.*, to look into a globular or egg-shaped glass),
and thereby to solve the gravest questions respecting the
future fortunes of those who consult them.   Nor is this
by any means an unprofitable pursuit.   The writer is
aware of several instances in which "casting nativities,"
&c., has proved a golden harvest to the professor.   One
individual gave up a well-paid occupation in order that he
might devote himself wholly to the still more lucrative
practice of astrology and fortune-telling.   He not only
predicted future events by means of the stars, but he gave
heads of families advice as to the recovery of stolen property and the detection of the thief; while impatient
maidens he counselled how to bring shy or dilatory lovers
to the point.   Another practitioner added to these practices the construction of sun-dials, in which he was very
ingenious, and thereby amassed considerable property after
a long and successful career.   Instances are very common
that credulity is not confined to the ignorant or uneducated classes.   An intelligent and well-meaning lady once
very seriously cautioned the writer against diving into the
secrets of astrology, as, she said, that pursuit had "turned
the head" of one of her acquaintance.   She not only had
a firm faith in the truth of all astrological predictions, but
(from apprehension engendered by this faith) she would
not on any account suffer any of these practitioners to
predict her fortune, nor would she on any account consult
them.   It seems that on one occasion she did commit
herself so far as to go to "a wise man," whom we
will call Mr. I., in company with Miss J., whose
marriage with Mr. K. was then somewhat doubtful;
and she afterwards solemnly affirmed that the astrologer
told her all her fortune.   She described him as first care-

fully drawing the requisite diagram, showing the state of the heavens at the hour of Miss J.'s birth; and after "charging his glass" he declared that the marriage would take place within a few months; "but," he added, "he was also very sorry to inform her that she would die young." Both these events did really happen within a limited period; and of course the lady's belief in the truth of astrological prediction was very powerfully strengthened and confirmed. Some time after these events, this identical Mr. I. was brought before the magistrates in petty sessions, charged with obtaining money under false pretences; with practising astrology, palmistry, &c., and he only narrowly escaped imprisonment through some technical error in the charge or summons. It was said that the charge was a vindictive one—hence there was great rejoicing amongst his friends when it was dismissed; but the inspector of police who had charge of the case did not hesitate to declare that there were many persons then present who had paid Mr. I. money for his predictions.

Another specimen of the fortune-teller we may notice from a rural district. In the hamlet of Roe Green, in the township of Worsley, in a humble cottage, a few years ago lived a man who held the position of overseer or head of one class of workmen in the employ of the Bridgewater Trust. In the language of the locality, "Owd Rollison [Rawlinson] was a *gaffer.*" But to this regular avocation he added the profession of fortune-telling, and in the evenings many were the applicants for a little knowledge of future events from the villages and hamlets for miles around. His stock-in-trade consisted of various books on astrology, &c., and of two magic glasses or crystals, one a small globular mass of common white glass, with a short stem by which to hold it; the other was about the size and shape of a large hen's egg, but without any stem or handle. His whole apparatus was for some months in the possession of the writer, and a list of his books may serve to show the sort of literature held in esteem amongst this class of planet rulers. 1. *The Three Books of Occult Philosophy* of Henry Cornelius Agrippa, translated by J. Freake (London, 1651, pp. 583).* 2. Lilly's *Christian Astrology*, in three books (London, 1659, pp. 832). 3. John Gadbury's *Thesaurus Astrologiæ* (Westminster, 1674, pp. 272). 4. *The Star*, by Ebn Shemaya (London, 1839, pp. 203). Zadkiel's *Grammar of Astrology* (London, 1849, pp. 178) : in this volume were also bound up "Tables for Calculating Nativities," by Zádkiel (London, 1850, pp. 64). 6. *A Plea for Urania* (London, 1854, pp. 387).

One or two MS. books, apparently blank copy-books, which had been used to draw diagrams, or, as the phrase goes, to " construct horoscopes," or " erect schemes," or " cast nativities," showed that " Owd Rollison" had dabbled a little in a sort of Astrology; but the rudeness of these attempts betrayed him to be but a mere tyro in the " celestial science." He had also a reputation for selling "charms" against the various ills that flesh is heir to; amongst others, one to stop hæmorrhage. One countryman told the writer that he remembered, when a boy, that his uncle having a very severe hæmorrhage, so

---

* There is another curious volume, which professes to contain a fourth book of Agrippa; but it is spurious. It includes five treatises— viz., 1. Henry Cornelius Agrippa's Fourth Book on Occult Philosophy and Geomancy; 2. The Magical Elements of Peter de Abano; 3. The Astronomical Geomancy of Gerard Cremonensis; 4. Isagoge, or the Nature of Spirits, by Geo. Victorius Villinganus, M.D.; and 5. Arbatel of Magick. Translated into English by Robert Turner, Philomathées. (London, 1665, 8vo, pp. 266.) Another version of this book appeared in 1783, 8vo. It would lead us too far to describe the strange contents of this book, which contains long lists of the names of good and evil spirits, and symbols representing their characters; also symbols of the archangels and angels, their sigils, planets, signs, &c.

that he was believed to be bleeding to death, this boy was told to run off as hard as he could to Owd Rollison to get something to stop the bleeding. He soon received a small piece of parchment containing sundry unintelligible characters upon it, which was to be sewed up in a small bag and worn continually, so that the bag should rest on the skin just over the heart. This was done, the bleeding stopped, and the man recovered. Another person, who had been a sort of confidant of the wise man, told the writer that at one period Rawlinson went at regular intervals, and on stated days, to Manchester, where at a quiet public-house he met other " wise men," and they assembled in an upper chamber, with locked door, and sometimes remained for hours in deliberation. Of the subject of such deliberations the informant said he knew nothing, for he was never admitted; he had the honour of remaining outside the door as watchman, guard, or sentinel, to prevent any prying listeners from approaching. He conjectured that what they were about was " magic and such like;" but more he knew not. " Owd Rollison" kept his situation under the Bridgewater Trust until his death, at a ripe old age; and though he left several sons and a daughter, the mantle of his astrological or fortune-telling wisdom does not seem to have fallen on any of them.

Much might be stated respecting the practice of the art of fortune-telling by wandering gipsies, especially in that branch of it termed palmistry—predicting the future from an examination of the " lines" of the palm of the left hand, each of which, in the jargon of palmists, has its own peculiar character and name, as the line of life, of fortune, &c.; but as these wanderers are not indigenous to Lancashire, but may be found in every county in England, it may suffice thus to name them. Of the old women who tell fortunes by cards chiefly, to silly women who are always wanting to know whether their future husband is to be denoted by the King of Hearts (a true-loving swain) or by the Monarch of Diamonds (as indicative of great wealth), it is enough to say that they may be found by scores or hundreds in every town in Lancashire.

MAGIC AND MAGICIANS.

Our forefathers had a strong faith in the power of magic, and even divided the knowledge of it into two opposite kinds—viz., "white magic," which was acquired from the communications of the archangels and angels, or at least from some of the good spirits who were allowed to aid human beings by their supernatural power in deeds of beneficence; and black magic, or "the black art," also termed "necromancy," which was derived from "dealings with the devil, or at least from commerce with his imps, or the evil spirits of wicked dead men. At one period the terms magician and conjuror had the same meaning— one who conjured, by magical power, spirits and demons to appear and do his bidding. Conjuror has since become a name for a professor of *legerdermain* or sleight-of-hand.

EDWARD KELLY THE SEER.

Edward Kelly, whose dealings in the Black Art, it is said, would fill a volume, was born at Worcester, and had been an apothecary. We have elsewhere noticed his doings as an alchemist. He was for a considerable time the companion and associate of "Dr." John Dee, per- forming for him the office of "Seer," by looking into the doctor's crystal or stone, a faculty not possessed by

Dee, who in consequence was obliged to have recourse to Kelly for the revelations he has published respecting the world of spirits. These curious transactions may be found in Casaubon's work, entitled, *A True and Faithful Relation of what Passed for many years between Dr. John Dèe and some Spirits*—opening out another dark page in the history of imposture and credulity. Dee says that he was brought into unison with Kelly by the mediation of the angel Uriel. Afterwards he found himself deceived by him, in his opinion that these spirits which ministered unto him were messengers of the Deity. They had had several quarrels before; but when Dee found Kelly degenerating into the worst species of the magic art, for the purposes of avarice and fraud, he broke off all connexion with him, and would never afterwards be seen in his company. Kelly, being discountenanced by the doctor, betook himself to the meanest practices of magic, in all which money and the works of the devil appear to have been his chief aim. Many wicked and abominable transactions are recorded of him.

In Lilly's Memoirs are the following passages relating to this Seer :—"Kelly outwent the Doctor, viz., about the Elixir and the Philosopher's Stone, which neither he nor his master attained by their own labour and industry. It was in this manner that Kelly obtained it, as I had it related from an ancient minister, who knew the certainty thereof from an old English merchant, resident in Germany, at what time both Kelly and Dee were there. Dee and Kelly, being on the confines of the Emperor's dominions, in a city where resided many English merchants, with whom they had much familiarity, there happened an old friar to come to Dr. Dee's lodgings, knocking at the door. Dee peeped down stairs : 'Kelly,' says he, 'tell the old man I am not at home.' Kelly

did so.   The friar said, ' I will take another time to wait
upon him.'   Some few days after, he came again.   Dee
ordered Kelly, if it were the same person, to deny him
again.   He did so; at which the friar was very angry.
' Tell thy master I came to speak with him, and to do
him good; because he is a great scholar, and famous :
but now tell him, he put forth a book, and dedicated it
to the Emperor.   It is called *Monas Hieroglyphicas.*
He understands it not.   I wrote it myself.   I came to
instruct him therein, and in some other more profound
things.   Do thou, Kelly, come along with me.   I will
make thee more famous than thy master Dee.'   Kelly
was very apprehensive of what the friar delivered, and
thereupon suddenly retired from Dr. Dee, and wholly
applied unto the friar, and of him either had the Elixir
ready made, or the perfect method of its preparation and
making.   The poor friar lived a very short time after :
whether he died a natural death, or was otherwise poisoned
or made away by Kelly, the merchant who related this,
did not certainly know."   "It was vulgarly reported that
he [Kelly] had a compact with the devil, which he out-
lived, and was seized at midnight by infernal spirits, who
carried him off in sight of his family, at the instant he
was meditating a mischievous design against the minister
of the parish, with whom he was greatly at enmity."*

RAISING THE DEAD AT WALTON-LE-DALE.

In the reign of Queen Elizabeth and the year 1560,
three judicial astrologers met in Preston, for the purpose
of raising a corpse by incantations.   They were Dr. Dee,
Warden of Manchester, Edward Kelly, his assistant, and
" seer," and Paul Wareing, of Dove Cotes, near Clayton

* See Roby's *Traditions of Lancashire.*

Brook. Casaubon, in his "True and faithful Account of what passed for many years between John Dee and some Spirits," (apparently quoting from Weever's *Funeral Monuments*) states that "The aforesaid Master Edward Kelly, a person well skilled in judicial astrology, with one Paul Wareing (who acted with him in these incantations and all these conjurations) and Dr. Dee, went to the churchyard of St. Leonard's, in Walton-le-Dale, near Preston, and entered the burial ground exactly at midnight, the moon shining brightly, for the purpose of raising the body of a person who had been interred there, and who had during his life hidden a quantity of money without disclosing the fact previous to his death. Having had the grave pointed out to them on the preceding day, they opened it, removed the coffin lid, and set to work by various exorcisms, until the body became animated, by the spirit entering it again. The body then rose out of the grave and stood upright before them. It not only satisfied their wicked desires, it is said, but delivered several strange predictions concerning persons in the neighbourhood, which were literally and exactly fulfilled. Sibley, in his *Occult Sciences,* relates a similar account of this transaction, and also gives an engraving representing the scene, which took place at the midnight hour in the church of Walton. Another account states that Dr. Dee was engaged with Kelly in this enterprise, August 12th, 1560, and that Paul Wareing, of Clayton Brook, was the other who gave assistance in endeavouring to obtain an intercourse with familiar spirits."—(*Whittle's Preston.*)

AN EARL OF DERBY CHARGED WITH KEEPING
A CONJUROR.

The loyal and munificent Edward (third) Earl of Derby, notwithstanding his great services to Queen Elizabeth, and

K

his long-proved loyalty, was maligned and accused of trai-
torous intentions. The Earl of Huntingdon wrote to Sir
William Cecil, then the Queen's Secretary of State (afterwards Lord Burghley, her Treasurer), a letter, commu-
nicating suspicions of the Earl of Derby, which the writer
asked should be burned as soon as read, but which has
been preserved (and printed) amongst Lord Burghley's
State Papers (I. 603.) Modernising the spelling, the letter
runs thus :—

Sir,—I am bolder to write to 'you on weighty matters, than I dare be
to some others ; the cause I leave to your consideration, and so to you
only I am bold to impart that I hear. The matter in short is this :—
Among the Papists of Lancashire, Cheshire, and the Cosynes (?), great
hope and expectation there is, that Derby will play as foul a part this
year as the two Earls did the last year. [See the Rising in the North.]
I hope better of him for my part, and for my respects, both general and
particular, I wish him to do better. I know he hath hitherto been loyal,
and even the last year, as you know, gave good testimony of his fidelity,
and of his own disposition, I think, will do so still ; but he may be
drawn by evil counsel, God knoweth to what. I fear he hath even at
this time many wicked counsellors, and some too near him. *There is
one Browne, a conjuror, in his house, kept secretly.* There is also one
Uphalle, who was a pirate, and had lately his pardon, that could tell
somewhat, as I hear, if you could get him. He that carried my Lord
Morley over, was also there within this se'ennight, kept secretly. He
with his whole family never raged so much against religion as they do
now, he never came to common prayer for this quarter or this year, as I
hear, neither doth any of the family, except five or six persons. I dare
not write what more I hear, because I cannot justify and prove it ; but
this may suffice for you in time to look to it. And surely, in my simple
opinion, if you send some faithful and wise spy, that would dissemble
to come from D'Alva, and dissemble popery, you might understand all ;
for if all be true that is said, there is a very fond company in the house
at this present. I doubt not but you can and will use this matter better
than I can advise you. Yet let me wish you to take heed to which of
your companions (though you be now but five together) you utter this
matter *ne forte* it be in Lathom sooner than you would have it ; for
some of you have men about you and friends attending on you, &c.,
that deal not always well. I pray God save our Elizabeth and confound
all her enemies ; and thus I take my leave, committing you to God his
tuition.

Your assured poor friend,
From Ashby, 24 Aug., 1570.   H. HUNTYNGDON.
P.S.—Because none there should know of my letter, I would not
send it by my servant, but have desired Mr. Ad. to deliver it to you

in secret. When you have read it, I pray you to burn it and forge the name of the writer. I pray God I may not hear any more of your coming to ——.

There seems to have been no substantial ground for suspecting the loyalty of the Earl of Derby, which remained unshaken through another ordeal, the conspiracy of the Duke of Norfolk to marry the Queen of Scots, and place her on the English throne. But the Bishop of Ross gave evidence, that in Mary's design, in 1571, to escape from Sheffield Castle to the Continent, she was aided by several Lancashire gentlemen; and adds, that she wrote a letter by a little priest of Rolleston's to Sir Thomas Stanley. Sir Thomas Gerrard and Rolleston devised a cypher for her; and they offered to convey her away, and willed the Bishop to ask the Duke of Norfolk's opinion therein. The prelate further stated that Hall told him that if the Queen [Mary] would get two men landed in Lancashire, Sir Thomas Stanley, and Sir Edward Stanley, along with Sir Thomas Gerrard, and Rolleston, would effect her escape to France or Flanders, &c. Upon this evidence Sir Thomas Stanley, Sir Thomas Gerrard, and Rolleston, were apprehended, and committed to the Tower as state prisoners.*

----◆----

MIRACLES, OR MIRACULOUS STORIES.

An age of credulity is naturally rich in miracles. Superstition is ever prone to explain the mysterious, or to account for the questionable, by hunting for some supernatural cause; and hence the popular love for and strong

---

* (*Lord Burghley's Papers,* vol. ii., p. 771.) The death of Edward Earl of Derby, "with whom (says Camden) the glory of hospitality hath in a manner been laid asleep," took place on the 24th October 1572.

faith in the miraculous. No church erected before the
Reformation but had its miraculous legend; no well or
spring of a remote antiquity but had its tradition, either
connected with its origin or with its marvellous and
miraculous powers of healing. The miracle of a past
age, preserved to the present in the form of a legend, is
equally entitled to a place in our Folk-Lore.

MIRACLES BY A DEAD DUKE OF LANCASTER AND KING.

One of the Harleian Manuscripts (Cod. 423), found
amongst the papers of Fox the Martyrologist, and entitled
" De Miraculis Beatissimi Militis Xpi Henrici Vj." (Of
the Miracles of the Most blessed Knight of Christ, Henry
VI.), consisting of about 150 closely written pages, con·
tains an account of a vast number of reputed miracles
performed by this weak and credulous monarch (who long
hoped to pay his large debts by the aid of two alchemists !)
and of which the following specimens will doubtless suffice
for our readers :—How Richard Whytby, priest of St.
Michael's, was long ill of a fever, and at last miraculously
cured by journeying to the tomb of Henry VI. John,
called Robynson, who had been blind ten years, recovered
his sight by visiting Henry's tomb. How Henry Lancaster
afflicted in fever, was miraculously cured in three days by
the appearance of the blessed prince Henry VI. in the sky.
How a girl called Joan Knyght, who was nearly killed
with a bone sticking in her throat, and considered dead, on
the bystanders invoking Henry VI., vomited the bone and
was restored to health. If these superstitions wanted a
crowning absurdity, that is not wanting in the fact that
Henry VII. actually sent an embassy to Rome, to impor-
tune the newly-elected Pope Julius II. to canonize Henry

VI. as a saint! His holiness referred the matter to certain cardinals, to take the verification of the deceased monarch's holy acts and miracles; but these were not sufficiently obvious to entitle him to the dignity of the calendar, and the negotiation was abandoned in despair.*

Mr. Monckton Milnes, M.P. (now Lord Houghton), in an interesting letter in *Notes and Queries*, I. 181, asks for information respecting this popular "saint," to whom the Church, however, denied canonization. He refers to Brady for an account of the miracle performed at the tomb of Thomas Earl of Lancaster, and of the picture or image of the Earl exhibited in St. Paul's, London, and the object of many offerings. Brady cites the opinion of an ecclesiastic, who doubted the propriety of this devotion being encouraged by the Church; the Earl, besides his political offences, having been a notorious evil-liver. In June 1327, a "King's letter" (of Edward III.) was given to Robert de Weryngton, authorizing him and his agents to collect alms throughout the Kingdom for the purpose of building a chapel on the hill where the Earl was beheaded; and praying all prelates and authorities to give him aid and heed. This sanction gave rise to imposture; and in the following December a proclamation appeared, ordering the arrest and punishment of unauthorized persons collecting money under this pretence and taking it for their own use. The chapel was constructed, and officiated in till the dissolution of the monasteries; the image in St. Paul's was always regarded with especial affection, and the cognomen of "*Saint* Thomas of Lancaster" was generally accepted and understood. Five hundred years after the execution of the Earl of Lancaster [in 1822], a large stone coffin, massive and roughly hewn, was found in

* Baines's *Lancashire.*

a field that belonged of old to the Priory of Pomfret, but
at least a quarter of a mile distant from the hill where the
chapel stood.   Within was the skeleton of a full-grown
man, partially preserved; the skull lay between the thighs.
There is no record of the decapitation of any person at
Pontefract of sufficient dignity to have been interred in a
manner showing so much care for the preservation of the
body, except the Earl of Lancaster.   The coffin may have
been removed here at the time the opposite party forbade
its veneration, from motives of precaution for its safety.—
R. M. M.—[The Editor of *Notes and Queries* adds, that
" The Office of St. Thomas of Lancaster," which begins
" *Gaude, Thoma, ducum decus, lucerna Lancastriæ*," is
printed in the volume of " *Political Songs* " edited by Mr.
Wright for the Camden Society, from a royal MS. in the
British Museum, *MS. Reg.* 12.   Another correspondent,
we believe Mr. James Thompson of Leicester, states that
at the dissolution of the monasteries in that town, several
relics of St. Thomas (who was Earl of Leicester, as well
as of Lancaster) were exhibited; amongst others his felt
hat, which was considered a great remedy for the head-
ache !]

A MIRACULOUS FOOTPRINT IN BRINDLE CHURCH.

Beneath the eastern gable of the chancel lies a huge
stone coffin, with a cavity for the head, but its history is
unknown.   In the wall just above it is a small indentation,
resembling the form of a foot, which, according to tradition, was made by the high-heeled shoe of a Popish dispu-
tant, who, in the ardour of debate, wished, if the doctrine
he advanced was not true, that his foot might sink into
he stone, " upon which the reforming stone instantly
softened and buried the papistical foot;" much in the

same way, no doubt, as the flag in Smithells Hall received the print of the foot of George Marsh, the martyr."*

THE FOOTPRINT AT SMITHELLS OF GEORGE MARSH, THE MARTYR.

George Marsh, one of the three Lancashire martyrs in the reign of Queen Mary, was the son of Mr. George Marsh, a yeoman of Dean, and was born about 1575. He was educated at the Bolton Free Grammar School, and for a time followed farming, and, marrying at twenty-five, settled there till the death of his wife; when, placing his children with his father, he became a student at Cambridge University, was ordained, and was appointed curate of Allhallows, Bread-street, London. He continued for some time preaching the reformed doctrines, and zealously supporting the Protestant faith, both in London and Lancashire; and while in his native county, in March 1555, he learned that he had been sought after by the servants of Mr. Barton of Smithells Hall, a magistrate; on which he went thither voluntarily, and was examined before Mr. Barton. In a passage near the door of the dining-room is a cavity in a flag, bearing some resemblance to the print of a man's foot, and this cavity is said by tradition to have been caused by the martyr stamping his foot to confirm his testimony, and it is shown to this day as a miraculous memorial of the holy man. The story goes, that " being provoked by the taunts and persecutions of his examiners, he stamped with his foot upon a stone, and, looking up to Heaven, appealed to God for the justness of his cause; and prayed that there might remain in that place a

* Baines's *Lancashire.*

constant memorial of the wickedness and injustice of
his enemies." It is said that about the beginning of
the eighteenth century this stone was removed by
two or three young men, of the family of Barton,
then living at the hall, during the absence of their
parents ; that they cast it into the clough behind the hall ;
but all the inmates of the house were so much disturbed
that same night by alarming noises, that they could not
rest. Inquiry led to confession, the stone was replaced,
and the noises ceased. It is also stated that in 1732, a
guest (John Butterworth, of Manchester,) sleeping alone
in the Green Chamber at Smithells Hall, saw an appari-
tion, in the dress of a minister with bands, and a book in
his hand. The ghost of Marsh (for so it was pronounced
to be) disappeared through the door-way, and on the
owner of Smithells hearing the story, he directed that
divine service (long discontinued) should be resumed at
the hall chapel every Sunday. Such are some of the
stories told about Smithells Hall ; and there is hardly an
old hall in the country that has not one or more such
traditions floating about its neighbourhood. It is as if
ghostly visitants scorned to honour with their presence any
house below the dignity of a hall. In this case, it may be
observed that neither in Marsh's own account of what
passed at Smithells, nor in Mr. Whatton's Biographical
notice of him in Baines's *History of Lancashire*, is any
mention made of the miraculous foot-print. But in a
volume of four or five tracts printed at Bolton (no year
stated) the third tract is "The Life and Martyrdom of
George Marshe," &c. "Also, the particulars respecting
the print of a foot on the flag shewn at Smithills Hall,
near Bolton ;" which latter is signed "W. D.," and dated
"August 22, 1787." Amongst other discrepancies, it
may be observed that W. D. makes Marsh's interrogator

" Sir Roger Barton ;" while Marsh, a native of the immediate neighbourhood " invariably writes of him as " Mr.
Barton."

———————

A LEGEND OF CARTMEL CHURCH.

Better than six hundred years ago (runs the story) some
monks came over to Lancashire from another country ;
and, finding all this part of the kingdom covered with
wood, they resolved to build a monastery in some part of
Cartmel Forest. In their rambles, they found a hill which
commanded a prospect so beautiful and extensive that they
were quite charmed with it. They marked out a piece of
ground on the summit, and were preparing to build the
church, when a voice spoke to them out of the air, saying
" Not there, but in a valley, between two rivers, where
the one runs north, and the other south." Astonished at
this strange command, they marvelled where the valley
could be, for they had never seen a valley where two
rivers ran in contrary directions. They set out to seek
this singular valley, and travelled throughout the North of
England, but in vain. Wearied with their fruitless search,
they were returning to the hill where they had heard the
strange voice. In passing through a valley covered with
wood, they came to a small river, the stream of which ran
north. They waded through it, and shortly after found
another, the stream of which ran south. They placed the
church midway between the two streams, upon a little
island, of hard ground, in the midst of a morass ; dedicat-
ing it to St. Mary. They also built a small chapel on the
hill where they had heard the voice, which they dedicated
to St. Bernard. The chapel has long since disappeared,
but the hill is still called Mount Bernard.*

* See *Lonsdale Magazine*, February, 1821.

THE PROPHET ELIAS, A LANCASHIRE FANATIC.

In 1562, a native of Manchester who called himself Elias, but whose real name was Ellys, pretended to possess the spirit of prophecy. He went to London, where he made some proselytes, uttering his "warning voice" in the public places. James Pilkington, D.D., a native of Rivington, in Lancashire, and an eminent Protestant divine, who was raised by Queen Elizabeth in 1560 to the See of Durham, preached before the Queen at Greenwich, against the supposed mission of this Manchester fanatic. The Bishop of London, three days afterwards, ordered the northern prophet to be put in the pillory in Cheapside. He was thence committed to Bridewell, where he died in or about 1565.

OMENS AND PREDICATIONS.

An intense desire to know future events, besides being the great encouragement of astrologers, sorcerers, and magicians, wise men, cunning women, fortune-tellers, &c., has given rise to a large class of small circumstances which are regarded as indicative of coming good or bad luck, of good or evil fortune, to the observer or the person experiencing their influence. Hence, nothing is more common than to hear amongst uneducated and credulous people predications from the most trivial occurrences of daily life. A winding-sheet in the candle, spilling the salt, crossing knives, and various other trifles, are omens of evil to thousands of lore-folk to this day. Should one of your children fall sick when on a visit at a friend's house, it is held to be sure to entail bad luck on that family for the rest of the year, if you stay over New Year's-day. Persons have been known to travel sixty miles with a sick child rather than run the risk. A flake of soot on the bars of the grate is said to indicate the approach of a stranger; a bright spark on the wick of a candle, or a long piece of stalk in the tea-cup, betokens a similar event. When the fire burns briskly, some lover smirks or is good-humoured. A cinder thrown out of the fire by a jet of gas from burning coals, is looked upon as a coffin, if its hollow be long; as a purse of gold, if the cavity be roundish. Crickets in a house are said to indicate good fortune; but should they forsake the chimney corner, it is a sure sign of coming misfortunes.

In the neighbourhood of Lancaster I know ladies who consider it "lucky" to find *old iron :* a horseshoe or rusty nail is carefully conveyed home and hoarded up. It is also considered lucky if you see the *head* of the first lamb in spring; to present his *tail* is the certain harbinger of misfortune. It is also said that if you have money in your pocket the first time you hear the cuckoo, you will never be without all the year.*

In Lancashire we still dislike the moaning or hooting of owls and the croaking of ravens, as much as the Romans did of old. In a large class of our population few would yet defy evil fate, by beginning a journey or any important undertaking, or marrying, on a Friday; on which day Lancashire, like other sailors, have a strong repugnance to beginning a voyage. This day of the week is regarded as of evil augury, because it was the day (Good Friday) when our Saviour's blood was shed. The auguries of dreams are so numerous, that a large class of chap-books are still to be found circulating in country places, from *Mother Shipton* to *Napoleon's Book of Fate.* Few young women in the country, farmers' daughters and servants,

* "T. D.," in *Notes and Queries.*

were without a favourite "Dream-Book." Again, the farmer or cottager deems it necessary, in order to secure a crop of onions, to sow the seed on St. Gregory's-day [March 12] named "Gregory-gret-Onion," (*i. e.*, Gregory the Great). Amongst the more pardonable longings to raise the veil of futurity are those of village maidens (and not a few of those in towns too, and of all ranks) to get a peep at the figure of the husband whom the future has in store for her. On All-Hallows Eve she strews the ashes which are to take the form of one or more letters of her lover's name; she throws hemp-seed over her shoulder and timidly glances to see who follows her. On the fast of St. Agnes she watches a small candle called a "pig-tail," to see the passing image of her future husband. The up-turned tea-cup, for its leaves, or the coffee-cup for its "grounds;" the pack of cards, with the desired King of Hearts or Diamonds, the sputterings and spurtings of a tallow-candle, all furnished to the omen-instructed damsel some sign by which to read the future, and to arrive at a knowledge of her lot in life, as to husband, children, fortune, &c. When leaving home to begin a journey, or to commence any future enterprise, it is deemed an important observance, necessary to insure good luck, to walk "withershins" (*i.e.*, as the weather or sun shines). In many country places this is always observed by a bridal party when advancing to the altar to have the marriage solemnized, and, of course, one particular aisle of the church is the only fortunate or lucky one to proceed by. Some, however, say that to walk "widdershins" is to take a direction contrary to the course of the sun, *i.e.*, from right to left.* Some persons more credulous than humane, will shut up a poor cat in the oven, to ensure their own

* See Halliwell's *Archaic Dictionary*, in voce.

good luck. Days have long been parcelled out between lucky and unlucky, for any important undertaking, as a journey, taking a partner in business or for life, buying land, or even for such trivial matters as blood-letting, taking physic, cutting the hair, or paring nails. Again, the moon's age is an important element in securing future weal or woe. For the first year of an infant's life many mothers will not have its hair or nails cut, and when the year is gone these operations must be performed when the moon is so many days old, to ensure good results. A tooth, as soon as it has been drawn, should be sprinkled with salt, and thrown into the fire; if it be lost, no rest or peace will be enjoyed till it is found again. The following are a few omens drawn from observing peculiarities about animals :—

CATS.

1. If a cat tear at the cushions, carpets, &c., with its claws, it is considered to be a sign of wind. Hence we say, " the cat is raising the wind." 2. If a cat in washing its face draw its paw quite over its forehead, it is a sign of fair weather. If not so, it betokens speedy rain. 3. Allowing cats to sleep with you is considered very unhealthy. They are said to " draw your health away." 4. Those who play much with cats have never good health. A cat's hair is said to be indigestible, and you will die if one get into your stomach. 5. It is counted unlucky to allow cats to die in a house. Hence when they begin to be ill they are usually drowned. A case of this kind occurred in Burnley a short time ago. 6. If a kitten come to a house, it is counted a lucky omen.

DOGS.

1. Dogs are said to sit down and howl before the door when any one is about to be sick, or die. A death is considered *certain* if the dog return as often as driven away. 2. Dogs are hence considered to be somehow acquainted with the spirit world, " or else," as one said, " how should they know when a person is going to die ?'' This is firmly believed in about Mellor and Blackburn. In Burnley and neighbourhood equally so at present. 3. The *life* of a dog is sometimes said to be *bound up* with that of its master or mistress. When either *dies* the other cannot *live*. Is this a remnant of the old belief in the transmigration of souls ? 4. The whining of a favourite dog is considered by many to betoken calamity to the family to which it belongs.

LAMBS.

It is very lucky for lambs to have their faces towards you when you first see them in Spring. The omen is much more favourable when they are looking towards the east.

BIRDS.

To kill or ill-use swallows, wrens, redbreasts, &c., is accounted unfortunate; for these all frequent our houses for good. There is a stanza common among us which declares that

> " A Cock Robin and a Jenny Wren
> Are God Almighty's cock and hen;
> A Spink and a Sparrow
> Are the Devil's bow and arrow."

Birds are supposed by some to be somehow cognizant of what is about to happen. A *jackdaw* is always an unwelcome visitor, if it alight on the window-sill of a sick chamber. A *white dove* is thought to be a favourable omen; its presence betokens recovery to the person within, or it is *an angel in that form* ready to convey the soul of a dying person to heaven. I once knew a Wesleyan' Methodist who was of opinion that "forgiveness of sins" was assured to her by a small bird, which flew across her path when she had long been praying for a token of this kind. When a *Canary-bird* sings cheerfully, all is well with the family that keeps it; when it becomes silent, and remains so, there is calamity in store for that household. If you hear the *cuckoo* shout towards the east, for the first time in any year, and have gold, silver, and copper coin in your pockets, you will never want money during that year.

SWALLOWS.

1. If swallows, or martins, begin to build their nests about a house or barn, it is looked upon as predicating good luck to the occupier. " The *more* birds the *better* luck." 2. On the contrary, when they forsake a haunt, the occupiers become apprehensive of misfortune. Hence farmers will always protect such birds, and often ill-use boys who may be stoning them, or attempting to rob their nests.

MAGPIES.

There are, at least in Lancashire and Yorkshire, many curious superstitions connected with this bird. Its appearance *singly* is still regarded in both these counties by many even of the educated representatives of the last generation, as an evil omen, and some of the customs supposed to break the charm are curious. One is simply to raise the

hat as in salutation, another to sign the cross on the breast,
and to make the same sign by crossing the thumbs.   This
last custom is confined to Yorkshire, and I know one
elderly gentleman who not only crosses his thumbs, but
spits over them when in that position, a practice which
was, he says, common in his youth.   The superstition
applies only to a single magpie, according to the old
nursery legend :—

> " One for sorrow,
> Two for mirth,
> Three for a wedding,
> And four for a birth." *

I met a person the other day who solemnly assured me
that he had seen a ' pynot' as he came along the road ;
but he had made the figure of a cross on the mire in the
road, in order to avert the evil omen."†

In Lancashire they say :—

> " One for anger,
> Two for mirth,
> Three for a wedding,
> Four for a birth,
> Five for rich,
> Six for poor,
> Seven for a witch :
> I can tell you no more."‡

But in Tim Bobbin it is expressly said that two magpies
are indicative of ill-fortune :—" I saigh two rott'n pynots,
hong 'um, that wur a sign of bad fashin ; for I heerd my
gronny say hoo'd as leef o' seen two Owd Harries os two

---

* " E. B." (Liverpool) in *Notes and Queries,* 3rd series, vol. IX., p. 187).
  † " T. T. W."
  ‡ Another version has the last four lines thus :—

> " Five for a fiddle,
> Six for a dance,
> Seven for England,
> Eight for France."

pynots."* " I shall catch none to-day," we heard a man advanced in life, exclaim in a melancholy tone, who was angling in the river Ribble. " Why ?" we asked, " the day is not inauspicious." " No ; but do you not see that magpie ?" In fact *pynots,* that is, magpies, according, to an old Lancashire superstition, are considered birds of ill-omen. In spring it is considered by old-fashioned anglers unlucky to see a single magpie ; but two are a favourable auspice, because in cold weather one bird only leaves the nest in search of food, the other remaining to keep the eggs or the young ones warm ; but when both are out together, the weather is warm, mild, and favourable for fishing."†

DREAMS.

This might well form a great division of itself, in any work on Folk-lore. Yet a little reflection will serve to show that it is only one branch, though a very large one, of the general subject of " Omens." Dreams are regarded by the superstitious simply for what they predicate as about to happen; in other words, they are important to the credulous only as *omens* of coming events. Itinerant hawkers and small village shops drive a considerable trade in " Dream Books," or " Books of Fate," which profess to interpret every dream and to explain every omen, whether of good or evil import. Of the great variety and extent of " Dream-Book literature " we cannot treat, for want of space. Hawkers and small shops sell a vast quantity of penny dream-books in Lancashire. One of the oldest specimens of these chap-books we have met with is a little 32mo. volume, entitled " *Mother Shipton's Legacy,*

----

* J. O. Halliwell's *Nursery Rhymes.*
† *Pictorial History of Lancashire.*

or a favourite Fortune-book, in which is given a pleasing interpretation of dreams, and a collection of prophetic verses, moral and entertaining." (York, 1797, price 4*d.*) Cap. I. treats of Lucky and Unlucky Days; II. of Moles on the Person; III. Miscellaneous; IV. Dreams; and V. a Magical Table. A few specimens of the dream portion may suffice:—To dream of joy denotes grief; of fine clothes, poverty; of sweetmeats, a whipping; of flying, falling down; of fire, anger; of serpents, private enemies; of money, loss; of weeping, joy; of bathing, ease from pain; of kissing, strife; of feasting, want; of many people, affliction; of singing, sorrow; of changing abode, sudden news; of fishing, good luck; of death, marriage; of finding money, bad luck; of gold, death; of embracing, death; of being bald, misfortune; of a long nose, death; of growing fat, wealth; of drinking water, good entertainment; of the sun rising, preferment; of flashes of fire, sudden death; of being among tombs, riches by the death of relations; of your teeth falling out, losses; of a lean ox, famine; of a fine garden, much pleasure.

[*Moral.*]

> Though plain and palpable each subject seems,
> Yet do not put your trust too much in dreams;
> Events may happen, which in dreams you see,
> And yet as often quite contrary be :
> This learned hint observe, for Shipton's sake—
> Dreams are but interludes which fancies make.

Many persons persuade themselves into the belief that events are revealed to them in dreams. Those who can neither *see* nor *hear* spirits generally presume to have this faculty. *One* dream is not taken much notice of, but if the dream be repeated substantially *three* times, the events of the dreams are supposed to be sure to come to pass. Some *see* all the circumstances as *realities* in their dreams, others only have dim recollections; they *hear* all but do not *see* the persons. This agrees with the supposed *prophetical* dreams of the ancient Greeks and Romans. (*Homer, Virgil, Ovid,* &c.) Morning dreams are more to be relied on than those of any other time. Those of the morning twilight are most valued. Horrid dreams, or those in which the dreamer feels very uneasy, are supposed to predict bad luck, or misfortune to the family. " Dreams," they say, " always go by contraries." There is a very general belief in dreams among the people of Lancashire. The following are a few not hitherto noticed by the writer:—1. Dreaming of *misfortune* betokens *prosperity.*

> " Content and happy may they be
> Who dream of cold adversity ;
> To married man and married wife
> It promises a happy life."

1. To dream of sickness betokens *marriage* to young persons. 3. Dreaming of being before an altar indicates sorrow and misfortune. 4. To see angels is a sure sign of coming happiness. 5. When you dream of being angry with any one, you may count that person amongst your best friends. 6. To dream of catching fish is very unfortunate ; every fish you take betokens the death of some valued friend. 7. Dreaming about balls, dances, &c., indicates coming good fortune. To the young we may say :—

> " Who dreams of being at a ball,
> No cause have they for fear;
> For soon they will united be
> To those they hold most dear."

8. When persons dream of losing their hair, it is a sign of loss of health, friends, or property. 9. If a person dream of losing *one,* or *more,* of his teeth, it is a sign that he will lose *one,* or *more,* lawsuits which he may happen to

be engaged in. I knew a person who had a case in our county court. The case was to come on on the Thursday; but on Wednesday night he dreamt he had lost a tooth. On the case being decided against him, he appealed to his dream as a sure indication of his non-success. 10. Dreaming of bees is counted lucky, because they are industrious.

> " Happy the man who dreaming sees
> The little humble busy bees
> Fly humming round their hive."

If the bees sting you, it is a sign of bad luck, crosses and difficulties. 11. Dreaming of marriage, brides, &c., is a sign of death, or long sickness. 12. To dream of a candle burning *brightly* betokens health, prosperity; and *vice versâ*. 13. Dreaming of cats betokens treachery; but if you kill the cat you will have revenge. 14. To dream of seeing a *coffin* is unlucky; but to dream of seeing a *corpse* betokens a speedy marriage. 15. Dreaming of *death* betokens long life and happiness. 16. To dream that you are *dirty* implies sickness for a longer or shorter period. 17. If you dream of being *drowned* you will experience some loss. 18. To dream of *falling* indicates loss. 19. To dream of *flying* implies that you will not succeed in accomplishing high things. 20. If you dream of the water in a river being very *clear* you will have good luck; if the water be *muddy* you will have misfortune. 21. When a widow dreams of seeing her husband, it is a sure sign that she will soon have an eligible offer. 22. If you dream that you are daubed with ink, you may be sure that some one is *writing* evil of you. 23. Dreaming of going a journey indicates a change in your circumstances. 24. To dream of flying kites, or playing with bunches of keys, betokens prosperity and advancement in business. 25. To dream of cutting yourself, or of being infested with lice, indi-

cates misfortune or disease. 26. It is very fortunate to
dream of milk. 27. To dream of being naked indicates
shame and misfortune. 28. To dream of the nose bleeding is a very sure sign of misfortune and loss. 29. Dreaming of seeing the ocean in a calm state betokens steadiness
of circumstances; and *vice versâ.* 30. To dream of rats
indicates difficulties; of snow, prosperity and success; of
a wedding, death; and of a widow, that your husband,
wife, or lover, will desert you.

All the preceding, and many more, are well-known to
every Lancashire lad and lass.

THE MOON.

Our farmers predict fair weather, or the reverse, according
as the new moon " lies on her back, "or " stands upright."
It is also very unlucky for anyone to look at the new moon,
for the first time, through the window.

HÆVER OR HIVER.

A " quarter " of the heavens, or compass, or direction;
" a lucky hæver " is a fortunate or desirable direction.
The origin of this word is somewhat difficult of explanation; nor is it certain whether its proper etymon has yet
been ascertained. It is still in common use among some
of the farmers in East Lancashire, and was much more
frequently used some thirty or forty years ago. " What
hæver is the wind in this morning?" was a common inquiry when any prediction respecting the weather for the
day was about to be hazarded. " I don't expect much
rain," would probably be the reply, " the wind is in a
good *hæver.*" There is generally most rain in these parts

of Lancashire when the wind blows from the south or south-west; and hence if the wind came from the eastward continued rain was not to be expected.

Most persons have a notion that the East is the most sacred point of the compass. The Star of the Nativity was seen in the east; the chancel, or most holy portion of a church is placed at the east; and the dead are buried so as to rise with their faces towards the east on the morning of the resurrection. These considerations have been applied to the *hæver* from which the wind may blow; and hence the proverb occasionally met with among those who live in the neighbourhood of Mellor and Ramsgreave, near Blackburn, to the effect that "the East is a lucky *hæver*."

A writer who signs himself "F. C. H." in *Notes and Queries*, 3rd series, vol. VII., p. 310, asks whether *hæver* is not "a peculiar pronunciation of *ever*, so that the above inquiry would be in plain English, *whatever* is the wind in this morning?" This derivation appears both too fanciful and insufficient; for when we consider that Lancashire formed part of the Danelagh, and was long a Danish kingdom, and that its dialect contains a large admixture of Danish words; we are naturally led to examine whether such a term may not be found in the Danish language. On examination this proves to be the fact, for "Hive," (pronounced "heeve," as "high" is pronounced "hee,") is the verb "to blow;" and hence "hiver" or "hæver," as applied to the place whence the wind is blowing. This derivation appears to be both natural and sufficient, since it fully accounts for the use of this peculiar term; which, by the way, is not found in Halliwell's *Dictionary of Archaic Words*, or in Wright's more recent work on the same subject.

DEASIL OR WIDERSINNIS.

These are Celtic names for going round by way of ensuring good fortune. The former name is derived from the Gaelic *deas* or *des,* the right hand, and *Syl,* the sun, and denotes a motion from east to west, or according to the apparent motion of the sun ; and is a custom of high antiquity in religious ceremonies. In the western isles fire was carried in the right hand in this course, about the house, corn, cattle, &c., about women before they were churched, and children before they were baptized. So the fishermen rowed the boat about first sun-wise to ensure a lucky voyage. On the other hand, the Highland *Widersinnis* (whence the Lancashire *Wither-shins*) was from left to right or west to east, or opposed to the course of the sun, a course used in magical ceremonies, and said to be the mode of salutation given by witches and warlocks to the devil.*—(See page 140 *suprâ.*)

OMENS OF WEATHER FOR NEW YEAR'S-DAY.

In a Saxon MS. we find that " If the Kalends, or first of January, fall on the Lord's-day, then will the winter be good, pleasant and warm."† Another Saxon MS. in the Cotton Library contains the omens to the following effect : —" If the Kalends of January be on the moon's day (Monday) then there will be a severe and confused winter, a good spring, windy summer, and a rueful year, in which there will be much sickness. If the Kalends fall on Tuesday, then the winter will be dreary and severe, a windy heat and rainy summer, and many women will die ; ships will voyage in danger, and kings and princes will die. If on Wednesday, there will be a hard winter and bad spring ;

---

* Hampson's *Medii Ævi Kalend.,* vol. I. 255.
† Hickes's *Thesaurus,* II. 194.

but a good summer. The fruits of the earth will be much
beaten down, honey will be scarce, and young men will die.
If on Thursday, there will be a good winter, windy spring,
good summer, and abundance of the fruits of the earth,
and the plough will be over the earth; but sheep and
children will die. If on Friday, there will be a variable
winter, good spring and summer, with great abundance,
and sheep's eyes will be tender in the year. If on Saturday, there will be a snowy winter, blowing spring, and
rainy summer; earth fruits will labour, sheep perish, old
men die, and other men be sick; the eyes of many will
be tender, and fires will be prevalent in the course of the
year. If the Kalends fall on Sunday, there will be a good
winter, windy spring, and dry summer; and a very good
year this year will be; sheep will increase, there will
be much honey, and plenty and peace will be upon the
earth."*

DEATH TICK OR DEATH WATCH.

The death tick is not yet forgotten in the district around
Burnley. Very recently the insect has disturbed the
imagination of a young lady, and its ticks have led
to more than one gloomy conjecture. It is a curious
circumstance that the *real* death tick must only tick *three*
times on each occasion.

SUPERSTITIONS, GENERAL AND MISCELLANEOUS.

There are great numbers of small superstitions, beliefs,
and practices which we must place under this general head.
Before entering on these at length, we may briefly notice

* *Bibl. Cott. MSS. Tiberius, A.* III., fol. 39 b., and 40.

the fact in many cases, the probability in a still greater number, that the origin of superstitions still held to the popular heart, is to be found in other countries and in remote times. Indeed Folk-lore superstitions may be said to be the *débris* of ancient mythologies; it may be of Egypt or India, Greece or Rome, Germany or Scandinavia. Many of the following superstitions have been already glanced at or briefly referred to in the introductory chapter.

POPULAR SUPERSTITIONS.

Lancashire, like all other counties, has its own peculiar superstitions, manners, and customs, which find no parallels in those of other localities. It has also, no doubt, many local observances, current opinions, old proverbs, and vulgar ditties, which are held and taken in common with the inhabitants of a greater extent of country, and differ merely in minor particulars,—the necessary result of imperfect oral transmission. The following are a few of these local superstitions :—

1. If a person's hair, when thrown into the fire, burns brightly, it is a sure sign that the individual will live long. The brighter the flame, the longer life ; and *vice versâ*.

2. A young person lightly stirs the fire with the poker to test the humour of a lover. If the fire blaze brightly, the lover is good-humoured; and *vice versâ*.

3. A crooked sixpence, or a copper coin with a hole through, is accounted a *lucky* coin.

4. Cutting or paring the nails of the hands or feet, on a Friday or Sunday, is very unlucky.

5. If a person's *left* ear burn, or feel hot, somebody is praising the party; if the *right* ear burn, then it is a sure sign that some one is speaking evil of the person.

6. Children are frequently cautioned by their parents

not to walk *backwards* when going an errand; it is a sure
sign that they will be unfortunate in their objects.

7. Belief in witchcraft is still strong in many of the
rural districts. Many believe that others have the power
to bewitch cows, sheep, horses, and even persons to whom
the witch has an antipathy. One respectable farmer
assured me that his horse was bewitched into a stable
through a loophole twelve inches by three! The fact, he
said, was beyond doubt, for he had locked the stable-door
himself when the horse was in the field, and had kept the
key in his pocket. Soon afterwards a party of farmers
went through the process known as " burning the witch
out," or "killing the witch" as some express it; the
person suspected soon died, and the neighbourhood became
free from his evil doings.

8. A horse-shoe is still nailed behind many doors to
counteract the effects of witchcraft. A *hogstone* with a
hole through, tied to the key of the stable-door, protects
the horses, and, if hung up at the bed's head, the farmer
also.

9. A hot iron put into the cream during the process of
churning, expels the witch from the churn. Dough in
preparation for the baker is protected by being marked
with the figure of a cross.

10. Warts are cured by being rubbed over with a black
snail; but the snail must afterwards be impaled upon a
hawthorn. If a bag, containing as many pebbles as a
person has warts, be tossed over the *left* shoulder, it will
transfer the warts to whomsoever is unfortunate enough
to pick up the bag.

11. If black snails are seized by the horns and tossed
over the *left* shoulder, the process will ensure good luck
to the person who performs it.

12. Profuse bleeding is said to be instantly stopped by

certain persons, who pretend to possess the secret of a certain form of words or charm.

13. The power of bewitching, producing evil to persons by *wishing* it, &c., is supposed to be transmitted from one possessor to another when one of the parties is about to die.

14. Cramp is effectually prevented by placing the shoes with the toes just peeping from beneath the coverlet; or by tying the garter round the *left* leg, below the knee.

15. Charmed rings are worn by many for the cure of dyspepsia; and so also are charmed belts for the cure of rheumatism.

16. A red-haired person is supposed to bring ill-luck, if he be the first to enter a house on New Year's Day. Black-haired persons [are on the contrary deemed so lucky that they] are rewarded with liquor or small gratuities for "taking in the New Year" to the principal houses in their respective neighbourhoods.

17. If any householder's fire does not burn *through* the night of New Year's Eve, it betokens bad luck through the ensuing year. If any one allow another to take a live coal, or to light a candle, on that eve, the bad luck extends to the grantor.*

Amongst other Lancashire popular superstitions are the following:—

That a man must never "go a courting" on a Friday. If an unlucky fellow is caught with his lady-love on that day, he is followed home by a band of musicians, playing on pokers, tongs, pan-lids, &c., unless he can rid himself of his tormentors by giving them money for drink.

That whooping-cough will never be taken by any child that has ridden upon a bear. The old bearward's profits arose in great part from the money given by parents whose

* T. T. W. in *Notes and Queries,* iii. 55.

children had had a ride. The writer knows of cases in
which the charm is said to have been effectual.

That whooping-cough may be cured by tying a hairy
caterpillar in a small bag round the child's neck, and as
the caterpillar dies the cough goes.

That Good Friday is the best day of all the year to
begin weaning children, which ought, if possible, to be
put off till that day.

That May cats are unlucky, and will suck the breath of
infants.

That crickets are lucky about a house, and will do no
harm to those who use them well ; but that they eat holes
in the worsted stockings of such members of the family as
kill them. I was assured of this on the experience of a
respectable farmer's family.

That ghosts or boggarts haunt certain neighbourhoods.
There is scarcely a dell in my vicinity where a running
stream crosses a road by a small bridge or stone plat,
where such may not be seen. Wells, ponds, gates, &c.,
have often this bad repute. I have heard of a calf with
" eyes like saucers," a woman without a head, a white
greyhound, a column of white foam like a large sugar loaf
in the midst of a pond, or group of little cats, &c., as the
shape of the boggart; and sometimes it took that of a
lady, who jumped behind hapless passengers on horseback.
It is supposed that a Romish priest can lay them, and that
it is best to cheat them to consent to being laid " while
hollies are green." Hollies being evergreens, the ghosts
can reappear no more.*

Mr. J. Eastwood, of Ecclesfield, adds to T. T. W.'s
seventeen superstitions the following six :—

1. If a cock near the door crows with his face towards
it, it is a sure prediction of the arrival of a stranger.

* P. P. in *Notes and Queries*, iii. 516.

2. If the cat frisk about the house in an unusually lively manner, windy or stormy weather is approaching.

3. If a dog howl under the window at night, a death will shortly happen in the house.

4. If a *female* be the first to enter a house on Christmas or New Year's Day, she brings ill-luck to the house for the coming year.

5. For whooping-cough, pass the child nine times over the back and under the belly of an ass. (This ceremony I once witnessed, but cannot vouch for its having had the desired effect.)

6. For warts, rub them with a cinder, and this tied up in paper, and dropped where four roads meet [*i.e.* where two roads cross] will transfer the warts to whoever opens the parcel.*

BONES OF ST. LAWRENCE, AT CHORLEY.

In the parish church of Chorley, within the porch of the chancel, which belongs to the Standish family of Duxbury, *four* bones were shown, apparently thigh bones, said to have belonged to Saint Lawrence, the patron saint, which were brought over from Normandy by Sir Rowland Standish, in 1442, along with the head of that saint, which skull has, amongst the *Harl. MSS.*,† a certificate of a vicar of Croston, to which Chorley was then subject, preserved with the arms of the knight (azure, 3 plates) rudely tricked :—" Be it known to all men that I, Thomas Tarlton [or Talbot] vicar of the church of Croston, beareth witness and certify, that Mr. James Standish, of Duxbury, hath delivered a relique of St. Laurence's head

* *Notes and Queries,* iii. p. 516.
† Harl. MSS. Cod. 2042, fol. 239 a.

unto the church of Chorley, the which Sir Rowland of
Standish, knight, brother of the said James, and Jane his
wife, brought out of Normandy, to the worship of God
and St. Lawrence, for the profit and avail of the said
church ; to the intent that the foresaid Sir Rowland
Standish, and Dame Jane his wife, with their predecessors
and successors, may be in the said church perpetually
prayed for. And in witness of the which to this my
present writing I have set my seal. Written at Croston
aforesaid, the 2nd day of March, in the year of our Lord
God, 1442." [20 Hen. VI.]* St. Lawrence's Day is
August 10. As his martyrdom was said to be roasting
alive upon a gridiron, it is not clear how his thigh bones
should be preserved. But when we find there are *four* of
them, the miraculous character of the relics is at once
exhibited.

THE DEAD MAN'S HAND.

At Bryn Hall, now demolished, once the seat of the
Gerards, was a Roman Catholic Chapel and a priest, who
continued long after the family had departed, having
in his custody "The Dead Man's Hand," which is still
kept by the same or another priest, now residing at Garswood. Preserved with great care, in a white silk bag, it
is still resorted to by many diseased persons, and wonderful cures are said to have been wrought by this saintly
relic. It is said to be the hand of Father Arrowsmith,—
a priest who is stated to have been put to death at Lancaster for his religion, in the time of William III. The
story goes, that when about to suffer, he desired his
spiritual attendant to cut off his right hand, which should
then have the power to work miraculous cures on those

* Harl. MSS. Cod. 2042, fol. 239.

who had faith to believe in its efficacy. Not many years ago, a female sick of the small-pox had this dead hand lying in bed with her every night for six weeks, in order to effect her recovery, which took place.* A poor lad, living in Withy Grove, Manchester, afflicted with scrofulous sores, was rubbed with it; and though it had been said he was miraculously restored, on inquiry the assertion was found incorrect, inasmuch as he died in about a fortnight after the operation.† Not less devoid of truth is the tradition that Arrowsmith was hanged for " witnessing a good confession."

Having been found guilty of a rape (says Mr. Roby), in all probability this story of his martyrdom, and of the miraculous attestation to the truth of the cause for which he suffered, were contrived for the purpose of preventing the scandal that would have come upon the church through the delinquency of an unworthy member. A subordinate tradition accompanies that already related. It is said that one of the family of the Kenyons attended as under-sheriff at the execution, and that he refused the culprit some trifling favour at the gallows; whereupon Arrowsmith denounced a curse upon him,—to wit, that whilst the family could boast of an heir, so long they should never want a cripple; which prediction was supposed by the credulous to have been literally fulfilled.‡

* Mr. Roby derived this statement from Thomas Barritt, the antiquary, who in one of his MSS. writes—" I was in company with a woman who had lain with a relation of hers sick of the small-pox. During all the time they had this hand lying with them every night, on purpose to effect a safe recovery of the afflicted person." Barritt does not say, however, that the recovery took place.

† This story Mr. Roby derived from the same MSS. of Barritt, and also the statement of the real crime for which Arrowsmith was executed, and his alleged prophecy as to the Kenyons. Barritt says the dead hand was brought to Manchester about the time of the troubles in 1745, to cure a poor Papist lad, who came with Hill.

‡ See Roby's *Traditions of Lancashire*.

Mr. Roby, professing to give the *fact* upon which he founded
one of his tales, accuses the unfortunate priest of rape,
and states that he was executed for that crime in the reign
of William III. All this Mr. Roby gives as from himself,
and mentions a curse pronounced by Father Arrowsmith
upon the under-sheriff who executed him, in the reign of
William III. Now Arrowsmith was hung, under sanction
of an atrocious law, for no other reason but because he
had taken orders as a Catholic priest, and had endeavoured
to prevail upon others to be of his own faith. For this
offence, and for this offence alone, in 1628,—in the reign
not of William III., but of Charles I.,—he was tried at
Lancashire Assizes, and hanged, drawn, and quartered, in
the same year that Edmund Ashton, Esq. was sheriff.
Mr. Roby must have seen what was the real state of the
case in the same history of Lancashire* as that which he
repeatedly quotes.†

The hand of Arrowsmith, having been cut off after his
death, was brought to Bryn Hall, where it was used by
the superstitious to heal the sick, sometimes by the touch,
and at others by friction : faith, however, is essential to
success, and a lack of the necessary quality in the patient,
rather than any decrease in the healing emission from the
relic, is made to account for the disappointment which
awaits the superstitious votaries of this fanatical operation.
The " dead man's hand," or, as the Irish harvestmen are
accustomed to call it, " the holy hand," was removed from
Bryn to Garrwood, and subsequently to the priest's house
at Ashton, near Lancaster, where it remains in possession
of the priest, if the light and knowledge of the present
age have not consigned it to the earth.‡   A Roman Catholic

---

* Baines's *Lancashire*, vol. iii. p. 638.
† *Pictorial History of Lancashire*.
‡ Mannex's *Hist. and Topog. of Lancashire*.

publication, issued in 1737, signed by nineteen witnesses, seventeen of whom were Protestants (the names being with-held, however, as it is alleged, for prudential reasons), attest, that in 1736, a boy of twelve years, the son of Caryl Ha-warden, of Appleton-within-Widness, county of Lancaster, was cured of what appeared to be a fatal malady by the application of Father Arrowsmith's hand, which, according to the narrative, was effected in the following manner :— The boy had been ill fifteen months, and was at length deprived of the use of his limbs, with loss of his memory, and impaired sight. In this condition, which the physicians had declared hopeless, it was suggested to his parents, that as wonderful cures had been effected by the hand of " the martyred saint," it was advisable to try its effects upon their afflicted child. The " holy hand " was accordingly procured from Bryn, packed in a box, and wrapped in linen. Mrs. Hawarden having explained to the invalid her hopes and intentions, applied the back part of the dead hand to his back, stroking it down each side the backbone, and making the sign of the cross, which she accompanied with a fervent prayer that Jesus Christ would aid it with his blessing. Having twice repeated this operation, the patient, who had before been utterly helpless, rose from his seat, and walked about the house, to the surprise of seven persons who had witnessed the "miracle." From that day the boy's pains left him, his memory was restored, and his health became re-established ! The witnesses add, that the boy, on being afterwards inter-rogated, said that he *believed* the hand would do him good, and that upon its first touch he felt something give a short or sudden motion from his back to the end of his toes !"*

Another account states that Father Edmund Arrow-smith, of the Society of Jesus, was a native of Haydock,

* Baines's *History of Lancashire*, vol. iii. pp. 638-9.

M

in the parish of Winwick, and was born in 1585. In
1605 he entered the Roman Catholic College of Douay,
where he was educated, and in 1612 he was ordained
priest. His father's name was Robert Arrowsmith, and
his mother, Margery, was a lady of the ancient family of
the Gerards. In 1613 Father Arrowsmith was sent upon
the English mission, and in 1628 (4th Charles I.) was
apprehended and brought to Lancaster on the charge of
being a priest, contrary to the laws of the realm. He was
tried, sentenced to death, and executed on the 28th of
August, 1628, his last words being "Bone Jesu!" He
was afterwards cut down, embowelled, and quartered.
His head was set upon a pole or stake amongst the
pinnacles of Lancaster Castle, and his quarters were hung
upon four separate places of the same building. The hand
of the martyr, having been cut off after his death, was
brought to Bryn Hall [amongst his maternal relatives],
where it was preserved as a precious relic, and by the application of which numerous miraculous cures are said to have
been effected. "The holy hand" was removed from Bryn
to Garswood [in Ashton, a seat of the Gerards], and subsequently to the priest's house at Ashton-in-Makerfield,
where it still remains.* While the relic remained at Garswood,
it was under the care of the Gerards' family-chaplain for the
time being, and a fee was charged for its application to all
who were able to pay, and this money was bestowed in
charity on the needy or distressed. It is believed that no
fee is now charged. The late Sir John Gerard had no
faith in its efficacy, and many ludicrous anecdotes are
current in the neighbourhood of pilgrims having been
rather roughly handled by some of his servants, who were
as incredulous as himself;—such as getting a good beating
with a wooden hand (used for stretching gloves), and other

* Mannex's *History and Topography of Lancashire.*

heavy weapons ; so that the patients rapidly retraced their steps, without having had the application of the "holy hand." The applicants usually provide themselves with a quantity of calico or flannel, which the priest of St. Oswald's, Ashton, causes to come in contact with the " dead hand ;" the cloth is then applied to the part affected. Many instances are recorded of persons coming upon crutches or with sticks, having been suddenly so far restored as to be able to leave behind them these helps, as memorials, and return home, walking and leaping ; praising the priest for his charity ; the holy hand, for being the means of obtaining a cure ; and God for giving such power to the dead hand. Persons have been known to come from Ireland, and other distant parts, to be cured. Some of these return home with a large piece of the cloth which has been in contact with the hand. This they tear into shreds, and dispose of them to the credulous neighbours who have not the means of undertaking so long a pilgrimage. About four years ago (writes our informant), I saw a poor maniac being dragged along by two or three of her relatives, and howling most piteously. I asked what they were going to do with her, when one of them (apparently her mother) replied : " And sure enough, master, we're taking her to the priest, to be rubbed with the holy hand, that the devi may leave her." A short time afterwards I saw them returning, but the rubbing had not been effectual. A policeman assisted to remove the struggling maniac to a neighbouring house, till a conveyance could be got to take her to Newton Bridge railway station.*

* From a Correspondent.

NINETEENTH CENTURY SUPERSTITION.

Will it be credited that thousands of people have, during the past week, crowded a certain road in the village of Melling, near Ormskirk, to inspect a sycamore tree, which has burst its bark, and the sap protrudes in a shape resembling a man's head ? Rumour spread abroad that it was the re-appearance of Palmer, who " had come again, because he was buried without a coffin !" Some inns in the neighbourhood of this singular tree reaped a rich harvest.*

PENDLE FOREST SUPERSTITION.

Pendle Forest, in the neighbourhood of Burnley, has long been notorious for its witches. [After referring to the cases of alleged witchcraft in the beginning of the 17th century, the writer continues :] Two hundred years have since passed away, and yet the old opinions survive ; for it is notorious that throughout the Forest the farmers still endeavour to

> " Chase the evil spirits away by dint
> Of sickle, horse-shoe, and hollow flint."

Clay or wax images, pierced through with pins and needles, are occasionally met with in churchyards and gardens, where they have been placed for the purpose of causing the death of the persons they represent. Consumptive patients and paralytics are frequently said to be bewitched ; and the common Lancashire proverb, " Draw blood of a witch, and she cannot harm you," has been many times practically verified upon quarrelsome females within my own experience. In extreme cases the " witch-killer" is resorted to, and implicit faith

* The *Tablet,* July 26, 1856.

in his powers is not a rare item in the popular creed. Such a person usually combines the practice of Astrology with his other avocations. He casts nativities; gives advice respecting stolen property; tells fortunes; and writes out "charms" for the protection of those who may consult him. . . . Even the wives of clergymen have been known to consult "wise men" on doubtful matters respecting which they desired more satisfactory information.—*T. T. W.*

EAST LANCASHIRE SUPERSTITION.

Strong minds often are unable to escape the thraldom of tradition and custom, with the help of liberal education and social intercourse. How then are the solitary farmers on the skirts of moorland wastes, to free themselves from hereditary superstition? The strength of such traditions is often secret and unacknowledged. It nevertheless influences the life; it lurks out of sight, ready to assert its power in any great crisis of our being. It is a homage to the unseen and the unknown, in fearful contradiction with the teaching of Christianity, for it creates, like the religion of the Jezzidies, a ritual of propitiation to malignant powers, instead of the prayer of faith to the All-merciful. The solitude of the life in the moorland farm-houses does not, however, foster the influence of superstitious madness, perhaps, so much as the wild, stormy climate, which holds its blustering reign through six months of every year, in this region of morass and fog, dark clough, and craggy chasm. Night shuts in early. The sun has gone down through a portentous gulf of clouds which have seemed to swallow up the day in a pit of darkness. The great sycamores stagger in the blast which rushes from the distant sea. The wind moans through the night like a troubled spirit, shakes the house as though it demanded admittance from the storm, and rushes down the huge chimney (built two centuries ago for the log fires, and large, hot heap of wood ashes), driving down a cloud of smoke and soot, as though by some wicked cantrip the witches careering in the storm would scatter the embers and fire the building. The lone watcher by some sick bed, shudders as the casements are battered by the tempest; or the bough of some tree, or a branch of ivy, strikes the panes like the hand of some unseen thing fumbling at the casement latch; or, awake from pain or care, restless with fever or fatigue, or troubled with superstitious horror, the lone shepherd waits for the day, as for a reprieve to conscious guilt, and even trembles while he mutters some charm to exorcise the evil that rides exulting on the storm. A year of ill-luck comes. The ewes are barren; the cows drop their untimely calves, though crooked sickles and lucky stones have been hung in the shippons. The milk is " bynged," or will not churn, though a hot poker has been used to spoil the witchery. The horses escape from the stable at night, though there is a horse-shoe over the door, and the hinds say they were carefully " heawsed an' fettled, and t'dooers o weel latched, bur t'feeorin (fairies) han 'ticed 'em eawt o' t' leawphooles, an' flown wi' em' o'er t'stone dykes, wi' o t'yates tynt (gates shut), an' clapp'd 'em reet i' t' meadow, or t' corn, just wheer tey shudna be." As the year advances, with such misadventures, apprehension grows. Is there some evil eye on the house? Will the hay be spoiled in the field? Will the oats ripen, or must they be cut green and given to the cattle? Or, if they ripen, will the stormy autumn wrap its mantle of mist and rain so closely about them, that they cannot be housed before they have sprouted, or have spoiled? The cold, bitter damp benumbs the strength of the feeble. Appetite and health fail; a fear creeps into the life. Fate seems to have dragged the sufferer into a vault of gloom, to whisper foreboding and inspire dread. These traditions of mischief wrought by malignant men inheriting the wicked craft and vindictive spite of the sorcerers, are uttered at the fireside, or if not so uttered, are brooded upon by a disturbed fancy.*

SUPERSTITIOUS FEARS AND CRUELTIES.

John Webster, the great exposer of shams and denouncer of superstitions in his day, and author of the " *Discovery of pretended Witchcraft*," speaking of a clear head and sound judgment as necessary to competent witnesses, says :—" They ought to be of a sound judgment, and not of a vitiated and distempered phantasy, nor of a melancholic constitution; for these will take a bush to be a bugbear, and a black sheep to be a demon; the noise of the wild swans flying high in the night, to be spirits ; or, as they call them here in the north, ' Gabriel Ratchets ;' the calling of a daker hen in the meadow, to be the Whistlers; the howlings of the female fox in a gill or clough for the male, to be the cry of fairies." The Gabriel Ratchets seem to be the same with the German Rachtvogel or Rachtraven. The word and the superstition are still known in Lancashire, though in a sense somewhat different; for the Gabriel Raches are supposed to be something like litters of puppies yelping in the air. Ratch is certainly a name for a dog in general (see *Junius, in voce*). The whistlers are supposed to be the green or

* Scarsdale.

whistling plovers, which fly very high in the night, uttering their characteristic note.   Speaking of the practices
of witch-finders, Webster says :—" By such wicked means
and unchristian practices, divers innocent persons have lost
their lives ; and these wicked rogues wanted not greater
persons (even of the ministry too) that did authorize and
encourage them in their diabolical courses.   And the like
in my time happened here in Lancashire, where divers,
both men and women, were accused of supposed witchcraft, and were so unchristianly and inhumanly handled,
as to be stripped stark naked and laid upon tables and beds
to be searched for their supposed witch-marks; so barbarous and cruel acts doth diabolical instigation, working
upon ignorance and superstition, produce."*

SUPERSTITIOUS BELIEFS IN MANCHESTER IN THE SIX-
TEENTH CENTURY.

At no period in the history of Manchester was there a
greater disposition to believe in witchcraft, demoniacal
possession, and the occult sciences, than at the close of the
sixteenth century.   The seer, Edward Kelly, was ranging
through the country, practising the black art.   Dr. Dee, the
friend and associate of this impostor, had recently obtained
the appointment of warden of the Collegiate Church of
Manchester, by favour of his royal patroness, Queen
Elizabeth, herself a believer in his astrological calculations ;
and the fame of the strange doings [the alleged demoniacal
possession of seven persons] in the family of Mr. Starkie,
had spread far and wide.   The new warden was really a
learned man, of the most inquisitive mind, addicted to
chemical pursuits, not wholly unconnected with those of

* Dr. Whitaker's *History of Whalley.*

alchemy, and not altogether detached from the practice of necromancy and magic, notwithstanding his positive asseverations to the contrary, in his petition to King James. His life was full of vicissitudes; though enjoying the patronage of princes, he was always involved in embarrassments, and was at length obliged to relinquish his church preferment at Manchester, owing to the differences that existed between himself and his ecclesiastical brethren. It does not appear that during his residence in Lancashire he encouraged the deceptions of the exorcists. On the contrary he refused to become a party in the pretended attempt to cast out devils at Cleworth, and he strongly rebuked Hartley, the conjuror, who was afterwards executed at Lancaster for his disgraceful practices.

WELLS AND SPRINGS.

Water, everywhere a prime necessity of life, is pre-eminently so in the hot and arid plains and stony deserts of Asia and Africa. We need not be surprised, therefore, to find that in all the ancient Eastern cults and mythologies, springs and wells were held in reverence, as holy and sacred gifts to man from the Great Spirit of the universe. The great Indo-European tide of migration, rolling ever westward, bore on its bosom these graceful superstitions, which were eagerly adopted by the old church of Christendom ; and there is scarcely an ancient well of any consequence in the United Kingdom which has not been solemnly dedicated to some saint in the Roman Catholic calendar.

WELLS NEAR LIVERPOOL.—At Wavertree, near Liverpool, is a well bearing the following inscription, " Qui non dat quod habet, dæmon infra videt : 1414 " (Who giveth not what he hath, the devil below, seeth—or, if the last word be not *videt* but *ridet*—laughs). Tradition says that at one period there was a cross above it, inscribed " Deus dedit, homo bibit" (God gave it, man drinks it) ; and that all travellers gave alms on drinking. If they omitted to do so, a devil who was chained at the bottom of the well, laughed. A monastic building stood near, and the occupants received the contributions.* A well at Everton, near Liverpool, has the reputation of being haunted, a fratricide having been committed there ; but it is not mentioned in the local history of Syer, which merely says,—" The water for this well is procured by direct access to the liquid itself, through the medium of a few stone steps : it is free to the public, and seldom dry." Being formerly in a lonely situation, it was a haunt of pickpockets and other disorderly characters. It is now built over, and in a few years the short subterranean passage leading to the well will be forgotten.†

PEGGY'S WELL.—Peggy's Well is near the Ribble, in a field below Waddow Hall, not far from Brunckerley stepping stones, in attempting to cross by which several lives have been lost, when the river was swollen by a rapid rise, which even a day's rain will produce. These calamities, as well as any other fatal accidents that occur in the neighbourhood, are usually attributed to Peggy, the evil spirit of the well. There is a mutilated stone figure by

* Mr. Baines, in his *History of Lancashire* (vol. iii. p. 760), says that in Wavertree is an ancient well with a rude, unintelligible inscription, of the date of 1414, which is thus *charitably* rendered by the villagers :—

" He that hath, and wont bestow,
The Devil will reckon with him below."

Or.

" He who here does not bestow,
The Devil laughs at him below."
† " Agmond," in *Notes and Queries,* vol. vi. p. 305.

the well, which has been the subject of many strange tales and apprehensions. It was placed there when turned out of the house at Waddow, to allay the terrors of the domestics, who durst not continue under the same roof with this mis-shapen figure. It was then broken, either from accident or design, and the head, some time ago, as is understood, was in one of the attic chambers at Waddow. Who Peggy of the Well was, tradition doth not inform us.

The writer of the *Pictorial History of Lancashire* states that going to Waddow Hall he inquired after the headless stone statue known as " Peg o' th' Well ;" and a neat, intelligent young woman, one of the domestics, showed him Peggy's head on the pantry table, and the trunk by a well in an adjacent field. He gives the following as the substance of the tradition :—The old religion had been supplanted in most parts of the country, yet had left memorials of itself and its rites in no few places, nor least in those which were in the vicinity of an old Catholic family, or a monastic institution. Some such relic may Peggy have originally been. The scrupulous proprietors of Waddow Hall regarded the innocuous image with distrust and aversion ; nor did they think themselves otherwise than justified in ascribing to Peggy all the evils and mischances that befel in the house. If a storm struck and damaged the house, Peggy was the author of the damage. If the wind whistled or moaned through the ill-fitting doors and casements, it was " Peggy at her work," requiring to be appeased, else some sad accident was sure to come. On one occasion Master Starkie—so was the host named— returned home very late with a broken leg. He had been hunting that day, and, report said, made too free with the ale afterwards. But, as usual, Peggy bore the blame : for some dissatisfaction she had waylaid the master of the

house and caused his horse to fall. Even this was for-
given. A short time afterwards a Puritan preacher was
overtaken by a fresh in the river, in attempting to cross
over on the stepping-stones which lay just above the Hall,
the very stones on which poor King Henry (VI.) was
captured. Now, Mrs. Starkie had a great attachment to
those preachers, and had indeed sent for the one in question, for him to exorcise and dispossess her youngest son,
a boy of ten years of age, who was grievously afflicted
with a demon, or, as was suspected, tormented by Peggy.
" Why does he not come ?" asked the lady, as she sat that
night in her best apparel, before a blazing fire and near a
well-furnished table. " The storm seems to get worse.
Hark ! heard ye no cry ? Yes ! there again. Oh, if the
dear man be in the river ! Run all of ye to his rescue."
In a few minutes two trusty men-servants returned, pant-
ing under the huge weight of the dripping parson. He
told his tale. " 'Tis Peg," she suddenly exclaimed, " at
her old tricks ! This way, all !" She hurried from the apart-
ment, rushed into the garden, where Peggy stood quiet
enough near a spring, and with one blow of an axe, which
she had seized in her passage, severed Peggy's head from
her body.

St. Helen's Well in Brindle.—Dr. Kuerden in
one of his MSS., describing the parish of Brindle in
Leyland, states that " Over against Swansey House, a
little towards the hill, standeth an ancient fabric, once the
manor-house of Brindle, where hath been a chapel belonging to the same ; and a little above it, a spring of very clear
water, rushing straight upwards into the midst of a fair
fountain, walled square about in stone and flagged in the
bottom, very transparent to be seen, and a strong stream
issuing out of the same. This fountain is called St.
Ellen's Well, to which place the vulgar neighbouring

people of the Red Letter [*i.e.*, Roman Catholics] do much resort with pretended devotion on each year upon St. Ellins-day—[St. Helen's-day is either on May 21, August 18, or September 3, the two first being days of a queen, and the last of an empress saint]—where and when, out of a foolish ceremony, they offer or throw into the well, pins, which there being left, may be seen a long time after by any visitor of the fountain."*

St. Helen's Well, near Sefton.—Mr. Hampson† notices the superstition of casting pins or pebbles into wells, and observing the circles formed thereby on the surface of the agitated water, and also whether the water were troubled or preserved its clearness and transparency; from which appearances they drew omens or inferences as to future events. He adds: " I have frequently seen the bottom of St. Helen's Well, near Sefton, Lancashire, almost covered with pins, which, I suppose, must have been thrown in for the like purposes."

————◆————

WITCHES AND WITCHCRAFT.

In the lore of these subjects no county in England is richer than Lancashire. The subject is a large one, and may even be said to include all the cases of demoniacal possession described in the earlier pages of this volume, since all these alleged possessions were the result of malice and (so-called) witchcraft. Indeed it is not easy to separate these two superstitious beliefs in their practical operation; witchcraft being the supposed cause, and demoniacal possession the imagined effect. The reader will find much, bearing on both branches of the subject, under both titles.

* Baines's *History of Lancashire*, vol. iii. p. 497.
† *Medii Ævi Kalendarium.*

WITCHCRAFT IN THE FIFTEENTH CENTURY.

The first distinct charge of witchcraft in any way connected with this county, is that of the wife of the good
Duke Humphrey, Eleanor, Duchess of Gloucester, the
associate of Roger Bolingbroke, the priest and necromancer,
and Margaret Jourdain, the witch of Eye. The Duke of
Gloucester, uncle and protector to the king, having become
obnoxious to the predominant party, they got up in 1441
a strange prosecution. The Duchess of Gloucester,
Eleanor, the daughter of Lord Cobham, a lady of haughty
carriage and ambitious mind, being attached to the prevailing superstitions of the day, was accused of the crime
of witchcraft " for that she, by sorcery and enchantment, intended to destroy the king, to the intent
to advance and promote her husband to the crown."*
It was alleged against her and her associates, Sir Roger
Bolingbroke, a priest, and chaplain to the Duke, (who
was addicted to astrology,) and Margery Jourdain,
the witch of Eye, that they had in their possession a wax
figure of the king, which they melted by a magical
device before a slow fire, with the intention of wasting
away his force and vigour by insensible degrees. The
imbecile mind of Henry was sensibly affected by this
wicked invention ; and the Duchess of Gloucester, on
being brought to trial (in St. Stephen's Chapel, before the
Archbishop of Canterbury) and found guilty of the design to
destroy the king and his ministers by the agency of witchcraft, was sentenced to do public penance in three places
within the city of London, and to suffer perpetual imprisonment. Her confederates were condemned to death and
executed, Margaret Jourdain being burnt to death in
Smithfield. The duchess, after enduring the ignominy

Hall's *Chronicle.*

of her public penance, rendered peculiarly severe by the
exalted state from which she had fallen, was banished to
the Isle of Man, where she was placed under the ward
of Sir Thomas Stanley. On the way to her place of
exile, she was confined for some time, first in Leeds Castle,
and afterwards in the Castle of Liverpool ;* the earliest
and the noblest witch on record within the county of
Lancaster. Another account states that amongst those
arrested as accomplices of the duchess were a priest and
canon of St. Stephen's, Westminster, named Southwell,
and another priest named John Hum or Hume. Roger
Bolingbroke, the learned astronomer and astrologer (who
died protesting his ignorance of all evil intentions), was
drawn and quartered at Tyburn ; Southwell died in prison
before the time of execution ; and John Hum received
the royal pardon. The worst thing proved against the
duchess was that she had sought for love-philters to
secure the constancy of her husband.† Shakspere, in the
Second Part of King Henry VI., Act 1, Scene 4, represents
the duchess, Margery Jourdain, Hume, Southwell, and
Bolingbroke, as engaged in raising an evil spirit in the
Duke of Gloucester's garden, when they are surprised and
seized by the Dukes of York and Buckingham and their
guards. The duchess, after remaining in the Isle of Man
some years, was transferred to Calais, under the ward of
Sir John Steward, knight, and there died.

* William of Worcester's *Annales Rerum Anglicarum*, pp. 460-61.
† *Pictorial History of England*, vol. ii. p. 81 ; also Hall's *Chronicle.*

THE FAMOUS HISTORY OF THE LANCASHIRE WITCHES:

Containing the manner of their becoming such; their enchantments,
spells, revels, merry pranks, raising of storms and tempests, riding
on winds, &c. The entertainments and frolics which have happened
among them. With the loves and humours of Roger and Dorothy.
Also, a Treatise of Witches in general, conducive to mirth and re-
creation. The like never before published.*

CHAPTER I.—*The Lancashire Witch's Tentation, and of the
Devil's appearing to her in sundry shapes, and giving
her money.*

Lancashire is a famous and noted place, abounding with
rivers, hills, woods, pastures, and pleasant towns, many of
which are of great antiquity. It has also been famous
for witches, and the strange pranks they played. Therefore, since the name of Lancashire Witches has been so
frequent in the mouths of old and young, and many imperfect stories have been rumoured abroad, it would doubtless tend to the satisfaction of the reader, to give some
account of them in their merry sports and pastimes.

Some time since lived one Mother Cuthbert, in a little
hovel at the bottom of a hill, called Wood-and-Mountain
Hill, in Lancashire. This woman had two lusty daughters, who both carded and spun for their living, yet was
very poor; which made them often repine at and lament
their want. One day, as Mother Cuthbert was sauntering
about the hill-side, picking the wool off the bushes, out
started a thing like a rabbit, which ran about two or three
times, and then changed into a hound, and afterwards into
a man, which made the old beldame to tremble, yet she
had no power to run away. So, putting a purse of money
in her hand, and charging her to be there the next day, he
immediately vanished away, and old Mother Cuthbert
returned home, being somewhat disturbed between jealousy
and fear.

* This is the title-page of an old 12mo chap-book, the date of publication of which is not shown.

Such is the first chapter of this marvellous story, which, it is clear, is a fiction based upon real narratives. It relates the witcheries of Mother Cuthbert and her two daughters, Margery and Cicely, under the auspices of an irch-witch, " Mother Grady, the Witch of Penmure [Penmaen-mawr] a great mountain of Wales." Here is " *The Description of a Spell.*—A spell is a piece of paper written with magical characters, fixed in a critical season of the moon, and conjunction of the planets; or sometimes by repeating mystical words. Of these there are many sorts." As showing what was the popular notion as to witches, take the following :—" About this time great search was made after witches and many were apprehended, but most of them gave the hangman and the gaoler the slip ; though some hold that when a witch is taken she hath no power to avoid justice. It happened, as some of them were going in a cart to be tried, a coach passed by, in which appeared a person like a judge, who, calling to one, bid her be of good comfort, for neither she nor any of her companions should be harmed. In that night all the prison locks flew open, and they made their escape; and many, when they had been cast into the water for a trial, have swam like a cork. One of them boasted she could go over the sea in an egg-shell. It is held on all hands they adore the devil, and become his bond-slaves, to have for a term of years their pleasure and revenge. And indeed many of them are more mischievous than others in laming and destroying cattle, and in drowning ships at sea, by raising storms. But the Lancashire witches, we see, chiefly divert themselves in merriment, and are therefore found to be more sociable than the rest." The closing chapter in this chap-book, contains "A short description of the famous Lapland Witches."

DR. DEE CHARGED WITH WITCHCRAFT.

On the usual proclamation of a general pardon, on the accession of James I., the crime of witchcraft was specially excepted from the general amnesty; and the credulous King's belief in this superstition encouraged witch-finders and numerous accusations in all parts of the country. Amongst others, it was remembered that Dr. Dee, then warden of the Collegiate Church of Manchester, had in the preceding reign predicted a fortunate day for the coronation of Queen Elizabeth, and had also undertaken to render innocuous the waxen effigy of that Queen, found in Lincoln's Inn-fields. He was also known to have made various predictions, to be the possessor of a magic crystal or stone,* and to have held a close intimacy with Edward Kelly, *alias* Talbot, a noted seer, conjuror and necromancer of the time. Accordingly Dr. Dee was formally accused of practising witchcraft, and a petition from him, dated 5th January, 1604, (preserved in the *Lansdowne MSS.,* Cod. 161,) praying to be freed from this revolting imputation, even at the risk of a trial for his life, sufficiently indicates the horror excited by the charge. The doctor's petition sets forth that "It has been affirmed that your Majesty's supplicant was the conjuror belonging to the most honourable privy council of your Majesty's predecessor of famous memory, Queen Elizabeth, and that he is, or hath been, a caller or invocater of devils or damned spirits. These slanders, which have tended to his utter undoing, can no longer be endured; and if, on trial, he is found guilty of the offence imputed to him, he offers himself willingly to the punishment of death, yea, either to be stoned to death, or to be buried quick, or to be burned unmercifully." He seems to have escaped scathe-

---

* This was sold by auction only a few years ago.

less, save in reputation; and in 1594, when applied to for
the purpose of exorcising seven demons who held possession of five females and two of the children of Mr
Nicholas Starkie, of Leigh, he refused to interfere advising they should call in some godly preachers, with whom
he would, if they thought proper, consult concerning a
public or private fast. He also sharply reproved Hartley
a conjuror, for his practices in this case.

THE LANCASHIRE WITCHES.

Come, gallant sisters, come along,
Let's meet the devil ten thousand strong;
Upon the whales' and dolphins' backs,
Let's try to choak the sea with wracks,
Spring leaks, and sink them down to rights.
            [*Line wanting.*]
And then we'll scud away to shour,
And try what tricks we can play more.

Blow houses down, ye jolly dames,
Or burn them up in fiery flames;
Let's rowse up mortals from their sleep,
And send them packing to the deep,
Let's strike them dead with thunder-stones,
With lightning search [? scorch] to skin and bones;
For winds and storms, by sea and land,
You may dispose, you may command.

Sometimes in dismal caves we lie,
Or in the air aloft we flie;
Sometimes we caper o'er the main,
Thunders and lightnings we disdain;

N 2

Sometimes we tumble churches down,
And level castles with the ground;
We fire whole cities, and destroy
Whole armies, if they us annoy.

We strangle infants in the womb,
And raise the dead out of their tomb;
We haunt the palaces of kings,
And play such pranks and pretty things ·
And this is all our chief delight,
To do all mischief in despight;
And when we've done, to shift away,
Untoucht, unseen, by night or day.

When imps do   *   *   *
We make them act unlucky feats;
In puppets' wax, sharp needles' points
We stick, to torture limbs and joints.
With frogs' and toads' most poys'nous gore
Our grizly limbs we 'noint all o'er,
And straight away, away we go,
Sparing no mortal, friend or foe.

We'll sell you winds, and ev'ry charm
Or venomous drug that may do harm;
For beasts or fowls we have our spells
Laid up in store in our dark cells;
For there the devils used to meet,
And dance with horns and cloven feet;
And when we've done, we frisk about,
And through the world play revel-rout.

We ride on cows' and horses' backs,
O'er lakes and rivers play nice knacks;

We grasp the moon and scale the sun,
And stop the planets as they run.
We kindle comets' whizzing flames,
And whistle for the winds by names;
And for our pastimes and mad freaks,
'Mongst stars we play at barley-breaks.*

We are ambassadors of state,
And know the mysteries of fate;
In Pluto's bosom there we ly,
To learn each mortal's destiny.
As oracles their fortunes show,
If they be born to wealth or wo,
The spinning Sisters' hands we guide,
And in all this we take a pride.

To Lapland, Finland, we do skice,
Sliding on seas and rocks of ice,
T'' old beldames there, our sisters kind,
We do impart our hellish mind;
We take their seals and hands in blood
For ever to renounce all good.
And then, as they in dens do lurk,
We set the ugly jades a-work.

We know the treasures and the stores
Lock'd up in caves with brazen doors;
Gold and silver, sparkling stones,
We pile on heaps, like dead men's bones.
There the devils brood and hover,
Keep guards, that none should them discover;
Put upon all the coasts of hell,
'Tis we, 'tis we, stand sentinel.

* For Sir Philip Sidney's poetical description of this old game, see
his *Arcadia*, or Brand's *Popular Antiquities* (Ed. 1841, vol. ii. p. 236).

SUPERSTITIOUS FEAR OF WITCHCRAFT.

During the sixteenth century whole districts in some
parts of Lancashire seemed contaminated with the presence of witches; men and beasts were supposed to
languish under their charm, and the delusion which
preyed alike on the learned and the vulgar did not allow
any family to suppose that they were beyond the reach of
the witch's power. Was the family visited by sickness?
It was believed to be the work of an invisible agency,
which in secret wasted the image made in clay before
the fire, or crumbled its various parts into dust. Did the
cattle sicken and die? The witch and the wizard were
the authors of the calamity. Did the yeast refuse to fer-
ment, either in the bread or the beer? It was the consequence of a "bad wish." Did the butter refuse to *come?*
The "familiar" was in the churn. Did the ship founder at
sea? The gale or hurricane was blown by the lungless
hag who had scarcely sufficient breath to cool her own
pottage. Did the Ribble overflow its banks? The floods
descended from the congregated sisterhood at Malkin
tower. The blight of the season, which consigned the
crops of the farmer to destruction, was the saliva of the
enchantress, or distillations from the blear-eyed dame who
flew by night over the field on mischief bent. To refuse
an alms to a haggard mendicant, was to incur maledictions
soon manifest in afflictions of body, mind, and estate, in
loss of cattle and other property, of health, and sometimes
even of life itself. To escape from evils like these no
sacrifice was thought too great. Superstitions begat cruelty
and injustice; the poor and the rich were equally interested in obtaining a deliverance; and the magistrate in
his mansion, no less than the peasant in his cot, was deeply
interested in abating the universal affliction. The Lanca-

shire witches were principally fortune-tellers and conjurors. The alleged securities against witchcraft were numerous, the most popular being the horse-shoe; hence we see. in Lancashire so many thresholds ornamented with this counter-charm. Under these circumstances the situation of the reputed witch was not more enviable than that of the individuals or families over whom she exerted her influence. Linked by a species of infernal compact to an imaginary imp, she was shunned as a common pest, or caressed only on the same principle which leads some Indian tribes to pay homage to the devil. The reputed witches themselves were frequently disowned by their families, feared and detested by their neighbours, and hunted by the dogs as pernicious monsters. When apprehended they were cast into ponds in the belief that witches swim; so that to sink or swim was almost equally perilous to them; they were punctured by bodkins to discover the witch imp or devil marks; they were subjected to hunger and kept in perpetual motion till confessions were obtained from a distracted mind. On their trials they were listened to with incredulity and horror, and consigned to the gallows with as little pity as the basest of malefactors. Their imaginary crimes created a thirst for their blood; and people of all stations, from the highest to the lowest, attended their trials at Lancaster with an intensity of interest that such mischievous persons, now divested of their sting, naturally excited. It has been said that witchcraft and kingcraft in England came in and went out with the Stuarts. This is not true. The doctrine of necromancy was in universal belief in the fourteenth and fifteenth centuries, and there was not perhaps a man in Lancashire who doubted its existence. The belief in witchcraft and in demoniacal possession was confined to no particular sect or persuasion; the Roman Catholics,

the members of the Church of England, the Presbyterians
Independents, and even the Methodists (though a sect of
more recent standing) have all fallen into this delusion;
and yet each denomination has upbraided the other with
gross superstition, and not unfrequently with wilful fraud.
It is due, however, to the ministers of the Established
Church to say that they were among the first of our
public writers to denounce the belief in witchcraft with
all its attendant mischiefs; and the names of Dr. Hars-
nett, afterwards Archbishop of York, of Dr. John Webster
(who detected Robinson, the Lancashire witch-hunter), of
Zach. Taylor, one of the king's preachers for Lancashire, and of Dr. Hutchinson, the chaplain in ordinary to
George I., are all entitled to the public gratitude for
their efforts to explode these pernicious superstitions. For
upwards of a century the sanguinary and superstitious laws
of James I. disgraced the English statute-book; but in the
ninth year of George II. (1735) a law was enacted
repealing the statute of James I., and prohibiting any
prosecution, suit, or proceeding against any person for
witchcraft, sorcery, enchantment, or conjuration. In this
way the doctrine of witchcraft, with all its attendant
errors, was finally exploded, except among the most
ignorant of the vulgar.*

A HOUSEHOLD BEWITCHED.

(From the *Late Lancashire Witches*, a comedy, by Thomas Heywood.)

My Uncle has of late become the sole
Discourse of all the country; for a man respected
As master of a govern'd family;
The house (as if the ridge were fix'd below,

* Baines's *History of Lancashire.*

And groundsills lifted up to make the roof),
All now's turn'd topsy turvy
In such a retrograde, preposterous way
As seldom hath been heard of, I think never.
The good man
In all obedience kneels unto his Son ;
He, with an austere brow, commands his Father.
The Wife presumes not in the Daughter's sight
Without a prepared curtsey ; the Girl, she
Expects it as a duty, chides her mother,
Who quakes and trembles at each word she speaks ;
And what's as strange, the Maid, she domineers
O'er her young Mistress, who is awed by her.
The Son, to whom the Father creeps and bends,
Stands in as much fear of the groom, his Man !
All in such rare disorder, that in some
As it breeds pity, and in others wonder,
So in the most part laughter.   It is thought
This comes by WITCHCRAFT !

THE LANCASHIRE WITCHES OF 1612.

King James VI. of Scotland, in 1594 (nine years before
he ascended the English throne as James I.), wrote and
published his disgracefully credulous and cruel treatise,
entitled " Dæmonologie," containing statements as to the
making of witches, and their practice of witchcraft, which,
if true, would only prove their revealer to be deep in the
councils of Satan, and a regular member or attendant of
assemblages of witches.   The royal witch-hater held that,
as witchcraft is an act of treason against the prince, the evidence of barnes [children] or wives [weak women], or ever
so defamed persons [*i.e.*, of character however infamous],

may serve for sufficient witnesses against them ; for [he asks], who but witches can be provers, and so witnesses of the doings of witches ? Besides evidence, "there are two other good helps that may be used for their trial; the one is the finding of their *mark,* and then trying the insensibleness thereof; the other is floating on the water" [or drowning], &c. Having thus opened the door by admitting the loosest evidence and the most absurd tests for the most unjust convictions, the royal fanatic adds, that all witches [*i.e.,* persons thus convicted] ought to be put to death, without distinction of age, sex, or rank. This "British Solomon" ascended the English throne in 1603, and, as might have been expected, witch-finders soon plied their infamous vocation with success. The wild and desolate parts of the parish of Whalley furnished a fitting scene for witch assemblies, and it was alleged that such meetings were held at Malkin Tower, in Pendle Forest, within that parish. At the assizes at Lancaster in the autumn of 1612, twenty persons, of whom sixteen were women of various ages, were committed for trial, and most of them tried for witchcraft. Their names were—
1. Elizabeth Southerne, widow, *alias* "Old Demdike" (aged eighty or more) ; 2. Elizabeth Device [probably Davies], *alias* "Young Demdike," her daughter; 3. James Device, son of No. 2 ; 4. Alizon Device, daughter of No. 2 ; 5. Anne Whittle, widow, *alias* "Chattox," *alias* Chatterbox [more probably Chadwicks], the rival witch of "Old Demdike" (and, like her, eighty or more years of age); 6. Anne Redferne, daughter of No. 5 ; 7. Alice Nutter; 8. Katherine Hewytt, *alias* "Mould-heels;" 9. Jane Bulcock, of the Moss End; 10. John Bulcock, her son; 11. Isabel Robey; and 12. Margaret Pearson, of Padiham. No. 12 was tried first for murder by witch-craft; 2nd for bewitching a neighbour; 3rd for bewitch-

ing a horse; and, being acquitted of the two former charges, was sentenced for the last to stand upon the pillory in the markets of Clitheroe, Padiham, Colne, and Lancaster for four successive market days, with a printed paper upon her head, stating her offence. The twelve persons already named were styled "Witches of Pendle Forest." The following eight were called "Witches of Samlesbury:"—13. Jennet Bierley; 14. Ellen Bierley; 15. Jane Southworth; 16. John Ramsden; 17. Elizabeth Astley; 18. Alice Gray; 19. Isabel Sidegraves; and 20. Lawrence Haye. The last four were all discharged without trial. The sensation produced by these trials was immense, not only in this, but throughout neighbouring counties, and Thomas Potts, Esq., the clerk of the court, was directed by the judges of assize, Sir Edward Bromley, Knt., and Sir James Altham, Knt., to collect and publish the evidence and other documents connected with the trial, under the revision of the judges themselves; and Potts's "Discovery of Witches," originally published in 1613, has been reprinted by the Chetham Society (vol. vi.), under the editorship of its president, Mr. James Crossley, F.S.A. According to Potts, Old Mother Demdike, the principal actress in the tragedy, was a general agent for the devil in all these parts; no man escaping her or her furies that ever gave them occasion of offence, or denied them anything they stood in need of. The justices of the peace in this part of the country, Roger Nowell and Nicholas Bannister, having learned that Malkin Tower [Malkin is a north-country name for a hare], in the Forest of Pendle, the residence of Old Demdike and her daughter, was the resort of the witches, ventured to arrest their head and another of her followers, and to commit them to Lancaster Castle. Amongst the rest of the voluntary confessions made by the witches, that of Dame Demdike is preserved. She confessed that, about twenty years ago, as she was coming home from begging, she was met near Gould's Hey, in the forest of Pendle, by a spirit or devil in the shape of a boy, the one half of his coat black and the other brown, who told her to stop, and said that if she would give him her soul, she should have anything she wished for. She asked his name, and was told *Tib*. She consented, from the hope of gain, to give him her soul. For several years she had no occasion to make any application to her evil spirit; but one Sunday morning, having a little child upon her knee, and she being in a slumber, the spirit appeared to her in the likeness of a brown dog, and forced himself upon her knee, and begun to suck her blood under her left arm, on which she exclaimed, "Jesus! save me!" and the brown dog vanished, leaving her almost stark mad for eight weeks. On another occasion she was led, being blind, to the house of Richard Baldwyn, to obtain payment for the services her daughter had performed at his mill, when Baldwyn fell into a passion, and bid them to get off his ground, calling them w——s and witches, and saying he would burn the one and hang the other. On this, *Tib* appeared, and they concerted matters to revenge themselves on Baldwyn; how, is not stated. This poor mendicant pretender to the powers of witchcraft, in her examination stated that the surest way of taking a man's life by witchcraft is to make a picture of clay, like unto the shape of the person meant to be killed, and when they would have the object of their vengeance suffer in any particular part of his body, to take a thorn or pin and prick it into that part of the effigy; and when they would have any of the body to consume away, then to burn that part of the figure; and when they would have the whole body to consume, then to burn the clay image; by which means the afflicted will

die. The substance of the examinations of the so-called
witches and others, may be given as follows :—Old
Demdike persuaded her daughter, Elizabeth Device, to
sell herself to the devil, which she did, and in turn
initiated her daughter, Alizon Device, in these infernal
arts. When the old witch had been sent to Lancaster
Castle, a grand convocation of seventeen witches and three
wizards was held at Malkin Tower on Good Friday, at
which it was determined to kill Mr. M'Covell, the
governor of the castle, and to blow up the building, to
enable the witches to make their escape. The other two
objects of this convocation were to christen the familiar
of Alizon Device, one of the witches in the castle, and
also to bewitch and murder Mr. Lister, a gentleman of
Westby-in-Craven, Yorkshire. The business being ended,
the witches, in quitting the meeting, walked out of the
barn, named Malkin Tower, in their proper shapes, but
on reaching the door, each mounted his or her spirit,
which was in the form of a young horse, and quickly
vanished. Before the assizes, Old Demdike, worn out by
age and trouble, died in prison. The others were brought
to trial. The first person arraigned before Sir Edward
Bromley, who presided in the criminal court, was Ann
Whittle, *alias* " Chattox," who is described by Potts as a
very old, withered, spent, and decrepit creature, eighty
years of age, and nearly blind, a dangerous witch, of
very long countenance, always opposed to Old Demdike,
for whom the one favoured, the other hated deadly, and
they accused each other in their examinations. This
witch was more mischievous to men's goods than to themselves; her lips ever chattered as she walked (hence,
probably, her name of Chattox or Chatterbox), but no
one knew what she said. Her abode was in the Forest of
Pendle, amongst the company of other witches, where the

woollen trade was carried on, she having been in her
younger days a wool-carder. She was indicted for having
exercised various wicked and devilish arts called witch-
crafts, enchantments, charms and sorceries, upon one
Robert Nutter, of Greenhead, in the Forest of Pendle,
and with having, by force thereof, feloniously killed him.
To establish this charge her own examination was read,
from which it appeared that fourteen or fifteen years ago,
a thing like " a Christian man " had importuned her to
sell her soul to the devil, and that she had done so, giving
to her familiar the name of *Fancy*. On account of an
insult offered to her daughter, Redfern, by Robert Nutter,
they two conspired to place a bad wish upon Nutter, of
which he died. It was further deposed against her that
John Device had agreed to give Old Chattox a dole of
meal yearly if she would not hurt him, and that when he
ceased to make this annual tribute, he took to his bed and
died. She was further charged with having bewitched
the drink of John Moore, and also with having, without
using the churn, produced a quantity of butter from a
dish of skimmed milk ! In the face of this evidence, and
no longer anxious about her own life, she acknowledged
her guilt, but humbly prayed the judges to be merciful to
her daughter, Anne Redfern ; but her prayer was in vain.
Against Elizabeth Device, the testimony of her own
daughter, a child nine years of age, was received ; and the
way in which her evidence was given, instead of filling
the court with horror, seems to have excited their applause
and admiration. Her familiar had the form of a dog and
was called *Bull*, and by his agency she bewitched to death
John and James Robinson and James Mitton ; the first
having called her a strumpet, and the last having refused to
give Old Demdike a penny when she asked him for charity.

To render her daughter proficient in the art, the prisoner taught her two prayers, by one of which she cured the bewitched, and by the other procured drink. The person of Elizabeth Device, as described by Potts, seems witch-like. " She was branded (says he) with a preposterous mark in nature ; her left eye standing lower than her right; the one looking down and the other up at the same time." Her process of destruction was by modelling clay or marl figures, and wasting her victims away along with them. James Device was convicted principally on the evidence of his child-sister, of bewitching and killing Mrs. Ann Towneley, the wife of Mr. Henry Towneley, of the Carr, by means of a picture of clay ; and both he and his sister were witnesses against their mother. This wizard (James Device), whose spirit was called *Dandy,* is described as a poor, decrepit boy, apparently of weak intellect, and so infirm, that it was found necessary to hold him up in court on his trial.

Upon evidence of this kind no fewer than ten of these unfortunate people were found guilty at Lancaster, and sentenced to suffer death. Eight others were acquitted; why, it is not easy to see, for the evidence appears to have been equally strong, or rather equally weak and absurd, against all. The ten persons sentenced were—Ann Whittle *alias* " Chattox," Elizabeth Device, James Device, Anne Redfern, Alice Nutter, Catherine Hewytt, John Bulcock, Jane Bulcock, Alizon Device, and Isabel Robey.

The judge, Sir Edward Bromley, in passing sentence on the convicted prisoners, said, " You, of all people, have the least cause of complaint; since on the trial for your lives there hath been much care and pains taken ; and what persons of your nature and condition were ever arraigned and tried with so much solemnity ? The court

hath had great care to receive nothing in evidence against
you but matter of fact (!)* As you stand simply (your
offence and bloody practices not considered) your fate
would rather move compassion than exasperate any man;
for whom would not the ruin of so many poor creatures
at one time touch, as in appearance simple, and of little
understanding ? But the blood of these innocent children,
and others his Majesty's subjects whom cruelly and bar-
barously you have murdered and cut off, cries unto the
Lord for vengeance. It is impossible that you, who are
stained with so much innocent blood, should either prosper
or continue in this world, or receive reward in the next."
Having thus shut the door of hope, both as to this life and
the future, the judge proceeded to urge the wretched
victims of superstition to repentance ! and concluded by
sentencing them all to be hanged. They were executed
at Lancaster on the 20th of August, 1612, for having
bewitched to death " by devilish practices and hellish
means " no fewer than sixteen inhabitants of the Forest
of Pendle. These were, 1. Robert Nutter, of Greenhead. 2. Richard Assheton, son of Richard Assheton,
Esq., of Downham. 3. A child of Richard Baldwin, of
Westhead, in the Forest of Pendle. 4. John Device, or
Davies, of Pendle. 5. Ann Nutter, daughter of Anthony
Nutter, of Pendle. 6. A child of John Moor, of Higham.
7. Hugh Moor, of Pendle. 8. John Robinson, *alias*
Swyer. 9. James Robinson. 10. Henry Mytton, of
Rough Lee. 11. Ann Towneley, wife of Henry Towneley,

---

* To prove the guilt of one of the prisoners, evidence was received
that it was the opinion of a man not in court, that she had turned his
beer sour. To prove the charge of murder, it was thought sufficient to
attest that the sick person had declared his belief that he owed his
approaching death to the maledictions of the prisoner. The bleeding
of the corpse on the touch of Jennet Preston, was received as an incon-
trovertible evidence of guilt. It would be nearer the truth to say that
nothing but fiction was received in evidence.

of Carr Hall, gentleman. 12. John Duckworth. 13. John Hargreaves, of Goldshaw Booth. 14. Blaize Hargreaves, of Higham. 15. Christopher Nutter. 16. Ann Folds, near Colne. John Law, a pedlar, was also bewitched, so as to lose the use of his limbs, by Alizon Device, because he refused to give her some pins without money, when requested to do so by her on his way from Colne. Alizon Device herself *was a beggar by profession*, and the evidence sufficiently proved that Law's affliction was nothing more than what would now be termed paralysis of the lower extremities.

In his *Introduction* to *Potts's Discovery of Witches*, Mr. Crossley observes that " the main interest in reviewing this miserable band of victims will be felt to centre in Alice Nutter. Wealthy, well conducted, well connected, and placed probably on an equality with most of the neighbouring families, and the magistrate before whom she was brought and by whom she was committed, she deserves to be distinguished from the companions with whom she suffered, and to attract an attention which has never yet been directed to her. That James Device, on whose evidence she was convicted, was instructed to accuse her by her own nearest relatives, and that the magistrate, Roger Nowell, entered actively as a confederate into the conspiracy, from a grudge entertained against her on account of a long-disputed boundary, are allegations which tradition has preserved, but the truth or falsehood of which, at this distance of time, it is scarcely possible satisfactorily to examine. Her mansion, Rough Lee, is still standing, a very substantial and rather fine specimen of the houses of the inferior gentry, *temp.* James I., but now divided into cottages."

———◆———

THE SAMLESBURY WITCHES.

The trials of these persons took place at the same assizes, and before the same judge. Against Jane and Ellen Bierley and Jane Southworth, all of Samlesbury, charged with having bewitched Grace Sowerbutts there, the only material evidence was that of Grace Sowerbutts herself, a girl of licentious and vagrant habits, who swore that these women (one of them being her grandmother), did draw her by the hair of the head and lay her upon the top of a hay-mow, and did take her senses and memory from her ; that they appeared to her sometimes in their own likeness, and sometimes like a black dog. She declared that they by their arts had induced her to join their sisterhood ; and that they were met from time to time by " four black things going upright and yet not like men in the face," who conveyed them across the Ribble, where they danced with them, &c. The prisoners were also charged with bewitching and slaying a child of Thomas Walshman's, by placing a nail in its navel ; and after its burial, they took up the corpse, when they ate part of the flesh, and made an " *unxious* ointment " by boiling the bones. This was more than even the capacious credulity of the judge and jury could digest. The Samlesbury witches were, therefore, acquitted, and a seminary priest named Thompson *alias* Southworth, was suspected by two of the county magistrates [the Rev. William Leigh and Edward Chisnall, Esq.,] to whom the affair was afterwards referred, of having instigated Sowerbutts to make the charge ; but this imputation was not supported by any satisfactory evidence.

WITCHCRAFT AT MIDDLETON.

About 1630, a man named Utley, a reputed wizard, was tried, found guilty, and hanged, at Lancaster, for having bewitched to death, Richard, the son of Ralph Assheton, Esq., of Downham, and Lord of Middleton.*

WITCHCRAFT IN 1633-34.

In 1633, a number of poor and ignorant people, inhabitants of Pendle Forest, or the neighbourhood, were apprehended, upon the information of a boy named Edmund Robinson, and charged with witchcraft. The following is a copy of Robinson's deposition :—

" The examination of Edmund Robinson, son of Edmund Robinson, of Pendle Forest, mason, taken at Padiham, before Richard Shuttleworth [of Gawthorpe, Esq., then forty-seven or forty-eight] and John Starkie, Esq. [one of the seven demoniacs of Cleworth, in 1595] two of his Majesty's Justices of the Peace, within the county of Lancaster, 10th of February, A.D. 1633 [1634]. Who informeth upon oath (being examined concerning the great outrages of the witches), and saith, that upon All Saints' Day last past [Nov. 1, 1633], he, this informer, being with one Henry Parker, a next door neighbour to him, in Wheatley-lane, desired the said Parker to give him leave to get some bulloes [? bullace], which he did. In which time of getting⁕ bulloes, he saw two greyhounds, viz., a black and a brown one, come running over the next field towards him ; he verily thinking the one of them to be Mr. Nutter's, and the other to be Mr. Robinson's, the said Mr. Nutter and Mr. Robinson having then such like. And the said greyhounds came to him and fawned on him, they having about their necks either of them a collar, and to either of which collars was tied a string, which collars, as this informant affirmeth, did shine like gold; and he thinking that some either of Mr. Rutter's or Mr. Robinson's family should have followed them, but seeing nobody to follow them, he took the said greyhounds, thinking to hunt with them, and presently a hare rise [rose] very near before him, at the sight of which he cried ' Loo ! loo !' but the dogs would not run. Whereupon being very angry he took them, and with the strings that were at their collars, tied either of them to a

------

* Dr. Whitaker's *Whalley*, p. 528.

little bush on the next hedge, and with a rod that he had in his hand he beat them. And instead of the black greyhound, one Dickonson wife stood up (a neighbour), whom this informer knoweth; and instead of the brown greyhound a little boy, whom this informer knoweth not. At which sight this informer being afraid, endeavoured to run away, but being stayed by the woman, viz., by Dickonson's wife, she put her hand into her pocket and pulled out a piece of silver much like to a fair shilling, and offered to give him to hold his tongue, and not to tell, which he refused, saying, 'Nay, thou art a witch.' Whereupon she put her hand into her pocket again, and pulled out a string like unto a bridle, that jingled, which she put upon the little boy's head that stood up in the brown greyhound's stead; whereupon the said boy stood up a white horse. Then immediately the said Dickonson's wife took this informer before her upon the said horse and carried him to a new house called Hoare-stones, being about a quarter of a mile off; whither when they were come there were divers persons about the door, and he saw divers others come riding upon horses of several colours towards the said house, which tied their horses to a hedge near to the said house, and which persons went into the said house, to the number of three score or thereabouts, as this informer thinketh, where they had a fire and meat roasting, and some other meat stirring in the house, whereof a young woman, whom he, this informer, knoweth not, gave him flesh and bread upon a trencher, and drink in a glass, which, after the first taste, he refused, and would have no more, and said it was nought. And presently after, seeing divers of the company going to a barn adjoining, he followed after, and there he saw six of them kneeling, and pulling at six several ropes, which were fastened or tied to the top of the house, at or with which pulling came then in this informer's sight flesh smoking, butter in lumps, and milk as it were syling [skimming or straining] from the said ropes, all which fell into basins which were placed under the said ropes. And after that these six had done, there came other six, which did likewise; and during all the time of their so pulling, they made such foul faces that feared this informer, so as he was glad to steal out and run home; whom, when they wanted, some of their company came running after him, near to a place in a highway called Boggard-hole, where this informer met two horsemen, at the sight whereof the said persons left following him; and the foremost of which persons that followed him, he knoweth to be one Loynd wife, which said wife, together with one Dickonson wife, and one Janet Davies, he hath seen at several times in a croft or close adjoining to his father's house, which put him in a great fear. And further this informer saith, upon Thursday after New Year's Day last past, he saw the said Loynd wife sitting upon a cross piece of wood being near the chimney of his father's dwelling-house: and he, calling to her, said, 'Come down, thou Loynd wife,' and immediately the said Loynd wife went up out of his sight. And further, this informer saith, that after he was come from the company aforesaid to his father's house, being towards evening, his father bade him go fetch home two kine to seal [cows to yoke], and in the way, in a field called the Ollers [*i.e.*, Alders,] he chanced to hap upon a boy who began to quarrel with him, and they fought so together till this informer had his ears made very bloody by fighting; and looking down, he saw the boy had a cloven foot, at which sight he was afraid, and ran away from him to seek the kine. And in the way he saw a light like a lantern, towards which he made haste, supposing it to be carried by some of Mr. Robinson's people; but when he came to the place he only found a woman standing on a bridge, whom, when he saw her, he knew to be Loynd wife, and knowing her he turned back again, and immediately he met with the aforesaid boy, from whom he offered to run; which boy gave him a blow on the back, which caused him to cry. And he further saith, that when he was in the barn, he saw three women take three pictures from off the beam, in the which pictures many thorns, or such like things, sticked; and that Loynd wife took one of the said pictures down; but the other two women that took the other two pictures down he knoweth not. And being further asked what persons were at the meeting aforesaid, he nominated these persons hereafter mentioned; viz., Dickonson wife, Henry Priestly wife and her son, Alice Hargreaves, widow, Jennet Davies, William Davies, the wife of Henry Jacks and her son John, James Hargreaves of Marsden, Miles wife of Dicks, James wife, Saunders as he believes, Lawrence wife of Saunders, Loynd wife, Boys wife of Barrowford, one Holgate and his wife as he believes, Little Robin wife of Leonards of the West Close.

" Edmund Robinson of Pendle, father of the said Edmund Robinson, the aforesaid informer, upon oath saith, that upon All Saints' Day he sent his son, the aforesaid informer, to fetch home two kine to seal, and saith that he thought his son stayed longer than he should have done, and went to seek him; and in seeking him heard him cry very pitifully, and found him so afraid and distracted, that he neither knew his father, nor did know where he was, and so continued very near a quarter of an hour before he came to himself; and he told this informer his father all the particular passages that are before declared in the said Edmund Robinson his son's information."

Upon such evidence as the above, these poor creatures, chiefly women and children, were committed by the two magistrates named, to Lancaster Castle, for trial. On their trials at the assizes, a jury, doubtless full of prejudice and superstitious fear, found seventeen of them guilty. The judge respited the convicts and reported the case to the king in council. They were next remitted to the Bishop of Chester (Dr. Bridgeman), who certified his opinion of the case, which, however, does not appear. Subsequently, four of these poor women, Margaret Johnson, Frances Dickonson, Mary Spencer, and the wife of one of the

Hargreaveses, were sent for to London, and examined, first by the king's physicians and surgeons, and afterwards by Charles I. in person. The strangest part of this sad story of superstition is that one of the four, who underwent examination before the magistrates, trial before " my lords the king's justices," a sifting question by the Right Rev. the Lord Bishop of Chester, aided, probably, by his chancellor, archdeacons, chaplains, proctors, &c., next before the lords of his majesty's privy council, and lastly, before his sacred majesty the king himself, whose very touch would remove the king's evil,—one of these foul women, doubtless after much badgering, bullying, and artful questioning, actually made a confession of her guilt as a witch. When this was made it does not appear; but here is the confession as preserved in Dodsworth's Collection of MSS., vol. lxi. p. 47 :—

"THE CONFESSION OF MARGARET JOHNSON.—That betwixt seven and eight years since, she being in her own house in Marsden in great passion of anger and discontent, and withal pressed with some want, there appeared unto her a spirit or devil in the proportion or similitude of a man, apparelled in a suit of black, tied about with silk points ; who offered that if she would give him her soul he would supply all her wants, and bring to her whatsoever she did need ; and at her appointment would in revenge either kill or hurt whom or what she desired, were it man or beast. And saith, that after a solicitation or two, she contracted and covenanted with the said devil for her soul. And that the said devil or spirit bade her call him by the name of Mamilian ; and when she would have him do anything for her, call in ' Mamilian,' and he would be ready to do her will. And saith, that in all her talk and confidence she calleth her said devil, ' Mamil, my God.' She further saith that the said Mamilian, her devil (by her consent) did abuse and defile * * * And saith that she was not at the great meeting at Hoare-stones, at the Forest of Pendle, upon All Saints' Day, where * * * * But saith she was at a second meeting the Sunday next after All Saints' Day, at the place aforesaid, where there was at the time between thirty and forty witches, who did all ride to the said meeting, and the end of the meeting was to consult for the killing and hurting of men and beasts. And that besides their private familiars or spirits, there was one great or grand devil or spirit, more eminent than the rest. And if any desire to have a great and more wonderful devil, whereby they may have more power to hurt, they may have one such.

And saith that such witches as have sharp bones given them by the devil to prick them, have no paps or dugs whereon the devil may suck ; but the devil receiveth blood from the place pricked with the bone ; and they are more grand witches than any that have marks. She also saith, that if a witch had but one mark, she hath but one spirit ; if two, then two spirits ; if three, yet but two spirits. And saith that their spirits usually have keeping of their bodies. And being desired to name such as she knew to be witches, she named, &c. And if they would torment a man, they bid their spirit go and torment him in any particular place. And that Good Friday is one constant day for a yearly general meeting of witches, and that on Good Friday last they had a meeting near Pendle water-side. She also saith that men witches usually have women spirits, and women witches men spirits. And their devil or spirit gives them notice of their meeting, and tells them the place where it must be. And saith, if they desire to be in any place upon a sudden their devil or spirit will, upon a rod, dog, or anything else, presently convey them thither ; yea, into any room of a man's house. But she saith, it is not the substance of their bodies, but their spirit [that] assumeth such form and shape as go into such rooms. She also saith that the devil (after he begins to suck) will make a pap or dug in a short time, and the matter which he sucks is blood. And saith that their devils can cause foul weather and storms, and so did at their meetings. She also saith that when her devil did come to suck her pap, he usually came to her in the likeness of a cat, sometimes of one colour and sometimes of another. And that since this trouble befel her, her spirit hath left her, and she never saw him since."

One cannot read this farrago of revolting absurdities without instinctively feeling that no uneducated woman could have dictated it; that it must have been prepared and dressed up for her to attach her mark, and that all she did was to make the cross to it, in fear, peradventure, of impending tortures. It is at least satisfactory to know that all these examinations of the poor women by legal, ecclesiastic, and regal authorities had a beneficial result. Strong presumption was afforded that the chief witness, the boy Robinson, had been suborned to accuse the prisoners falsely; and they were accordingly discharged. The boy afterwards confessed that he was suborned. The story excited, at the time, so much interest in the public, that in the following year, 1634, was acted and published a play entitled " The Witches of Lancashire," which Steevens cites in illustration of Shakspeare's witches. *Dr. Whitaker's Whalley.* [Reference is probably made here to Heywood and Broome's play of " The late Lanca- shire Witches" (London, 1634, quarto). There was a much later play entitled "The Lancashire Witches," by Shadwell (London, 1682)].

THE LANCASHIRE WITCHES OF 1633-4.

Sir Wm. Pelham writes, May 16, 1634, to Lord Con- way :—" The greatest news from the country is of a huge pack of witches, which are lately discovered in Lancashire, whereof, 'tis said, 19 are condemned, and that there are at least 60 already discovered, and yet daily there are more revealed : there are divers of them of good ability, and they have done much harm. I hear it is suspected that they had a hand in raising the great storm, wherein his Majesty [Charles I.] was in so great danger at sea in Scotland." The original is in the State Paper Office.*

LANCASHIRE WITCH-FINDERS.

Dr. Webster, in his " Display of Witchcraft," depicts the consternation and alarm amongst the old and decrepit, from the machinations of the witch-finders. Of the boy Robinson, who was a witness on several trials of witches, he says—" This said boy was brought into the church at Kildwick [in Yorkshire, on the confines of Lancashire], a large parish church, where I, being then curate there, was preaching in the afternoon, and was set upon a stool to look about him, which moved some little disturbance in the con- gregation for a while. After prayers, I enquired what the

* " W.N.S.," in *Notes and Queries*, 2nd series, vol.iv., p. 365.

matter was : the people told me that it was the boy that discovered witches; upon which I went to the house where he was to stay all night, and here I found him and two very unlikely persons, that did conduct him and manage the business. I desired to have some discourse with the boy in private, but that they utterly refused. Then, in the presence of a great many people, I took the boy near me and said : ' Good boy, tell me truly and in earnest, didst thou see and hear such strange things at the meeting of witches as is reported by many thou didst relate ?' But the two men, not giving the boy leave to answer, did pluck him from me, and said he had been examined by two *able* justices of the peace, and *they did never ask him such a question.* To whom I replied, the persons accused had therefore the more wrong." Dr. Webster subsequently adds, that "The boy Robinson, in more mature years, acknowledged that he had been instructed and suborned to make these accusations against the accused persons, by his father and others, and that, of course, the whole was a fraud. By such wicked means and unchristian practices, divers innocent persons lost their lives ; and these wicked rogues wanted not greater persons (even of the ministry too) that did authorise and encourage them in their diabolical courses ; and the like in my time happened here in Lancashire, where divers, both men and women, were accused of supposed witchcraft, and were so unchristianly and inhumanly handled, as to be stript stark naked, and laid upon tables and beds to be searched for their supposed witch-marks ; so barbarous and cruel acts doth diabolical instigation, working upon ignorance and superstition, produce."

THE FOREST OF PENDLE—THE HAUNT OF THE
LANCASHIRE WITCHES.

The Forest of Pendle is a portion of the greater one of
" Blackburnshire," and is so called from the celebrated
mountain of that name, over the declivity of which it extends, and stretches in a long but interrupted descent of
five miles to the Water of Pendle, a barren and dreary
tract.   Dr. Whitaker observes of this and the neighbouring
forests, and the remark even yet holds good, " that they still
bear the marks of original barrenness and recent cultiva-
tion ; that they are still distinguished from the ancient
freehold tracts around them, by want of old houses, old
woods, high fences (for these were forbidden by the forest
laws) ; by peculiarities of dialect and manners in their
inhabitants ; and lastly, by a general air of poverty which
all the opulence of manufactures cannot remove." He con-
siders that " at an uncertain period during the occupancy
of the Lacies, the first principle of population (in these
forests) commenced ;" it was found that these wilds, bleak
and barren as they were, might be occupied to some advantage in breeding young and depasturing lean " cattle,
which were afterwards fattened in the lower domain.
Vaccaries, or great upland pastures, were laid out for this
purpose ; *booths* or mansions erected upon them for the
residence of herdsmen; and at the same time that herds
of deer were permitted to range at large as heretofore,
lawnds, by which are meant parks within a forest, were
enclosed, in order to chase them with greater facility, or by
confinement to produce fatter venison.   Of these lawnds
Pendle had New and Old Lawnd, with the contiguous
Park of Ightenhill."   In the early part of the 17th century
the inhabitants of this district must have been, with few
exceptions, a wretchedly poor and uncultivated race, having little communication with the occupants of the more

fertile regions around them, and in whose minds superstition, even yet unextinguished, must have had absolute and
uncontrollable domination. Under the disenchanting influence of steam, still much of the old character of its
population remains. The " parting genius" of superstition
still clings to the hoary hill tops and rugged slopes and
mossy water sides, along which the old forest stretched its
length, and the voices of ancestral tradition are still heard
to speak from the depth of its quiet hollows, and along
the course of its gurgling streams. He who visits Pendle
will find that charms are yet generally resorted to amongst
the lower classes ; that there are hares which, in their
persuasion, never can be caught, and which survive only
to baffle and confound the huntsman; that each small
hamlet has its peculiar and gifted personage, whom it is
dangerous to offend ; that the wise man and woman (the
white witches of our ancestors) still continue their in-
vestigations of truth, undisturbed by the rural police or
the progress of the schoolmaster; that each locality has
its haunted house ; that apparitions still walk their ghostly
rounds,—and little would his reputation for piety avail that
clergyman in the eyes of his parishioners, who should refuse to lay those " extravagant and erring spirits," when
requested, by those liturgic ceremonies which the orthodoxy
of tradition requires. In the early part of the reign of
James I., and at the period when his execrable statute
against witchcraft might have been sharpening its appetite
by a temporary fast for the full meal of blood by which it
was eventually glutted—for as yet it could count no recorded victims—two wretched old women with their
families resided in the Forest of Pendle. Their names
were Elizabeth Southernes and Ann Whittle, better
known, perhaps, in the chronicles of witchcraft by the
appellations of Old Demdike and Old Chattox [perhaps,

Chadwick]. Both had attained, or reached the verge of the advanced age of eighty, and were evidently in a state of extreme poverty, subsisting with their families by occasional employment, by mendicancy, but principally, perhaps, by the assumption of that unlawful power which commerce with spirits of evil was supposed to procure, and of which their sex, life, appearance, and peculiarities might seem to the prejudiced neighbourhood in the Forest to render them not unsuitable depositaries.*

[For the details of the witchcraft alleged to be practised by these old crones and their families, with their trials and fate, see an article (page 185 *supra*) in the present volume, entitled " The Lancashire Witches of 1612."]

PENDLE HILL AND ITS WITCHES.

(From Rev. Richard James's *Iter Lancastrense.*)

" Penigent, Pendle Hill, and Ingleborough,
Three such hills be not in all England thorough."†

I long to climb up Pendle‡ : Pendle stands
Round cop, surveying all the wild moor lands,
And Malkin's Tower,§ a little cottage, where
Report makes caitiff witches meet, to swear

---

* Mr. James Crossley's introduction to *Potts's Discovery of Witches.*

† This is an old local proverb, amongst the Yorkshire proverbs in Grose's *Provincial Glossary.* Ray gives it thus :—

" Ingleborough, Pendle, and Penigent,
Are the highest hills between Scotland and Trent."

‡ Pendle Hill, or *Pen hull* (*i.e.,* the head hill) is situated on the borders of Lancashire, in the northern part of Whalley, and rises about 1800 feet above the level of the sea. The views from the summit are very extensive, including the Irish sea on one side, and York Minster (at a distance of nearly sixty miles) on the other. Notwithstanding the boast of the old proverb above, there are several hills round it of higher elevation.

§ Malkin Tower, in the Forest of Pendle, and on the declivity of Pendle Hill, was the place where, according to vulgar belief, a sort of assembly or convention of reputed witches took place on Good Friday in

Their homage to the devil, and contrive
The deaths of men and beasts. Let who will dive
Into this baneful search, I wonder much
If judges' sentence with belief on such
Doth pass: then sure, they would not for lewd gain
Bad clients favour, or put good to pain
Of long pursuit; for terror of the fiend
Or love of God, they would give causes end
With equal justice. Yet I do confess
Needs must strange fancies poor old wives possess,
Who in those desert, misty moors do live,
Hungry and cold, and scarce see priest to give
Them ghostly counsel. Churches far do stand
In laymen's hands, and chapels have no land
To cherish learned curates,* though Sir John
Do preach for four pounds unto Haslingden.
Such yearly rent, with right of begging corn,
Makes John a sharer in my Lady's horn:
He drinks and prays, and forty years this life
Leading at home, keeps children and a wife.†
These are the wonders of our careless days:
Small store serves him who for the people prays.

1612, which was attended by seventeen pretended witches and three wizards, who were afterwards brought to trial at Lancaster Assizes, and ten of these unfortunate creatures being found guilty, were executed.

* The laymen here referred to were not the patrons, but the persons officiating, who were called readers, and had no orders. Nearly every chapel in the parish of Whalley was destitute of land in 1636.

† The Sir John was probably John Butterworth, clerk, curate of Haslingden about this period. "Sir John" was a designation frequently applied to an illiterate priest. The old allowance to the priest in Haslingden, according to Bishop Gastrell, was 4*l*. Formerly parish clerks (and perhaps the priests of poor cures also) claimed once a year a bowl of corn from each parishioner of substance

WITCHCRAFT ABOUT 1654.

Dr. Webster, in his *Display of Witchcraft*, dated February 23, 1673, mentions two cases somewhat vaguely, in the following terms :—" I myself have known two supposed witches to be put to death at Lancaster, within these eighteen years [*i.e.*, between 1654 and 1673] that did utterly deny any league or covenant with the devil, or even to have seen any visible devil at all ; and may not the confessions of those (who both died penitent) be as well credited as the confessions of those that were brought to such confessions by force, fraud, or cunning persuasion and allurement ?"

A LIVERPOOL WITCH IN 1667.

In the MS. *Rental of Sir Edward More* (p. 62), dated in the year 1667, it is gravely recorded that one of his tenants residing in Castle-street, Liverpool, was a witch, descended from a witch, and inheriting the faculty of witchcraft in common with her maiden sister :—" Widow Bridge, a poor old woman, her own sister Margaret Ley, being arraigned for a witch, confessed she was one, and when she was asked how long she had so been, replied, since the death of her mother, who died thirty years agone, and at her decease she had nothing to leave her and this widow Bridge, that were sisters, but her two spirits, and named then the elder spirit to this widow, and the other spirit to her, the said Margaret Ley. God bless me and all mine from such legacies. Amen."*

* The *Moore Rental*, p. 62.

THE WITCH OF SINGLETON.

The village of Singleton [in the Fylde] is remarkable only for having been the residence of " Mag Shelton," a famous witch in her day. Her food, we are told, was *haggis* (at that time commonly used in the district) made of boiled groats, mixed with thyme or parsley. Many are the wild tales related of her dealings in the black art. The cows of her neighbours were constantly milked by her ; the pitcher in which she conveyed the stolen milk away, walking before her in the shape of a goose. Under this disguise her depredations were carried on till a neighbour, suspecting the trick, struck the seeming goose, and lo! immediately it was changed into a broken pitcher, and the vaccine liquor flowed. Once only was this witch foiled by a powerful spell, the contrivance of a maiden, who, having seated her in a chair, before a large fire, and stuck a bodkin, crossed with two weaver's healds, about her person, thus fixed her irremoveably to her seat.*

WITCHCRAFT AT CHOWBENT IN THE EIGHTEENTH CENTURY.

In the beginning of this [the eighteenth] century, one Katherine Walkden, an old woman of the township of Atherton, Chowbent, was committed to Lancaster as a witch. She was examined at Hulton Hall, where the magistrate then resided, by a jury of matrons, by whom a private teat was discovered, and upon this and other evidence (I suppose of equal importance) her *mittimus* was made out, but she died in gaol before the ensuing assizes.†

* Rev. W. Thomber's *History of Blackpool*, p. 308.
† *MS. Description of Atherton and Chowbent in* 1787, by Dorning Rasbotham, Esq.

KILLING A WITCH.

Some years ago I formed the acquaintance of an elderly gentleman who had retired from business, after amassing an ample fortune by the manufacture of cotton. He was possessed of a considerable amount of general information —had studied the world by which he was·surrounded— and was a leading member of the Wesleyan connexion. The faith element, however, predominated amongst his religious principles, and hence both he and his family were firm believers in witchcraft. On one occasion, according to my informant, both he and the neighbouring farmers suffered much from loss of cattle, and from the unproductiveness of their sheep. The cream was *bynged* [soured] in the churn, and would bring forth no butter. Their cows died mad in the shippons, and no farrier could be found who was able to fix upon the diseases which afflicted them. Horses were bewitched out of their stables through the loopholes, after the doors had been safely locked, and were frequently found strayed to a considerable distance when they ought to have been safe in their stalls. Lucky-stones had lost their virtues; horseshoes nailed behind the doors were of little use; and sickles hung across the beams had no effect in averting the malevolence of the evil-doer. At length suspicion rested upon an old man, a noted astrologer and fortune-teller, who resided near New Church, in Rossendale, and it was determined to put an end both to their ill-fortune and his career, by performing the requisite ceremonials for " killing a witch." It was a cold November evening when the process commenced. A thick fog covered the valleys, and the wild winds whistled across the dreary moors. The farmers, however, were not deterred. They met at the house of one of their number, whose cattle were then supposed to

be under the influence of the wizard; and having procured a live cock-chicken, they stuck him full of pins and
burnt him alive, whilst repeating some magical incantation. A cake was also made of oatmeal, mixed with the
urine of those bewitched, and, after having been marked
with the name of the person suspected, was then burnt in
a similar manner. . . . . . The wind suddenly rose to a
tempest and threatened the destruction of the house.
Dreadful moanings as of some one in intense agony, were
heard without, whilst a sense of horror seized upon all
within. At the moment when the storm was at the
wildest, the wizard knocked at the door, and in piteous
tones desired admittance. They had previously been
warned by the " wise man " whom they had consulted,
that such would be the case, and had been charged not to
yield to their feelings of humanity by allowing him to
enter. Had they done so, he would have regained all his
influence, for the virtue of the spell would have been dis-
solved. Again and again did he implore them to open the
door, and pleaded the bitterness of the wintry blast, but no
one answered from within. They were deaf to all his
entreaties, and at last the wizard wended his way across
the moors as best he could. The spell, therefore, was
enabled to have its full effect, and within a week the
Rossendale wizard was locked in the cold embrace of
death.*

A RECENT WITCH, NEAR BURNLEY.

Not many years ago there resided in the neighbourhood
of Burnley an old woman, whose malevolent practices
were supposed to render themselves manifest by the inju-
ries she inflicted on her neighbours' cattle; and many a

---

* See *Transactions of Lancashire and Cheshire Historical Society.*

lucky-stone, many a stout horse-shoe and rusty sickle may now be found behind the doors or hung from the beams in the cow-houses and stables belonging to the farmers in that locality, which date their suspension from the time when this " witch " in reputation held the country-side in awe. Not one of her neighbours ever dared to offend her openly ; and if she at any time preferred a request, it was granted at all hazards, regardless of inconvenience and expense. If, in some thoughtless moment, any one spoke slightingly, either of her or her powers, a corre-sponding penalty was threatened as soon as it reached her ears, and the loss of cattle, personal health, or a general " run of bad luck " soon led the offending party to think seriously of making peace with his powerful tormentor. As time wore on, she herself sickened and died ; but before she could " shuffle off this mortal coil " she must needs *transfer her familiar spirit* to some trusty successor. An intimate acquaintance from a neighbouring township was consequently sent for in all haste, and on her arrival was immediately closeted with her dying friend. What passed between them has never fully transpired, but it is confidently affirmed that at the close of the interview this associate *received the witch's last breath into her mouth, and with it the familiar spirit.* The dreaded woman thus ceased to exist, but her powers for good or evil were transferred to her companion ; and on passing along the road from Burnley to Blackburn, we can point out a farm-house at no great distance, with whose thrifty matron no one will yet dare to quarrel.

"LATING" OR "LEETING" WITCHES.

All-hallows Eve, Halloween, &c. (from the old English *halwen*, saints), denote the vigil and day of All

Saints, October 31 and November 1, a season abounding in superstitious observances. It was firmly believed in Lancashire that the witches assembled on this night at their general rendezvous in the Forest of Pendle,—a ruined and desolate farm-house, called the *Malkin Tower* (*Malkin* being the name of a familiar demon in Middleton's old play of *The Witch;* derived from *maca,* an equal, a companion). This superstition led to another, that of *lighting, lating,* or *leeting* the witches (from *leoht,* A.-S. light). It was believed that if a lighted candle were carried about the fells or hills from eleven to twelve o'clock at night, and burned all that time steadily, it had so far triumphed over the evil power of the witches, who, as they passed to the Malkin Tower, would employ their utmost efforts to extinguish the light, and the person whom it represented might safely defy their malice during the season; but if, by any accident the candle went out, it was an omen of evil to the luckless wight for whom the experiment was made. It was also deemed inauspicious to cross the threshold of that person until after the return from *leeting,* and not then unless the candle had preserved its light. Mr. Milner describes this ceremony as having been recently performed.*

* *Year Book,* part xiii. col. 1558.

PART II.

LOCAL CUSTOMS AND USAGES AT VARIOUS SEASONS.

Every greater or lesser festival of the church had its popular no less than its ecclesiastical observances. The three great events of human birth, marriage, and death, with their church rites of baptism, wedding, and burial, naturally draw towards them many customs and usages deemed fitting to such occasions. There are many customs in connexion with the free and the inferior tenants of manors, and their services to the manorial lord. Another class of customs will be found in observance in agricultural districts amongst the owners, occupiers, and labourers of farms and the peasantry generally. Lastly, as has been observed of the English generally, every great occasion, collective or individual, must have its festal celebration by eating and drinking in assembly. The viands and the beverages proper to particular occasions, therefore, constitute a not unimportant part of the local customs and usages of the people; and hence demand a place in a volume of Folk-Lore. To these subjects the present Part of this book is appropriated, and it is believed that they will be found not less strikingly illustrative of the manners and habits of the people of Lancashire, than the Superstitious Beliefs and Practices recorded in the first Part of this little work.

CHURCH AND SEASON FESTIVALS.

The feasts of dedication of parish churches to their particular tutelary saints, of course are much too numerous to be more than named in a work of this nature. The eve of such anniversary was the yearly wake [or watching] of the parishioners; and originally booths were erected in the churchyards, and feasting, dancing, and othei revelry continued throughout the night. The parishioners attended divine service on the feast day, and the rest of that day was then devoted to popular festivities. So great grew the excesses committed during these prolonged orgies, that at length it became necessary to close the churches against the pageants and mummeries performed in them at these anniversaries, and the churchyards against the noisy, disorderly, and tumultuous merry-makings of the people. Thenceforth the great seat of the revels was transferred from the church and its grave-yard, to the village green or the town market-place, or some space of open ground, large enough for popular assemblages to enjoy the favourite sports and pastimes of the period. Such were the general character and features of the wakes and feasts of country parishes, changing only with the name of the patron saint, the date of the celebration. But the great festivals of the church, celebrated alike in city and town, in village and hamlet, wherever a church " pointed its spire to heaven," were held with more general display, as uniting the cere-monials and rites of the church, with the popular festivities outside the sacred precincts. Of these great festivals the chief were New Year's Day, Twelfth Night (Jan. 5), Shrove or Pancake Tuesday, Ash-Wednesday or the first day of Lent, Mid-Lent or Mothering Sunday, Palm Sunday, Good Friday, Easter, Whitsuntide or Pentecost, May-Day, Midsummer Day (St. John's Eve and Day, June 23 and 24), Michaelmas Day (Sept. 29), and Christmas Day, with the Eve of the New Year. Of these we propose to notice various customs and practices as observed in Lanca-shire from the beginning to the close of the year.

NEW YEAR'S DAY.

In the church calendar this day is the festival of the Circumcision ; in the Roman church it is the day of no fewer than seven saints. But it is much more honoured as a popular festival. Many families in Lancashire sit up on New Year's Eve till after twelve o'clock midnight, and then drink "a happy New Year" to each other over a cheerful glass. The church bells, too, in merry peals ring out the Old Year, and ring in the New. In the olden time the wassail-bowl, the spiced ale called "lamb's wool," and currant bread and cheese, were the viands and liquor in vogue on New Year's Eve and Day. A turkey is still a favourite dish at dinner on New Year's Day.

FIRE ON NEW YEAR'S EVE.

My maid, who comes from the neighbourhood of Pendle, informs me that an unlucky old woman in her native village, having allowed her fire to go out on New Year's Eve, had to wait till one o'clock on the following day before any neighbour would supply her with a light.*

NEW YEAR'S LUCK.

Should a female, or a light-haired male, be the first to enter a house on the morning of New Year's Day, it is supposed to bring bad luck for the whole of the year then commencing. Various precautions are taken to prevent this misfortune : hence many male persons with black or dark hair, are in the habit of going from house to house, on that day, "to take the New Year in ;" for which they

* Hermentrude in *Notes and Queries,* 3rd ser. vol. ii. p. 484.

are treated with liquor, and presented with a small gratuity. So far is the apprehension carried, that some
families will not open the door to any one until satisfied
by the voice that he is likely to bring the house a year's
good luck by entering it. Then, the most kindly and
charitable woman in a neighbourhood will sternly refuse
to give any one a light on the morning of New Year's
Day, as most unlucky to the one who gives away light.

NEW YEAR'S FIRST CALLER.

For years past, an old lady, a friend of mine, has regularly reminded me to pay her an early visit on New Year's
Day; in short, to be her first caller, and to " let the New
Year in." I have done this for years, except on one occasion. When I, who am of fair complexion, have been
her first visitor, she has enjoyed happy and prosperous
years; but on the occasion I missed, some dark-com-
plexioned, black-haired gentleman called;—sickness and
trouble, and commercial disasters, were the result.* [This
is at variance with the preceding paragraph as to the
favourite colour of the hair, &c. Perhaps this differs in
different localities; but of this at least we are assured,
that any male, dark or fair, is regarded as a much more
lucky " letter-in " of the New Year, than any girl or
woman, be she blonde or brunette.]

In Lancashire, even in the larger towns, it is considered
at this time of day particularly fortunate if " a black
man" (meaning one of a dark complexion) be the first
person that enters the house on New Year's Day.†

* Prestoniensis in *Notes and Queries*, 2nd ser. vol. ii. p. 326.
† Hampson's *Medii Ævi Kalendarium*, vol. i. p. 98.

NEW YEAR'S DAY AND OLD CHRISTMAS DAY.

Some persons still keep Old Christmas Day. They always look for a change of weather on that day, and never on the 25th December. The common people have long begun their year with the 1st of January. The Act of 1752, so far as they were concerned, only caused the Civil and the Ecclesiastical Year to begin together. In Hopton's *Year Book* for A.D. 1612, he thus speaks of *January 1st:*—" January. New-yeares day in the morning being red, portends great tempest and warre."

AULD WIFE HAKES.

Christmas and New Year's tea parties and dances are called " Auld Wife Hakes" in the Furness district of Lancashire. The word *hake* is never used in the central part of the county.* Can this be from *hacken* (? from *hacking*, chopping small), a pudding made in the maw of a sheep or hog. It was formerly a standard dish at Christmas, and is mentioned by N. Fairfax, *Bulk and Selvedge,* 1674, p. 159.† [To *hake*, is to sneak, or loiter about.†]

NEW YEAR'S GIFTS AND WISHES.

It was formerly a universal custom to make presents, especially from superiors to dependents, and *vice versâ.* Now the custom is chiefly confined to parents and elders giving to children or young persons. The practice of making presents on New Year's Day existed among the Romans, and also amongst the Saxons; from one or both of which peoples we have doubtless derived it. The

---

* Prestoniensis, in *Notes and Queries,* 2nd series, vol. iii. p. 50.
† Halliwell's *Archaic and Provincial Dictionary.*

salutation or greeting on New Year's Day is also of great antiquity. Pieces of Roman pottery have been found inscribed "A happy new year to you," and one inscriber wishes the like to himself and his son. In country districts, the homely phrase is: "A happy New Year t'ye, and monny on 'em." In more polished society, and in correspondence, "I wish you a happy New Year," or "The compliments of the season to you."

SHROVETIDE.

This name, given to the last few days before Lent, is from its being the custom for the people to go to the priest to be *shriven*, *i.e.* to make their confession, before entering on the great fast of Lent, which begins on Ash-Wednesday. *Tide* is the old Anglo-Saxon word for time, and it is still retained in Whitsuntide. After the people had made the confession required by the ancient discipline of the church, they were permitted to indulge in festive amusements, though restricted from partaking of any repasts beyond the usual substitutes for flesh: hence the Latin and continental name *Carñaval,*—literally "Carne, vale," "Flesh, farewell." In Lancashire and other Northern counties, three days in this week had their peculiar dishes, viz.: "Collop Monday," "Pancake Tuesday," and "Fritters Wednesday." Originally, collops were simply slices of bread, but these were long ago discarded for slices or rashers of bacon. Fritters were thick, soft cakes, made from flour batter, with or without sliced apples intermixed. Shrovetide was anciently a great time for cock-throwing and cock-fighting, and indeed of many other loose and cruel diversions, arising from the indulgences formerly granted by the church, to compensate for

the long season of fasting and humiliation which commenced on Ash-Wednesday. As Selden observes—" What
the church debars us on one day, she gives us leave to take
on another; first we feast, and then we fast; there is a
carnival, and then a Lent."

SHROVE-TUESDAY, OR PANCAKE TUESDAY.

The tossing of pancakes (and in some places fritters)
on this day was a source of harmless mirth, and is still
practised in the rural parts of Lancashire and Cheshire,
with its ancient accompaniments :—

> It is the day whereon the rich and poor,
> Are chiefly feasted on the self-same dish,
> When every paunch till it can hold no more,
> Is fritter-filled, as well as heart can wish ;
> And every man and maid do take their turn
> And toss their pancakes up for fear they burn,
> And all the kitchen doth with laughter sound,
> To see the pancakes fall upon the ground."*

Another wr er gives this injunction :—

> " Maids,t ritters and pancakes enow see ye make,
> Let Slut have one pancake for company's sake."†

COCK-THROWING AND COCK-FIGHTING.

Cock-fighting was a barbarous pastime of high an-
tiquity, being practised by the Greeks and Romans. In
England it may be traced back to the twelfth century,
when it appears to have been a childish or boyish sport.
FitzStephen, in his description of London in the time of
Henry II., says : " Every year, on the morning of Shrove-

---

* Pasquil's *Palinodia.*
† *Ploughman's Feasting Days*, stanza 3.

Tuesday, the schoolboys of the city of London, and of other cities and great towns, bring game cocks to their masters, and in the fore-part of the day, till dinner-time, are permitted to amuse themselves with seeing them fight." The school was the cock-pit, and the master the comptroller or director of the pastime. The victor, or hero of the school, who had won the greatest number of fights was carried about upon a pole by two of his companions. He held the cock in his hands, and was followed by other boys bearing flags, &c. Cock-throwing was a sport equally cruel; but only one cock was needed. The poor bird was tied to a peg or stake, by a string, sometimes long, sometimes short, and the boys from a certain distance, in turn, threw a stick at the cock. The victor in this case was he whose missile killed the poor bird. Amongst the recognised payments by the boys at the old Free Grammar Schools, was a penny yearly to the master for the privilege of cock-fighting or cock-throwing on Shrove-Tuesday. The statutes of the Manchester Free Grammar School, made about 1525, show a creditable desire to abolish these barbarous sports. One of these statutes, as to the fees of the master, provides that " he shall teach freely and indifferently [not carelessly, but impartially] every child and scholar coming to the same school, without any money or other reward taking therefor, as cock-penny, victor-penny," &c. Another is still more explicit:— "The scholars of the same school shall use no cock-fights, nor other unlawful games, and riding about for victors, &c., which be to the great let [hindrance] of virtue, and to charge and cost of the scholars, and of their friends." At a much later period, however, the scholars seem to have been allowed, on Easter Monday, to have archery practice at a target, one of the prizes being a dunghill-cock; but this was abolished by the late **Dr.** Smith, when high master.

COCK-FIGHTING ABOUT BLACKBURN.

About thirty years ago cock-fighting formed a common pastime about Mellor and Blackburn. A blacksmith, named Miller, used to keep a large number of cocks for fighting purposes. He was said to have "sold himself to the devil" in order to have money enough for betting; and it was remarked that he rarely won! If the practice is still followed, it is done *in secret;* but the number of game-cocks one sees kept by "sporting characters" can scarcely admit of any other inference.

COCK-PENNY AT CLITHERO.

In the Clithero Grammar School an annual present at Shrovetide is expected from the scholars, varying in amount according to the circumstances of the parents. With the exception of this *cock-penny,* the school is free. The origin of this custom it is now difficult to trace. Shrove Tuesday, indeed, was a sad day for cocks. Cock-fighting and throwing at cocks were among its barbarous sports. Schoolboys used to bring game-cocks to the master, and delight themselves in cock-fighting all the forenoon. In Scotland, the masters presided at the fight, and claimed the runaway cocks called "forgers" [? 'fugees] as their perquisites. The "cock-penny" may have been the substitute devised by a less cruel age for the ordinary gratuity.*

COCK-FIGHTING AT BURNLEY.

The head master of Burnley Grammar School used to derive a portion of his income from "cock-pence" paid

* *Pictorial History of Lancashire.*

to him by his pupils at Shrovetide. This has been disused for half a century. Latterly it degenerated into a "clubbing together" of pence by the pupils for the purpose of providing themselves with materials for a carouse. This was, therefore, at last prohibited.

SHROVETIDE CUSTOMS IN THE FYLDE.

Shrove Tuesday was also called "Pancake Day," pancakes being the principal delicacy of the day. At eleven o'clock in the forenoon, the "pancake bell" rang at Poulton church, and operations were immediately commenced. Great was the fun in "tossing" or turning the pancake by a sudden jerk of the pan; while the appetites of the urchins never flagged. Amongst the sports on Shrove Tuesday, was pre-eminently cock-fighting; though bull and bear baiting were also among the rude and savage pastimes of the season.* In Poulton, on Shrove Tuesday, the pancake bell still warns the apprentice to qui. his work, not indeed to go to the confessional and be *shriven,* but to prepare for the feast of the day.†

LENT.—ASH-WEDNESDAY.

The forty days' fast at the beginning of spring, in commemoration of the temptation and fast of our Saviour in the wilderness, was called Lent, from the Saxon name for Spring, *lengten-tide.* The fast, as prescribed by the church, consisted in abstaining from flesh, eggs, preparations of milk, and wine, and in making only one meal, and that in the evening. Fish was not forbidden, though

* See Rev. W. Thornber's *History of Blackpool.*
† See also, under BELLS, the Pancake Bell.

many restricted themselves to pulse and fruit.   Ash-Wednesday, the first day in Lent, was one of severe discipline
in the Roman church ; and to remind the faithful, at the
beginning of the long penitential fast, that men are but
" dust and ashes," the priest, with ashes of the wood of
the palm-tree, marked the sign of the cross on the forehead of each confessing worshipper ; whence the name.
Since the Reformation the observance of Lent by fasting
is not general in Lancashire.

MID-LENT SUNDAY, OR " MOTHERING SUNDAY."

The fourth or middle Sunday between Quadragesima
(the first Sunday in Lent) and Easter Sunday.   It was of
old called *Dominica Refectionis,* or the Sunday of Refreshment, from the gospel of the day treating of the miraculous
feeding of the five thousand.   It was originally called
" Mothering Sunday," from the ancient usage of visiting
the mother or cathedral churches of the dioceses, when
Lent or Easter offerings were made.   The public processions have been discontinued ever since the middle of the
thirteenth century ; but the name of Mothering Sunday
is still retained, a custom having been substituted amongst
the people of Lancashire, Cheshire, Yorkshire, and other
counties, of those who have left the paternal roof visiting
their natural mother, and presenting to her small tokens
of their filial affection, in money, trinkets, frumenty, or
cakes.   In some parts of Lancashire, the particular kind
of cakes have long been fixed by old custom, being what
are called " simnels," or, in the dialect of the district,
" simlins ;" and with these sweet-cakes, it was, and in
places is still, the custom to drink warm, spiced ale, called
" bragot."   Another viand especially eaten on Mid-Lent
Sunday was that of fig or fag-pies.

SIMNEL CAKES.

In days of yore, there was a little alleviation of the severities of Lent permitted to the faithful, in the shape of a cake called " Simnel." Two English towns claim the honour of its origin,—Shrewsbury and Devizes. The first makes its simnel in the form of a warden-pie, the crust being of saffron and very thick ; the last has no crust, is star-shaped, and the saffron is mixed with a mass of currants, spice, and candied lemon. Bury, in Lancashire, is almost world-famous for its simnels and its bragot (or spiced sweet ale), on Mothering Sunday, or Mid-lent. As to the name, Dr. Cowell, in his *Law Directory or In- terpreter* (folio, 1727), derives *simnell* (Lat. *siminellus*), from the Latin *simila*, the finest part of the flour : "*panis similageneus*," simnel bread,—"still in use, especially in Lent." The English *simnel* was the purest white bread, as in the Book of Battle Abbey: "Panem regiæ mensæ apsum, qui *simenel* vulgo vocatur." (Bread fit for the royal table, which is commonly called *simenel*.) Dr. Cowell adds that it was sometimes called *simnellus*, as in the "Annals of the Church of Winchester," under the year 1042, "conventus centum *simnellos*" (the convent 100 *simnels*). He also quotes the statute of 51 Henry III. (1266-7), which enacts that "bread made into a *sim- nel* should weigh two shillings less than wastel bread ;" and also an old manuscript of the customs of the House of Farendon (where it is called "bread of symenel"), to the same effect. Wastel was the finest sort of bread. Herrick, who was born in 1591, and died in 1674 (?) has the following in his *Hesperides :*—

TO DIANEME.

A Ceremony in Gloucester.

I'll to thee a *Simnell* bring
'Gainst thou go'st a *mothering* ;

So that when she blesseth thee,
half that blessing thou'lt give me.

Bailey, in his Dictionary (folio 1764), says *simnel* is
probably derived from the Latin *simila,* fine flour, and
means, " a sort of cake or bun, made of fine flour, spice,
&c." It will thus appear that *simnel* cakes can boast a
much higher antiquity than the reign of Henry VII.
(Lambert *Simnel* probably taking his name from them,
as a baker, and not giving his name to them), and that
they were not originally confined to any particular time
or place.*

In the *Dictionarius* of John de Garlande, compiled at
Paris in the thirteenth century, the word *simineus* or *simnels,* is used as the equivalent to the Latin *placentæ,* which
are described as cakes exposed in the windows of the
hucksters, to sell to the scholars of the University and
others.†

BURY.

There is an ancient celebration in Bury, on Mid-lent
Sunday, there called " Simblin Sunday," when large cakes
called " simblins" (*i.e.,* simnels), are sold generally in the
town, and the shops are kept open the whole day, except
during Divine Service, for the purpose of vending this
mysterious aliment.‡ These cakes are a compound of currants, candied lemon, sugar, and spice, sandwich-wise, between crust of short or puff paste. They are in great
request at the period, not only in Bury, but in Manchester
and most of the surrounding towns. A still richer kind,
approaching the bride-cake in character, are called " Al-
mond Simnels."

* *Notes and Queries,* 2nd ser. V.
† For the Simnel cakes of Shrewsbury, &c., see *Book of Days,* I. 336.
‡ Baines's *History of Lancashire.*

BRAGOT-SUNDAY.

Formerly it was the practice in Leigh to use a beverage on Mid-lent Sunday, called "bragot," consisting of a kind of spiced ale; and also for the boys to indulge themselves by persecuting the women on their way to church, by secretly hooking a piece of coloured cloth to their gowns. A similar custom prevails in Portugal, at Carnival time, when many persons that walk the streets on the three last days of the Intrudo, have a long paper train hooked to their dress behind, on which the populace set up the cry of "Raboleve," which is continued till the butt of the joke is divested of his "tail." As to "Bragot," or more properly "Braget" Sunday, it is a name given in Lancashire to the fourth Sunday in Lent, which is in other places called "Mothering Sunday." Both appellations arise out of the same custom. Voluntary oblations, called *Quadragesimalia* (from the Latin name of Lent, signifying forty days), were formerly paid by the inhabitants of a diocese to the Mother Cathedral Church, and at this time prevailed the custom of processions to the Cathedral on Mid-lent Sunday. On the discontinuance of processions, the practice of "mothering," or visiting parents, began; and the spiced ale used on these occasions was called *braget*, from the British *bragawd*, the name of a kind of metheglin. Whitaker* observes that this description of liquor was called "Welsh ale" by the Saxons. Since his time, the liquor drunk on this day is principally *mulled ale*, of which there is a large consumption in Lancashire on Mid-lent Sunday.†

* *History of Manchester*, II. 265. † Baines's *History of Lancashire.*

FAG-PIE SUNDAY.

Fig-pies—(made of dry figs, sugar, treacle, spice, &c., and by some described as "luscious," by others as "of a sickly taste")—or, as they are locally termed, "fag-pies," are, or were at least till recently, eaten in Lancashire on a Sunday in Lent [? Mid-lent Sunday], thence called "Fag-pie Sunday."*

In the neighbourhood of Burnley Fag-pie Sunday is the second Sunday before Easter, or that which comes between Mid-lent and Palm Sunday. About Blackburn fig-pies are always prepared for Mid-lent Sunday, and visits are usually made to friends' houses in order to partake of the luxury.

———◆———

GOOD FRIDAY.

This name is believed to be an adoption of the old German *Gute* or *Gottes Freytag*, Good or God's Friday, so called on the same principle that Easter Day in England was at no very remote period called "God's Day." The length of the Church Services in ancient times, on this day, occasioned it to be called Long Friday. In most parts of Lancashire, buns with crosses stamped upon them, and hence called "cross buns," are eaten on this day at breakfast; and it is in many places believed that a cross bun, preserved from one Good Friday to another, will effectually prevent an attack of the whooping-cough. Some writers declare that our cross buns at Easter are only the cakes which our pagan Saxon forefathers ate in honour of their goddess Eostre, and from which the Christian clergy, who were unable to prevent people from eating them, sought to expel the paganism by marking them

* H. T. Riley in *Notes and Queries*, 2nd Ser. ii. 320.

with the cross. On the Monday before Good Friday the youths about Poulton-le-Fylde and its neighbourhood congregate in strange dresses, and visit their friends' houses, playing antics, on which occasion they are styled "the Jolly Lads."* It is stated that in some places in Lancashire, Good Friday is termed "Cracklin' Friday," as on that day it is a custom for children to go with a small basket to different houses, to beg small wheaten cakes, which are something like the Jews' Passover bread ; but made shorter or richer, by having butter or lard mixed with the flour. "Take with thee loaves and cracknels." (1 Kings xiv.)

———◆———

EASTER.

This name is clearly traced to that of Eostre, a goddess to whom the Saxons and other Northern nations sacrificed in the month of April, in which our Easter usually falls. Easter Sunday is held as the day of our Lord's resurrection. Connected with this great festival of the Church are various local rites and customs, pageants and festivities ; such as *pace* or *Pasche* [*i.e.* Easter] egging, lifting or heaving, Ball play, the game of the ring, guisings or disguisings, fancy cakes, "old hob," "old Ball," or hobby horse, &c.

Easter-Day is a moveable feast, appointed to be held on the first Sunday after the full moon immediately following the 21st of March; but if the moon happen to be at the full on a Sunday, then Easter is held on the following Sunday and not on the day of the full moon. Thus, Easter-Day cannot fall earlier than the 22nd of March, nor later than the 25th of April, in any year.

* *Pictorial History of Lancashire.*

PASCHE, PACE, OR EASTER EGGS.

In Lancashire and Cheshire children go round the village and beg eggs for thę Easter dinner, accompanying their solicitation by a short song, the burthen of which is addressed to the farmer's dame, asking for " an egg, bacon, cheese, or an apple, or any good thing that will make us merry;" and ending with

And I pray you, good dame, an Easter egg.

In the North of Lancashire, Cumberland, Westmorland, and other parts of the North of England, boys beg on Easter Eve eggs to play with, and beggars ask for them to eat. These eggs are hardened by boiling and tinged with the juice of herbs, broom-flowers, &c. The eggs being thus prepared, the boys go out and play with them in the fields, rolling them up and down like bowls, or throwing them up like balls into the air.*

PACE EGGING IN BLACKBURN.

The old custom of " pace egging" is still observed in Blackburn. It is an observance limited to the week before Easter-Day, and is said to be traceable up to the theology and philosophy of the Egyptians, Persians, Gauls, Greeks, and Romans; among all of whom an egg was an emblem of the universe, the production of the Supreme Divinity. The Christians adopted the egg as an emblem of the resurrection, since it contains the elements of a future life.

The immediate occasion of the observance may have been in the resumption on the part of our forefathers of eggs as a food at Easter on the termination of Lent; hence

* Hone's *Every-Day Book,* ii. 450; Brand's *Popular Antiquities, &c.*

the origin of the term *pace* or *pasque* [rather from *Pasche*]
that is, Easter egg. In a curious roll of the expenses
of the household of Edward I., communicated to the
Society of Antiquaries, is the following item in the
accounts for Easter Sunday: "For four hundred and a
half of eggs, eighteen pence." The following prayer,
found in the ritual of Pope Paul V., composed for the use
of England, Ireland, and Scotland, illustrates the meaning
of the custom : " Bless, O Lord, we beseech thee, this
Thy creation of eggs, that it may become a wholesome
sustenance to Thy faithful servants, eating it in thankful-
ness to Thee, on account of the resurrection of our Lord."
In Blackburn at the present day, pace egging commences on
the Monday and finishes on the Thursday before the Easter-
week.   Young men in groups varying in number from
three to twenty, dressed in various fantastic garbs, and wearing masks—some of the groups accompanied by a player
or two on the violin—go from house to house singing,
dancing, and capering.   At most places they are liberally
treated with wine, punch, or ale, dealt out to them by the
host or hostess.   The young men strive to disguise their
walk and voice; and the persons whom they visit use their
efforts on the other hand to discover who they are ; in
which mutual endeavour many and ludicrous mistakes are
made.   Here you will see Macbeth and a fox-hunter arm
in arm ; Richard the Third and a black footman in familiar
converse; a quack doctor and a bishop smoking their pipes
and quaffing their "half and half;" a gentleman and an
oyster-seller ; an admiral and an Irish umbrella-mender ;
in short, every variety of character, some exceedingly well-
dressed, and the characters well sustained.   A few years
ago parties of this description were much subject to an-
noyance from a gang of fellows styled the " Carr-laners,'"

(so-called, because living in Carr-lane, Blackburn,) armed
with bludgeons, who endeavoured to despoil the pace-
eggers. Numerous fights, with the usual concomitants of
broken eggs and various contusions, were amongst the results. This lawless gang of ruffians is now broken up,
and the serious affrays between different gangs of pace-
eggers have become of comparatively rare occurrence.
An accident, however, which ended fatally, occurred last
year [? 1842]. Two parties had come into collision, and
during the affray one of the young men had his skull
fractured, and death ensued. Besides parties of the sort
we have attempted to describe, children, both male and
female, with little baskets in their hands, dressed in all the
tinsel-coloured paper, ribbons, and " doll rags" which they
can command, go up and down from house to house; at
some receiving pence, at others eggs, at others gingerbread, some of which is called *hot* gingerbread, having in
it a mixture of ginger and Cayenne, causing the most
ridiculous contortions of feature in the unfortunate being
who partakes of it. Houses are literally besieged by these
juvenile troops from morning till night. " God's sake !
a pace-egg," is the continual cry. There is no particular
tune, but various versions of pace-egging and other songs
are sung. The eggs obtained by the juveniles are very
frequently boiled and dyed in logwood and other dyes, on
the Easter Sunday, and rolled in the fields one egg at
another till broken. Great quantities of mulled ale are
drunk in this district on Easter Sunday. The actors do
not take the eggs with them ; they are given at the places
where they call. The actors are mostly males; but in the
course of one's peregrinations on one of these evenings
it is not unusual to discover one or two of the fair sex in
male habiliments, and supporting the character admirably.
This old custom of pace-egging was again observed this

year [? 1843] notwithstanding the fatal accidents we have mentioned, without any molestation from the authorities, and without any accident occurring.*

———◆———

PACE OR PEACE EGGING IN EAST LANCASHIRE.

The week before Easter is a busy one for the boys and girls in East Lancashire. They generally deck themselves up in ribbons and fantastic dresses, and go about the country begging for money or eggs. Occasionally they go out singly, and then are very careful to provide themselves with a neat little basket, lined with moss. Halfpence or eggs, or even small cakes of gingerbread, are alike thankfully received. Sometimes the grown young men are very elaborately dressed in ribbons, and ornamented with watches and other jewellery. They then go out in groups of five or six, and are attended by a "fool" or "tosspot," with his face blackened. Some of them play on musical instruments while the rest dance. Occasionally young women join in the sport, and then the *men* are dressed in women's clothing, and the *women* in men's.

———◆———

EASTER SPORTS AT THE MANCHESTER FREE GRAMMAR SCHOOL.

A gentleman, using the initials G. H. F., some years ago communicated to a local paper the following facts relative to the sports of the scholars at Easter in the early part of the nineteenth century:—" On Easter Monday the senior scholars had a treat and various festivities. On the morning of that day, masters and scholars assembled in the school-room, with a band of music, banners, &c. One

* *Pictorial History of Lancashire.*

essential thing was a target, in a square frame, to which were suspended one or more pairs of silver buckles, constituting the chief archery prize, the second being a good dunghill-cock. These were the only prizes, and they were duly contended for by the scholars, the whole being probably devised in the old times, with a view to keep the youth of Manchester in the practice of the old English archery, which on the invention of gunpowder and fire-arms fell rapidly into desuetude. The gay procession thus provided, the scholars, bearing their bows and arrows, set out from the Grammar School, headed by some reverend gentleman of the Collegiate church, by the masters of the school, the churchwardens, &c.—the band playing some popular airs of the day—and took its route by Long Millgate, to Hunt's Bank, and along the Walkers' [*i.e.* fullers'] Croft, to some gardens, where it was then the custom for artizans on Sunday mornings to buy 'a penny posy.' Here the targets were set up, and the 'artillery practice,' as it was the fashion to call archery, . commenced. At its close the prizes were awarded, and the procession returned in the same order, along Hunt's Bank, the Apple Market, Fennel Street, Hanging Ditch, and Old Millgate, to the Bull's Head, in the Market Place,—in those days a very celebrated house, where the junior boys were treated with *frumenty*—wheat stewed, and then boiled in milk with raisins, currants, and spices, till it forms a thick, porridge-like mess, exceedingly palatable to young folk. The masters and assistants, and the senior scholars, partook of roast beef, plum pudding, &c. The abolition of this Easter Monday custom, said to have been by Dr. Smith, was by no means relished by the Grammar School boys."

"LIFTING" OR "HEAVING" AT EASTER.

This singular custom formerly prevailed in Manchester, and it is now common in the neighbourhood of Liverpool, in the parish of Whalley, at Warrington, Bolton,· and in some other parts of Lancashire, especially in rural districts, though it is by no means general, and in some places is quite unknown. A Manchester man, in 1784, thus describes it:—"*Lifting* was originally designed to represent our Saviour's resurrection. The men lift the women on Easter Monday, and the women the men on Tuesday. One or more take hold of each leg, and one or more of each arm, near the body, and lift the person up, in a horizontal position, three times. It is a rude, indecent, and dangerous diversion, practised chiefly by the lower class of people. Our magistrates constantly prohibit it by the bellman, but it subsists at the end of the town; and the women have of late years converted it into a money job. I believe it is chiefly confined to these northern counties."

The following [translated] extract from a document entitled *Liber Contrarotulatoris Hospicii,* 13 Edward I. [1225], shows the antiquity of the custom:—"To the Ladies of the Queen's Chamber, 15th of May; seven ladies and damsels of the queen, because they took [or lifted] the king in his bed, on the morrow of Easter, and made him pay fine for the peace of the king, which he made of his gift by the hand of Hugh de Cerr [or Kerr], Esq., to the lady of Weston, £14."*

On Easter Monday, between Radcliffe and Bolton, we saw a number of females surround a male, whom they mastered, and fairly lifted aloft in the air. It was a merry scene. What humour in the faces of these Lancashire

* Baines's *History of Lancashire.*

witches! What a hearty laugh! What gratification in
their eyes! The next day would bring reprisals: the
girls would then be the party to be subjected to this rude
treatment.*

EASTER GAME OF THE RING.

In his *History of Lancashire,* Mr. Baines states that the
Easter Game of the Ring, little known in other parts of
Lancashire, prevails at Padiham, in the parish of Whalley,
on the Sunday, Monday, and Tuesday in Easter week;
when young people, having formed themselves into a
ring, tap each other repeatedly with a stick, after the
manner of the holiday folks at Greenwich. The stick
may be a slight difference; but the game of Easter ring,
with taps of the hand, or the dropping of a handkerchief
at the foot, the writer has seen played at Easter and at
Whitsuntide in many villages and hamlets round Manchester.

PLAYING "OLD BALL."

This is an Easter custom. A huge and rude represen-
tation of a horse's head is made; the eyes are formed of
the bottoms of old broken wine or other "black bottles";
the lower and upper jaws have large nails put in them to
serve as teeth; the lower jaw is made to move by a contrivance fixed at its back end, to be operated on by the
man who plays "Old Ball." There is a stick, on which
the head rests, which is handled and used by the operator,
to move "Old Ball" about, and as a rest. Fixed to the
whole is a sheet of rough sacking-cloth, under which the
operator puts himself, and at the end of which is a tail.

* *Pictorial History of Lancashire.*

The operator then gets into his position, so as to make the whole as like a horse as possible. He opens the mouth by means of the contrivance before spoken of. Through the opening he can see the crowd, and he runs first at one and then another, neighing like a horse, kicking, rising on his hind legs, performing all descriptions of gambols, and running after the crowd; the consequence is, the women scream, the children are frightened, and all is one scene of the most ridiculous and boisterous mirth. This was played by sundry " Old Balls " some five years ago, at the pace-egging time, at Blackburn; but it has gradually fallen into disuse. This year [? 1843] our informant has not heard it even mentioned. [It is still continued in various parts of Lancashire, amongst others at Swinton, Worsley, &c.] The idea of this rude game may have been taken from the hobby-horse in the ancient Christmas mummings.—*Pictorial History of Lancashire.* [From the editor of the above work calling this " playing the old ball," and never marking the word ball by a capital B, he seems to have supposed it meant a spherical ball; whereas " Old Ball " throughout Lancashire is a favourite name for a cart-horse.—See a further notice of " Old Ball " under Christmas.—EDS.]

ACTING WITH " BALL."

This is a curious practice, and is often substituted for " pace-egging." The bones of a horse's head are fixed in their natural position by means of wires. The bottoms of glass bottles do duty for eyes; and the head is covered with the skin of a calf. A handle is then fixed in the upper portion of the head, and the whole skull is supported on a stout pole shod with an iron hoop. A sack is then made to fit the skull neatly, and to hang low enough down so as to hide the person who plays "Ball." The sack, or cover, is also provided with a tail so as to look as nearly like a horse's tail as possible. Some five or six then take "Ball" about the country and play him where they can obtain leave. Sometimes a doggrel song is sung, while "Ball" prances about and snaps at the company. As soon as the song is finished, "Ball" plays his most boisterous pranks, and frequently hurts some of the company by snapping their fingers between his teeth when they are defending themselves from his attacks. The writer has seen ladies so alarmed as to faint and go into hysterics :—on this account "Ball" is now nearly extinct in the neighbourhoods of Blackburn, Burnley, &c.

EASTER CUSTOMS IN THE FYLDE.

Children and young people as Easter approached, claimed their "pace-eggs" [from Pasche, the old term for Easter] as a privileged "dow" [dole]. On the afternoon of Easter Sunday the young of both sexes amused themselves in the meadows with these eggs, which they had dyed by the yellow blossoms of the "whin," or of other colours by dyeing materials. Others performed a kind of Morris or Moorish dance or play, called "*Ignagning*," which some have supposed to be in honour of St. Ignatius; but more probably its derivation is from "*ignis Agnœ*," a virgin and martyr who suffered at the stake about this time of the year. "Ignagning," says the Rev. William Thornber,* "has almost fallen into disuse, and a band of boys, termed 'Jolly Lads,' has succeeded, who, instead of reciting the combat of the

* *History of Blackpool*, p. 92.

Turk and St. George, the champion of England, the death of the former, and his restoration to life by the far-travelled doctor, now sing of the noble deeds of Nelson and Collingwood; retaining, however, the freaks and jokes of ' Old Toss-pot,' the fool of the party, who still jingles the small bells hung about his dress." Easter Monday was a great day for the young people of the neighbourhood going to the yearly fair at Poulton. Happy was the maiden who could outvie her youthful acquaintance in exhibiting a greater number of " white cakes," the gifts of admiring youths ; thereby proving beyond dispute the superior effects of her charms. Then the excitement and exertion of the dance ! At that time dancing consisted in the feet beating time to a fiddle, playing a jig in double quick time ; one damsel succeeding another, and striving to outdo her companions in her power of continuing this violent exercise, for much honour was attached to success in this respect, the bystanders meanwhile encouraging their favourites, as sportsmen do their dogs, with voice and clapping of hands. Such was—

> " The dancing pair that simply sought renown,
> By holding out, to tire each other down."

On Good Friday a jorum of *browis* and roasted wheat or *frumenty* was the treat for dinner ; white *jannocks*, introduced by the Flemish refugees, and *throdkins** were also then eaten with great zest by the hungry labourer.†

---

* *Browis* or *brewis* is broth or pottage; *frumenty*, is hulled wheat boiled in milk, and flavoured with cinnamon, sugar, allspice; and *jannocks*, oaten bread in large, coarse loaves; *throdkins*, a cake made of oatmeal and bacon.
† Rev. W. Thornber's *History of Blackpool.*

MAY-DAY CUSTOMS.

The Romans commenced the festival of Flora on the 28th April, and continued it through several days in May, with various ceremonies and rejoicings, and offerings of spring flowers and the branches of trees in bloom, which, through the accommodation of the Romish church to the pagan usages, remain to us as May-day celebrations to the present time. It was formerly a custom in Cheshire [and Lancashire] for young men to place birchen boughs on May-day over the doors of their mistresses, and mark the residence of a scold by an alder bough. There is an old rhyme which mentions peculiar boughs for various tempers, as an owler (alder) for a scolder, a nut for a slut, &c. Ormerod thinks the practice is disused; but he mentions that in the main street of Weverham are two May-poles, which are decorated on May-day with all due attention to the ancient solemnity; the sides are hung with garlands, and the top terminated by a birch, or other tall slender tree with its leaves on; the bark being peeled off and the stem spliced to the pole, so as to give the appearance of one tree from the summit.* The principal characteristics of May-day celebrations and festivities are of rejoicing that the reign of winter is at an end, and that of early summer with its floral beauties, has come. The hawthorn furnishes its white blossoms in profusion; and the tall May-poles, gaily decorated with garlands of leaves and flowers, and festoons of ribbons of the brightest colours, are centres of attraction on the village green, for the youth of both sexes to dance the May-pole dance, hand-in-hand, in a ring.

* Hone's *Every-Day Book,* ii. 597.

MAY SONGS.

Amongst the old customs of rural Lancashire and Cheshire is that of a small party of minstrels or carollers going round from house to house during the last few evenings of April, and singing a number of verses, expressive of rejoicing that "cold winter is driven away," and that the season is "drawing near to the merry month of May." The singers are generally accompanied by one or two musical instruments, a violin and clarionet for instance, and the tunes are very quaint and peculiar. Of course for their good wishes for the master of the house, with his "chain of gold," for the mistress, with "gold along her breast," and the children "in rich attire," a trifling gift in money is made.*

MAY-DAY EVE.

The evening before May-day is termed "Mischief Night" by the young people of Burnley and the surrounding district. All kinds of mischief are then perpetrated. Formerly shopkeepers' sign-boards were exchanged; "John Smith, grocer," finding his name and vocation changed, by the sign over his door, to "Thomas Jones, tailor," and *vice versâ ;* but the police have put an end to these practical jokes. Young men and women, however, still continue to play each other tricks, by placing branches of trees, shrubs, or flowers under each others' windows, or before their doors. All these have a symbolical meaning, as significant, if not always as complimentary, as "the Language of Flowers." Thus, "a thorn" implies "scorn;" "wicken" (the mountain ash) "my dear chicken;" a

---

* For the words of these songs, see Harland's *Ballads and Songs of Lancashire,* p. 116; and for words and music, Chambers's *Book of Days,* i. 546.

" bramble," for one who likes to " ramble," &c.   Much
ill-feeling is at times engendered by this custom.

MAY-DAY CUSTOM.

On the 1st of May the following custom is observed
in some parts of Lancashire, though now very nearly
obsolete.   Late on the preceding night, or early on that
morning, small branches of trees are placed at the doors of
houses in which reside any marriageable girls.   They are
emblematical of the character of the maidens, and have
a well-understood language of their own, which is
rhythmical.   Some speak flatteringly; others quite the
reverse; the latter being used when the character of
the person for whom it is intended is not quite " above
suspicion."   A malicious rustic wag may sometimes put a
branch of the latter description where it is not deserved;
but I believe this is an exception.   I only remember a few
of the various trees which are laid under contribution for
this purpose.   *Wicken* is the local name for mountain ash.

Wicken, sweet chicken.

Oak, for a joke.

Gorse, in bloom, rhymes with " at noon " (I omit the
epithet given here to an unchaste woman) and used for a
notorious delinquent.*

PENDLETON AND PENDLEBURY MAY-POLE AND GAMES.

The people of these townships for centuries celebrated
May-day (a relic of the ancient heathen festival of the
goddess Flora) by the May-pole, to which the watchful
care of Charles I. and his royal progenitor extended,
when they printed in their proclamation and " Book of

* A.B., Liverpool, in *Notes and Queries,* v. 581.

Sports," that after the end of divine service on Sundays, their "good people be not disturbed, letted, nor discharged from the having of May-games, and the setting up of the May-poles," &c. The ancient practice was to erect the pole on May-day, and to surround it with a number of verdant boughs, brought from " Blakeley Forest," which were decked usually with garlands and flowers, and around which the people assembled to dance and celebrate their May-games. " Pendleton Pole " is of much higher antiquity than the Reformation; for in the will of Thomas del Bothe, who died 47 Edw. III. (1373) the sum of 30*s.* is bequeathed towards making the causeway at Pendleton near "le Poll." In the time of the Commonwealth the Pendleton Pole was taken down, in virtue of an ordinance of Parliament against May-poles, and such other " hea- thenish vanities ;" but it was re-erected at the Restoration, and still presents its lofty head, surmounted by a Royal Crown; though much of the spacious field of the ancient May-games is now occupied by buildings [in 1780 the township was little more than a fold of cottages, with its May- pole and green], and much of the spirit of the rural sports of our ancestors has subsided. In Pasquil's " *Palinodia*," (published in 1654) the decay of May-games two centuries ago, is recorded and lamented :—

> " Happy the age, and harmless were the days
>   (For then true love and amity was found);
> When every village did a May-pole raise,
>   And Whitsun ales and May-games did abound,
> And all the lusty younkers in a rout,
> With merry lasses, danced the rod about;
> Then friendship to their banquets bid the guests,
> And poor men fared the better for their feasts.
>
> The lords of castles, manors, towns, and towers,
>   Rejoiced when they beheld the farmers flourish,
> And would come down unto the summer bowers,
>   To see the country gallants dance the Morice.
>   *   *   *   *   *

R

> But since the summer poles were overthrown,
>   And all good sports and merriments decay'd,
> How times and men are changed, so well is known,
>   It were but labour lost if more were said."

MAY CUSTOM IN SPOTLAND.

A custom of high antiquity and of primitive simplicity prevails in the district of Spotland, in the parish of Rochdale. On the first Sunday in May the young people of the surrounding country assemble at Knott Hill yearly, for the purpose of presenting to each other their mutual greetings and congratulations on the arrival of this cheering season, and of pledging each other in the pure beverage which flows from the mountain springs.*

MAY-DAY CUSTOMS IN THE FYLDE.

On the morning of the first day of May, many a May-bough† ornamented the villages and towns of the Fylde, inserted by some mischievous youngsters, at the risk of life or limb, in the chimney-tops of their neighbours' houses. Then came a most imposing piece of pageantry, that of "bringing-in May;" when a king and queen, with their royal attendants and rustic band of music, mummers, &c., attracted the attention and admiration of the country side. May-day with its pageants, sports, games, dances, garlands, and May-poles, was peculiarly a season of hilarity, merry-making, and good humour. The pageant of "bringing-in May," was a favourite pastime at Poulton

---

* Baines's *History of Lancashire.*
† These boughs, says Mr. Thornber, in his *History of Blackpool*, were emblematical of the character of the maiden thus conspicuously distinguished; an elder-bough for a scold, one of ash for a swearer, &c.

about fifty years ago [*i.e.*, about 1787] ; the causeways were strewed with flowers, and at the door of the house of each respectable inhabitant, sweetmeats, ale, and even wine, were handed about as a treat and refreshment to the young, who were thus affording them amusement. By degrees the pageant ceased ; a vigorous attempt, however, was made to revive it in 1818, with all its honours ; but the age-worn custom proved to be utterly incapable of resuscitation. Another writer,* however, states that at Poulton-le-Fylde and in its neighbourhood, some of the customs of the olden time are still observed. Very recently May-day was ushered in with a dance round the May-pole, and the lavish exhibition of garlands and merriment.

THE MAY-POLE OF LOSTOCK.

The May-pole of Lostock, a village near Bolton, is probably the most ancient upon record. It is mentioned in a charter by which the town of Westhalchton [? Westhaughton] was granted to the Abbey of Cockersand, about the reign of King John. The pole, it appears, had superseded a cross, and formed one of the landmarks which defined the boundaries, and it must therefore have been a permanent and not an annual erection. The words of the charter are:—" De Lostock meypull, ubi crux situ fuit, recta linea in austro, usque ad crucem super le Tunge." † (From Lostock Maypole, where the cross was formerly, in a straight line to the south, as far as to the cross upon the Tunge.)

* *Pictorial History of Lancashire.*
† Dugdale's *Monast. Anglic.* vol. vi. p. 906.

ROBIN HOOD AND MAY-GAMES AT BURNLEY, IN 1579.

In a letter from Edmond Assheton, Esq., then a magistrate of Lancashire, and aged 75, to William Farington, Esq. (who was also in the commission of the peace), dated Manchester, May 12, 1580, the writer thus complains of "lewd sports" and sabbath-breaking :—" I am sure, Right Worshipful, you have not forgotten the last year stirs at Burnley about Robin Hood and the May-games. Now, considering that it is a cause that bringeth no good effect, being contrary to the best, therefore a number of the justices of the peace herein in Salford Hundred have consulted with the [Ecclesiastical] Commission [of Queen Elizabeth] to suppress those lewd sports, tending to no other end but to stir up our frail natures to wantonness; and mean not to allow neither old custom. Then their excuse in coming to the church in time of divine service, for every man may well know with what minds, after their embracings, kissings, and unchaste beholding of each other, they can come presently prepared to prayer. A fit assembly to confer of worse causes, over and besides their marching and walking together in the night time. But chiefly because it is a profanation of the Sabbath-day, and done in some places in contempt of the gospel and the religion established, I pray God it be not so at Burnley. It is called in the Scriptures the Lord's Day, and was not lawful under the old law to carry a pitcher of water on the Sabbath, or to gather sticks, but it was death. Such regard was had in the time of the law to keeping holy the Sabbath. And do not we withdraw even the practice and use of good and godly works upon the same day ? Then in reason the other should cease. Tell me, I pray you, if you can find in the presence of the foresaid lewd pastimes, good example or profit to the commonwealth, the defence of the realm, honour to the prince, or to the glory of God ? Then, let them continue; otherwise, in my opinion, they are to be withdrawn. For to that end I address these contents unto you, because we would not deal for any reformation within the limits of your walk ; and for the better credit of the consent of the Commissioners, you may peruse how they mean to proceed against them of Burnley who have revived their former follies, if you redress not the same. . . . Your assured always to use, EDMOND ASSHETON. It will not be long afore [there] will be order taken for this dancing, either by the Privy Council or by the Bishops by their commandment. My meaning is, I would have you to do it yourself, which will with one word be brought to pass. . . . If you would set your hand to this precept with us, I think it would end these disorders within prescribed." *

MAY-DAY IN MANCHESTER.

In the now olden days of coaching, this was a great day in Manchester. The great coaching establishments, those of the royal mails, north, south, east, and west, and all the highflyers, &c., turned out all their spare vehicles and horses for a grand procession through the principal streets of the town. Many of the mail and other coaches were newly painted for the occasion ; all the teams were provided with new harness and gearing ; the coachmen and guards had new uniforms ; Jehu wore a great cockade of ribbons, and a huge bouquet of flowers, and he handled the new ribbons with a dignity and grace peculiar to this almost defunct race. The guard, in bright scarlet uniform, blew on his Kent bugle some popular tune of the time ; and the horses wore cockades and nosegays about their heads and ears ;

* *Farington Papers,* p. 128.

almost every coach on this occasion was drawn by four horses, their coats shining with an extra polish for May-day; and the cavalcade was really a pretty sight on a bright May-day morning. Second only to it in decorative splendour, and in horseflesh, was the display of lurries, waggons, drays, and carts, with their fine draught-horses. Then came the milk-carts, with their drivers in dresses covered with ribbons. These equine and asinine glories have passed away, extinguished by the rail.

QUEEN OF THE MAY, &c.

The custom of choosing a May King and Queen is now disused. May-games, and the May-pole, were kept up at the quiet little village of Downham when all other places in the neighbourhood had ceased to celebrate May-day. Nothing is now made of May-day, if we except the custom of carters dressing their horses' heads and tails with ribbons on that day.

WHITSUNTIDE.

The Feast of Pentecost, or Whitsuntide, was formerly kept as a high church festival, and by the people was celebrated by out-door sports and festivities, and especially by the drinking assemblies called "Whitsun-Ales." One writer (inquiring whether the custom of "lifting at Easter" is a memorial of Christ being raised up from the grave) observes that, "there seems to be a trace of the descent of the Holy Ghost on the heads of the Apostles, in what passes at Whitsuntide Fair, in some parts of Lancashire; where one person holds a stick over the head of another, whilst a third, unperceived, strikes the stick, and thus gives a smart

blow to the first. But this probably is only local." *
"Whit-week," as it is generally called, has gradually
grown to be the great yearly holiday of the hundred of
Salford, and the manufacturing district of which Manchester is the centre. This seems to have arisen from the
yearly races at Manchester being held from the Wednesday to the Saturday inclusive, in that week. After the
rise of Sunday-schools, their conductors, desiring to keep
youth of both sexes from the demoralizing recreations of
the racecourse, took them to fields in the neighbourhood
and held anniversary celebrations, tea-parties, &c., in the
schools. The extension of the railway system has led to
"cheap trips" and " school excursion trains" during Whitsuntide ; which are occasionally taken to Wales, the Lakes,
and other great distances. Canal boats take large numbers
of Sunday scholars to Dunham Park, Worsley, &c. Short
excursions are made in carts, temporarily fitted with seats.
It is customary for the cotton-mills, &c., to close for Whitsuntide week to give the hands a holiday ; the men going
to the races, &c., and the women visiting Manchester on
Whit-Saturday, thronging the markets, the Royal Ex-
change, the Infirmary Esplanade, and other public places ;
and gazing in at the "shop windows," whence this day is
usually called "Gaping Saturday." The collieries, too,
are generally closed in Whit-week ; and in some the
underground horses are brought to the surface to have a
week's daylight, the only time they enjoy it during the
year. The mills, coalpits, &c., generally have the requisite
repairs of machinery, &c., made during this yearly holiday
—those at least which would necessitate the stoppage of
the work at another time.

* *Gent. Mag.* vol. liii., for July, 1783, p. 578.

WHIT-TUESDAY.—KING AND QUEEN AT DOWNHAM.

The last rural queen chosen at Downham is still living in Burnley. The lot always fell to the prettiest girl in the village, and certainly it must be admitted that in this instance they exercised good judgment. A committee of young men made the selection; then an iron crown was procured and dressed with flowers. The king and queen were ornamented with flowers, a procession was then formed, headed by a fiddler. This proceeded from the Inn to the front of "Squire Assheton's," Downham Hall, and was composed of javelin men, and all the attendants of royalty. Chairs were brought out of the Hall for the king and queen, ale was handed round, and then a dance was performed on the lawn, the king and queen leading off. The procession next passed along through the village to the green, where seats were provided for a considerable company. Here again the dancing began, the king and queen dancing the first set. The afternoon was spent in the usual games, dances, &c. On the next night all the young persons met at the inn, on invitation from the king and queen—each paid a shilling towards the "Queen's Posset." A large posset was then made and handed round to the company. After this the evening was spent in dancing and merry-making.

ROGATIONS OR GANG DAYS.

These days are so named from the Litanies or Processions of the Church, before Holy Thursday or Ascension Day. It was a general custom in country parishes to "gang" or go round the boundaries and limits of the parish, on one of the three days before Holy Thursday, or the Feast of our Lord's Ascension; when the minister, accompanied by

his churchwardens and parishioners, was wont to depre-
cate the vengeance of God, beg a blessing on the fruits of
the earth, and preserve the rights and properties of the
parish. In some parishes this perambulation took place
on Ascension Day itself. In a parochial account-book,
entitled " A Record of the Acts and Doings of the thirty
men of the parish of Kirkham," Lancashire, is the following entry under the year 1665 : " Spent on going peram-
bulations on Ascension Day, 1s. 6d."

OATMEAL CHARITY AT INCE.

Under the name of Richardson's Charity, a distribution
takes place annually on the Feast of the Ascension or
Holy Thursday (ten days before Whit-Sunday) of *five
loads of oatmeal*, each load weighing 240 lb. Three loads
are given to the poor of the township of Ince, one to the
poor of Abram, and the other to the poor of Hindley;
adjacent townships, all in the parish of Wigan. The
Charity Commissioners, in their twenty-first report, state
that the meal is provided by Mr. Cowley, of Widnes, the
owner of an estate in Ince, formerly the property of
Edward Richardson, who, as the commissioners were informed, directed by his will that this distribution should
be made for fifty years from the time of his death. The
year 1784 was given as the date of this benefaction, in the
Returns made to Parliament in 1786. Mr. Cowley has
himself had the disposal of this charity. The charity
would, according to this statement, legally cease in 1836.

NAMES FOR MOONS IN AUTUMN.

In Lancashire, as well as in the South of Scotland and the South of Ireland, the moon of September is commonly called " the harvest moon," that of October " the huntsman's moon."*

"GOOSE INTENTOS."

In " An Universal Etymological English Dictionary," by N. Bailey, London, 1745, I read :—" Goose-intentos, a goose claimed by custom by the husbandmen in Lancashire, upon the sixteenth Sunday after Pentecost, when the old Church prayers ended thus: ' ac bonis operis jugiter præstat esse *intentos*.' " These words occur in the old Sarum books, in the Collect for the sixteenth Sunday after Pentecost; in the present Liturgy, in that for the seventeenth Sunday after Trinity.†

Blount, in his *Glossographia*, says that " in Lancashire the husbandmen claim it as a due to have a goose-intentos on the sixteenth Sunday after Pentecost: which custom takes its origin from the last word of the old Church prayer of that day :—" Tua nos Domine, quæ sumus, gratia semper et præveniat et sequatur ; ac bonis operibus jugiter præstet esse *intentos*." The vulgar people called it "a goose with ten toes." Beckwith, in his new edition of Blount's *Fragmenta Antiquitatis* (London, 4to, 1815, p. 413), after quoting this passage, remarks :—" But besides that the sixteenth Sunday after Pentecost, or after Trinity rather, being movable, and seldom falling upon Michaelmas Day, which is an immovable feast, the service for that day could very rarely be used at Michaelmas, there does not appear to be the most distant allusion to a goose

---

* M. F. in *Notes and Queries*, 3rd series, ii. 397.
† Aquinas, in *Notes and Queries*, 3rd series, v., April 2, 1864.

in the words of that prayer.   Probably no other reason
can be given for this custom, but that Michaelmas Day
was a great festival, and geese at that time most plentiful.
In Denmark, where the harvest is later, every family has
a roasted goose for supper on St. Martin's Eve" [Nov.10].
It must be borne in mind that the term *husbandman* was
formerly applied to persons of a somewhat higher position
in life than an agricultural labourer, as for instance to the
occupier and holder of the land.   In ancient grants from
landlords of manors to their free tenants, among other
reserved rents, boons, and services, the landlord frequently
laid claim to a good stubble goose at Michaelmas.   After
all, the connexion between the goose and the collect is
not apparent.*

ALL SOULS' DAY.—NOV. 2.

So named, because in the Church of Rome prayers are offered on
this day for "all the faithful deceased."

There is a singular custom still kept up at Great Marton,
in the Fylde district, on this day.   In some places it is
called "soul-caking," but there it is named "psalm-
caking,"—from their reciting psalms for which they receive
cakes.   The custom is changing its character also—for in
place of collecting cakes from house to house, as in the
old time, they now beg for money.   The term "psalm"
is evidently a corruption of the old word "sal," for soul ;
the mass or requiem for the dead was called "Sal-mas,"
as late as the reign of Henry VI.

GUNPOWDER PLOT AND GUY FAWKES.

The anniversary of the Gunpowder Plot of November
5, 1605, is still more or less kept in many parts of Lanca-

* Ed. *Notes and Queries.*

shire, in towns by the effigy of Guy Fawkes being paraded about the streets, and burnt at night with great rejoicing; and by the discharge of small cannon, guns, pistols, &c., and of fireworks. In the country the more common celebration is confined to huge bonfires, and the firing of pistols and fireworks. In some places, especially about Blackburn, Burnley, and that district, as well as in villages about Eccles, Worsley, &c., it is customary for boys for some days before the 5th of November, to go round to their friends and neighbours to beg for coals. They generally take their stand before the door, and either say or sing some doggerel, to the following effect:—

> "Remember, remember,
> The Fifth of November,
>   The gunpowder treason and plot;
> A stick and a stake,
> For King George's sake,
>   We hope it will ne'er be forgot."

CHRISTMAS.

In the olden time, before the Reformation, Christmas was the highest festival of the Church. In some rural parts of Lancashire it is now but little regarded, and many of its customs are observed a week later,—on the eve and day of the New Year. But still there linger in many places some relics of the old observances and festivities, as the carols, the frumenty on Christmas Eve, the mummers, with "old Ball," or the hobby-horse, and the decoration of churches and dwellings with boughs of evergreen shrubs and plants; in the centre of which is still to be found, in many country halls and kitchens, and in some also in the towns, that mystic bough of the mistletoe, beneath whose white berries, it is the custom and licence of the season to steal a kiss from fair maidens, and even from matrons "forty, fat, and fair."

CREATURES WORSHIPPING ON CHRISTMAS EVE.

I have been told in Lancashire, that at midnight on Christmas Eve the cows fall on their knees, and the bees hum the Hundredth Psalm. I am unwilling to destroy the poetry of these old superstitions; but their origin can, I think, be accounted for. Cows, it is well known, on rising from the ground, get up on their knees first; and a person going into the shippon at midnight would, no doubt, disturb the occupants, and by the time he looked around, they would all be rising on their knees. The buzzing of the bees, too, might easily be formed into a tune, and, with the Hundredth Psalm running in the head of the listener, fancy would supply the rest.*

CHRISTMAS MUMMING.

Mr. J. O. Halliwell, in his *Nursery Rhymes of England*, relates the following as a Christmas custom in Lancashire :—The boys dress themselves up with ribands, and perform various pantomimes, after which one of them, who has a blackened face, a rough skin coat, and a broom in his hand, sings as follows :—

> Here come I,
> Little David Doubt;
> If you don't give me money,
> I'll sweep you all out.
> Money I want,
> Money I crave;
> If you don't give me money,
> I'll sweep you all to the grave.

---

* Wellbank in *Notes and Queries,* 2nd series, viii. 242.

THE HOBBY HORSE, OR OLD BALL.

In an old painted window at Betley, Staffordshire, exhibiting in twelve diamond-octagon panes, the mummers and morris-dancers of May-day, the centre pane below the May-pole represents the old hobby-horse, supposed to have once been the King of the May, though now a mere buffoon. The hobby (of this window) is a spirited horse of pasteboard, in which the master dances and displays tricks of legerdemain, &c. In the horse's mouth is stuck a ladle, ornamented with a ribbon ; its use being to receive the spectators' pecuniary donations. In Lancashire the old custom seems to have so far changed, that it is the head of a dead horse that is carried about at Christmas, as described amongst the Easter customs. "Old Ball" bites everybody it can lay hold of, and holds its victims till they buy their release with a few pence.

CHRISTMAS CUSTOMS IN THE FYLDE.

The Rev. W. Thornber* describes the Christmas gambols and customs in the Fylde nearly a century ago, as having been kept up with great spirit. The midnight carols of the church-singers†—the penny laid on the hob by the fireside, the prize of him who came first to the outer door, to "let Christmas in,"—the regular round of visits—the

---

* See *History of Blackpool.*

† Here is the specimen of one sung from house to house during Christmas:—

> We're nather cum to yare hase to beg nor to borrow,
> But we're cum to yare hase to drive away o sorrow;
> A suop o' drink, as yau may think, for we're varra droy,
> We'll tell yau what we're cum for—a piece o' Christmas poye.

treat of mince pies*—in turn engrossed their attention. Each farm-house and hut possessed a pack of cards, which were obtained as an alms from the rich, if poverty forbade the purchase. Night after night of Christmas was consumed in poring over these dirty and obscured cards. Nor were the youngsters excluded from a share in the amusements of this festal season. Early, long before dawn, on Christmas morning, young voices echoed through streets and lanes, in the words of the old song—

> Get up old wives,
> And bake your pies,
> 'Tis Christmas-day in the morning;
> The bells shall ring,
> The birds shall sing,
> Tis Christmas-day in the morning.

Many an evening was beguiled with snap-dragon, bobbing for apples, jack-stone, blind-man's buff, forfeits, hot cockles, hunting the slipper, hide lose my supper, London Bridge, turning the trencher, and other games now little played. Fortune-telling by cards, &c., must not be omitted. In the bright frost and moonshine, out-door sports were eagerly pursued, guns were in great request, to shoot the shore-birds, and many found pleasure in "watching the fleet;" others played at foot-ball in the lanes or streets ; or engaged in the games of prison-bars, tee-touch-wood, thread-my-needle, horse-shoe, leap-frog, black-thorn, cad, bandy, honey-pot, hop-scotch, hammer and block, bang about and shedding copies. Cymbling for larks† was a very

---

* The mince-pie, made of a compound of Eastern productions, represented the offerings of the wise men who came from far to worship the Saviour, bringing spices. Its old English coffin-shape was in imitation of the manger in which the infant Jesus was laid.

† We have not been able to find any account of this mode of catching larks, at least, under the name here given.

common pastime; now it is scarcely known by name, and few have retained any of the implements or instruments requisite to practise the art. Tradesmen presented their customers with the Yule-loaf,* or two mould candles for the church, or some other Christmas-box. The churches and house-windows were decked with evergreens; a superstition derived probably from the Druids, who decked their temples and houses with evergreens in December, that the Sylvan Spirits might avoid the chilly frosts and storms of winter, by settling in their branches. For some weeks before Christmas, a band of young men called "Mutes," roused at early morn the slumbering to their devotions, or to activity in their domestic duties. The beggar at the door, craving an *awmas* [? alms] or *saumas* [soul-mass] cake, reminded the inmates that charity should be a characteristic of the season. The Eve of Christmas Day was named "Flesh Day," from the country people flocking to Poulton to buy beef, &c., sufficient to supply the needs of the coming year. On the morning of Christmas Day the usual breakfast was of black puddings, with jannock, &c.

CELEBRATION OF CHRISTMAS AT WYCOLLER HALL.

At Wycoller Hall, the family usually kept open house the twelve days at Christmas. The entertainment was [in] a large hall of curious ashlar work, [on] a long table, plenty of *frumenty*, like new milk, in a morning, made of husked wheat boiled, roasted beef, with a fat goose and

---

* The baker formerly gave his customers a baby of paste; and in my own recollection a cake, decorated with the head of a lamb, named "the Ewe loaf," was the Christmas present of bakers at Poulton. On Christmas Eve the houses were illuminated with candles of an enormous size.—W.T.

a pudding, with plenty of good beer for dinner. A round-about fire-place, surrounded with stone benches, where the young folks sat and cracked nuts, and diverted them-selves; and in this manner the sons and daughters got matching, without going much from home.*

CAROLS, &c.

" Carol" is supposed to be derived from *cantare* to sing, and *rola*, an interjection of joy. Amongst our Christmas customs that of carol-singing prevails over great part of Lancashire. It is the old custom of celebrating with song the birth of the Saviour, even as the angels are said to have sung " Glory to God in the highest," &c., at this great event. Almost every European nation has its carols. Our earliest Christian forefathers had theirs; one or two Anglo-Norman carols have been preserved, and some of every century from the thirteenth to the eighteenth. Numerous books containing carols have been printed (one by Wynkin de Worde), and it would occupy too much space to insert even the most popular of these carols here. A verse of one common to Lancashire and Yorkshire must suffice :—

> God rest you all, merry gentlemen,
> Let nothing you dismay;
> Remember Christ our Saviour
> Was born on Christmas-day.

The town or the village waitts go about after midnight, waking many a sleeper with their homely music, which sounds all the sweeter for being heard in the stilly night. Various items of payment to the Manchester waitts occur in

* From a family MS. of the Cunliffes, quoted in Baines's *Lancashire*, iii. 244.

the Church Leet Books of that manor. A dance tune called "The Warrington Waitts" occurs in a printed Tune-Book of 1732. Hand-bell ringing, a favourite Lancashire diversion, is much practised about Christmas.

EATING AND DRINKING CUSTOMS.

In many instances of particular Church Festivals, and of popular celebrations, we have already enumerated various viands appropriated to special occasions, as the turkey to New Year's Day; the pancake to Shrove Tuesday; the simnel, carlins, bragot, and fig-pie to Mid-Lent Sunday; the goose to Michaelmas; frumenty, mince-pies, &c., to Christmas. A few remain, however, for notice here:—Eccles cakes, Ormskirk gingerbread, Everton toffy, and other sweet cates have "all seasons for their own." The two rival shops in Eccles, on opposite sides of Church-street, the one called "The genuine Eccles cake shop, from over the way," and the other "The real Eccles cake shop, never removed," so much puzzle the stranger and visitor, that purchases are often made at both in order to secure the real, genuine, original article.

THE HAVERCAKE LADS.

Formerly the bread eaten by the labouring classes in the parish of Rochdale and others in the east of Lancashire was oat-cake, which was also pretty generally in use in the west of Yorkshire. A regiment of soldiers raised in these two adjoining districts at the beginning of the last war took the name of the "Havercake Lads," assuming as their badge an oat cake [oats are called havers], which was placed (for the purpose of attracting recruits) on the

point of the recruiting sergeant's sword.   Oat bread is still
eaten in various manufacturing and hilly districts of Lancashire, but not nearly so generally as half a century ago.*

WOODEN SHOES AND OATEN BREAD OR JANNOCKS.

Both these are said to have been introduced by the
Flemish immigrant weavers about the year 1567.   Their
sabots, however, were made entirely of wood, lined with
a little lamb's skin, to protect the top of the foot; while
the *clogs* of the present day have strong leather tops [often
brass clasps] and thick wooden soles.   The kind of bread
introduced by the Flemings into Bolton and other manufacturing districts of Lancashire was made of oatmeal in
the form of a loaf, and called *jannock;* but the gradual
change in manners and improvement in social condition
have almost banished this food, and wheaten-bread and
oat-cakes have almost altogether taken its place.

In the *Shepherd's Play*, performed at Chester in 1577,
in honour of the visit to that city of the Earl of Derby, the
third Shepherd says :—

> And brave ale of Halton I have,
> And what meat I had to my hire;
> A pudding may no man deprave,
> And a *jannock* of Lancaster-shire.

Jannock is now used in Leigh more commonly than in
most other parts of Lancashire.   Warrington ale was no
less celebrated than Halton ale, and a song in praise of the
former is printed in Harland's *Lancashire Ballads*.†

* Baines's *Lancashire.*
† P. 199.

S 2

PORK PASTIES.

In West Houghton, at the annual feast or wakes, there is a singular local custom of making large flat pasties of pork, which are eaten in great quantities on the Wakes Sunday, with a liberal accompaniment of ale; and people resort to the village from all places for miles round, on this Sunday, just as they rush into Bury on Mid-Lent or Mothering Sunday to eat simnels and drink bragot ale.

BIRTH AND BAPTISMAL CUSTOMS.

Many of the customs attending child-bearing, church-ing, and christening are not peculiar to Lancashire, but common nearly all over England. The term "the lady in the straw," merely meant the lady confined to her bed, as all beds were anciently stuffed with straw. It was for-merly the custom in Lancashire, as elsewhere, for the husband against the birth of the child to provide a large cheese and a cake. These were called "the groaning" cheese and cake; and throughout the north of England the first cut of the sick wife's cheese, or groaning cheese, is taken and laid under the pillows of young women to cause them to dream of their lovers. Amongst customs now obsolete was the giving a large entertainment at the churching. Now it is usually given at the christening.

PRESENTS TO WOMEN IN CHILDBED.

In a note on an entry of *Nicholls's Assheton's Journal,* Dr. Whitaker and its Editor, the Rev. Canon Raines, say that the custom of making presents to women in child-bed, is yet called "presénting" in Craven. It is now quite obsolete in South Lancashire, although it continued to be observed to the middle of the eighteenth century. In a MS. journal of 1706 is an entry " John Leigh brought my wife a groaning-cake: gave him 6*d.*" Other entries in the same journal show that money gifts ranged from 1*s.* 6*d.* to 5*s.* (the last being to the minister's wife) ; besides smaller gifts to maids and mid-wives, and bottles of wine, syrup of ginger, and other creature comforts to the person confined.

TEA-DRINKING AFTER CHILDBIRTH.

In some parts of North Lancashire it is customary to have a tea-drinking after the recovery from childbirth. All the neighbours and friends are invited—sometimes many more than can be comfortably accommodated—and both tea and rum are plentifully distributed. After tea, each visitor pays a shilling towards the expense of the birth feast; and the evening is spent in the usual gossip.

TURNING THE BED AFTER CHILDBIRTH.

An attendant was making a bed occupied by the mother of a child born a few days previously. When she attempted to turn it over, to give it a better shaking, the nurse ener-getically interfered, peremptorily forbidding her doing so till a month after the confinement, on the ground that it was decidedly unlucky ; and said that she never allowed it to be done till then, on any account whatever.*

* A. B., Liverpool, in *Notes and Queries,* vi. 432.

AN UNBAPTIZED CHILD CANNOT DIE.

The *Morning Herald* of the 18th June, 1860, notices a case of attempted infanticide near Liverpool. The wretched mother, having gained access to a gentleman's grounds, laid her child on the ground and covered it with sods. The child was happily discovered and its life saved. The mother was apprehended and charged with having attempted to murder her child. She confessed that she was guilty, and added [" the tender mercies of the wicked are cruel"] that she had previously succeeded in getting the child baptized, as she believed it could not otherwise have died. This is a strange bit of folk-lore.*

GIFTS TO INFANTS.

It is a custom in some parts of Lancashire, as well as in Yorkshire, Northumberland, and other counties, that when an infant first goes out of the house, in the arms of the mother or the nurse, in some cases the first family visited, in others every neighbour receiving the call, presents to or for the infant an egg, some salt, some bread, and in some cases a small piece of money. These gifts are to ensure, as the gossips avow, that the child shall never want bread, meat, or salt to it, or money, throughout life. The old custom of sponsors giving the child twelve tea-spoons, called "Apostle Spoons," is now obsolete. The gift of a coral with bells, is supposed to have had its origin in a very ancient superstition. Coral, according to Pliny, was deemed an amulet against fascination ; and it was thought to preserve and fasten the teeth. The coral-bells (especially if blest by the priest) would scare away evil spirits from the child.

* W. S. Simpson, in *Notes and Queries*, 2nd series, x. p. 184.

CHANGELINGS.

There is even yet in some parts of Lancashire a strong dread of the fairies or witches coming secretly and exchanging their own ill-favoured imps, for the newly born infant; and various charms are used to prevent the child from being thus stolen away.

BETROTHING AND BRIDAL OR WEDDING CUSTOMS.

BETROTHING CUSTOMS.

The common custom of breaking a piece of silver or gold (if it be crooked, so much the luckier) between lovers of the humbler classes, especially when the man is going to a distance, is believed to have had its origin in a sort of betrothal or promise of marriage, much practised amongst the ancient Danes, called *Hand-festing*, which is mentioned by Ray in his Collection or Glossary of Northumbrian Words. It means hand-fastening or binding. In betrothal it was also the custom to change rings, formed of two links or hoops, called gemmel rings, from *gemelli*, twins.

CURIOUS WEDDING CUSTOM.

An ancient custom at weddings of the poorer classes in Lancashire, and in some parts of Cumberland, is thus described:—The Lord of the Manor, in whose jurisdiction the marriage takes place, allowed the parties a piece of ground for a house and garden. All their friends assembled on the wedding-day, and the bridegroom having provided a dinner and drink, they set to work and constructed a dwelling for the young couple, of clay and wood, what is called post and petrel, or wattle and daub. Many of these " clay biggins " still remain in the Fylde district

and the northern parts of Lancashire. The relatives of
the pair supplied the most necessary part of the furniture,
and thus they were enabled to "start fair" in the world.*

———◆———

COURTING AND WEDDING CUSTOMS IN THE FYLDE.

On the occasion of a marriage, a christening, or a
churching, each guest either sent or presented some offering of money or food; thus providing a sufficient stock of
provisions for the entertainment without much, if any, cost
to the host. The preliminaries before marriage, the ad-
dresses paid by the swain to his sweetheart after the day's
labour was done, were styled "the sitting-up," the night
being the time allotted to courtship, by the kitchen fire,
after the other members of the family had retired to rest.
This "sitting-up" was regularly observed every Saturday
night if the lover was faithful; if otherwise, the price of
the "lant" (?) of the forsaken fair was transmitted by her
to the rival preferred by her inconstant swain. On the
wedding-day, when a bride and her "groom" left the
house to have the marriage rites solemnized, some relative
or servant threw at or after the smiling pair a "shuffle"
(*Pantoufle*, an old shoe or slipper)—a custom in its origin
said to be Jewish—as a preventive of future unhappiness,
an omen of good-luck and prosperity. At the church-
door an idle crowd was always ready for the "perry,"—
that is, to contest for the dole of scattered half-pence, or
if disappointed, to deprive the bride of her shawl or shoes,
till some largess was bestowed. The day was spent
in the company of a merry party of friends, who, after the
ceremony of "throwing the stocking" over the bed of the
wedded pair was performed, retired to their homes.†

* Hampson's *Medii Ævi Kalend.* i. 289.
† See Rev. W. Thornber's *History of Blackpool.*

ANCIENT BRIDAL CUSTOM.—THE BRIDE'S CHAIR AND THE FAIRY HOLE.

On the lower declivity of Warton Crag, in the parish of Warton (which abuts on Morecambe Bay and the Westmorland border), commanding a beautiful and extended prospect of the bay, a seat called " The Bride's Chair" was resorted to on the day of marriage by the brides of the village ; and in this seat they were enthroned with due solemnity by their friends ; but the origin and the object of the custom, which has now fallen in disuse, are unknown. Not far from Warton Crag are three rocking-stones placed in a line, about forty feet asunder, the largest stone lying in the middle. A cave is also mentioned by Lucas, named " The Fairy Hole," where dwarf spirits called Elves or Fairies, were wont to resort.*

BURNLEY.

An ancient custom prevails at Burnley Grammar School, by which all persons married at St. Peter's Church in that town are fined by the boys. As soon as a wedding is fixed the parish clerk informs the boys, and on the day appointed they depute two of their number to wait upon the groomsman and demand a fee. There is no fixed sum named ; but enough is got to purchase books and maintain a tolerable library for the use of the pupils. Former pupils always pay a liberal fine.

MARRIAGES AT MANCHESTER PARISH CHURCH.

" Th'owd Church," as the collegiate church of Manchester was provincially designated before it attained the

* Baines's *History of Lancashire.*

dignity of a cathedral, was known and celebrated far and wide over the extensive parish. Its altar has witnessed the joining together of thousands of happy [and unhappy] couples. The fees here being less than those demanded at other churches, which had to pay tribute to it, it was of course the most popular sanctuary in the whole parish for the solemnization of matrimony. At the expiration of Lent (during which the marriage fees are doubled) crowds of candidates for nuptial honours present themselves; indeed so numerous are they that the ceremony is performed by wholesale on Easter Monday. A chaplain of facetious memory [the Rev. Joshua Brookes] is said to have on one of these occasions accidentally united the wrong parties. When the occurrence was represented to him, his ready reply was, "Pair as you go out; you're all married; pair as you go out." This verbal certificate appeared to give general satisfaction, and each bridegroom soon found his right bride. Sir George Head, in his *Home Tour through the Manufacturing Districts, in the summer of* 1835, thus describes what he saw of these wholesale Monday marriages :—" I attended the Old Church at Manchester one Monday morning, in order to witness the solemnization of several marriages, which I had reason to suppose were then and there to take place. I had heard on the preceding Sunday the banns proclaimed as follows :—' For the first time of asking, 65; for the second time, 72; for the third time, 60. Total, 197.' Having been informed that it would be expedient to be on the spot at eight in the morning I repaired thither at that hour. Operations, however, did not commence before ten. The latter is the usual time of proceeding to business, although in cases of persons married by licence 8 o'clock is the hour. When all was ready and the church doors opened, the clergyman and clerk betook themselves to the vestry; and the people who were about to be married, and their friends, seated themselves in the body of the church opposite the communion table, on benches which were placed there for the purpose. Not less than fifty persons were assembled, among whom I took my seat quietly, without being noticed. A party who had arrived in a narrow *vis à vis* fly, most exclusively paraded in the meantime up and down (as if unwilling to identify themselves with the humbler candidates of matrimony) in another part of the church. The people at first took their seats in solemn silence, each one inquisitively surveying his neighbour; but as the clergyman and clerk were some time in preparation, the men first began to whisper one to another and the women to titter, till by degrees they all threw off their reserve, and made audible remarks on the new comers. There was little *mauvaise honte* among the women, but of the men, poor fellows! some were seriously abashed; while among the hymeneal throng there seemed to prevail a sentiment that obtains pretty generally among their betters, namely, inclination to put shy people out of conceit with themselves. Thus, at the advance of a sheepish-looking bridegroom, he was immediately assailed on all sides with 'Come in, man; what art thou afraid of? Nobody 'll hurt thee!' And then a general laugh went round in a repressed tone, but quite sufficient to confound and subdue the new comer. Presently a sudden buzz broke out, 'The clergyman's coming;' and all was perfectly silent. About twelve couples were to be married; the rest were friends and attendants. The former were called upon to arrange themselves all together around the altar. The clerk was an adept in his business, and performed the duties of his office in a mode admirably calculated to set the people at their ease and direct the proceedings. In appointing them to their proper places, he

addressed each in an intonation of voice perfectly soft and soothing, and which carried with it more of encouragement as he made use of no appellative but the Christian name of the person spoken to. Thus he proceeded:—
' Daniel and Phœbe; this way, Daniel, take off your gloves, Daniel. William and Anne; no, Anne; here, Anne; t'other side, William. John and Mary; here, John; oh John.' And then addressing them all together, ' Now, all of you give your hats to some person to hold.' Although the marriage service appeared to me (adds Sir George) to be generally addressed to the whole party, the clergyman was scrupulously exact in obtaining the accurate responses from each individual."

Many wedding customs, as the bridesmaids and bes men, the wedding-ring, the nuptial kiss in the church, the bouquet borne in the hand of the bride, &c., the scattering of flowers in her path, the throwing of an old shoe after her for luck, the giving gloves, &c., are of ancient origin and are the relics of Anglo-Saxon or Danish usages.

DYING, DEATH-BED, AND FUNERAL CUSTOMS.

DYING HARDLY.

Persons are said to "die hardly," as the phrase is meaning to be unable to expire, when there are pigeons feathers in the bed. Some will not allow dying persons to lie on a feather-bed, because they hold that it very much increases their pain and suffering, and actually retards their departure. On the other hand, there is a superstitious feeling that it is a great misfortune, nay, even a *judgment*, not to die in a bed.

BURYING IN WOOLLEN.

By a statute of 30 Car. II., stat. 1, cap. 3 (1678), entitled "An act for the lessening the importation of linen from beyond the seas, and the encouragement of the woollen and paper manufactures of the kingdom," it is enacted that the curate of every parish shall keep a register, to be provided at the charge of the parish, wherein to enter all burials and affidavits of persons being buried in woollen; the affidavit to be taken by any justice of the peace, mayor, or such like chief officer, in the parish where the body was interred; and if there be no officer, then by any curate within the city where the corpse was buried (except him in whose parish the corpse was buried), who must administer the oath and set his hand gratis. No affidavit to be necessary for a person dying of the plague. It imposes a fine of £5 for every infringement; one half to go to the informer, and the other half to the poor of the parish. This act was repealed by the 54 Geo. III. cap. 108 (1814). In the parish of Prestwich, the first entry in the book provided for such purposes was in August, 1678; and there is no entry later than 1681, which appears also to be the limit of the act's observance in the adjacent parish of Radcliffe; where the entries immediately follow the record of the burial itself in the registers, and not in a separate book as at Prestwich. Under the year 1679, is the following entry in the parish register of Radcliffe:—

"An orphan of Ralph Mather's, of Radcliffe, was buried the 9th day of April, and certified to be wound up in woollen only, under the hand of Mr. William Hulme."

In the churchwardens' accounts of Prestwich, for the year 1681, is the following item of receipt:—

"Received a fine of James Crompton, for burying his son, and not bringing in an affidavit, according to the act for burying in woollen, £2 10s."*

———◆———

FUNERAL DOLE AND ARVAL CAKE.

In Lancashire, the funeral was formerly celebrated with great profusion in meats and drinks, to which was added in those of the richer sort, what was called a penny dole, or promiscuous distribution of that sum, anciently delivered in silver to the poor. The effect of this custom, says Lucas (as quoted by Dr. Whitaker†) was such, that he had seen many "who would rather go seven or eight miles to a penny dole, than earn sixpence in the same time by laudable industry." This custom of distributing a small money alms or dole at funerals still existed in parts of Lancashire within the last fifty years. One sexagenarian informant told the writer that, when a lad, he went to the funeral of a Mr. D., in the hamlet of Swinton, parish of Eccles, and there was what he called "a *dow*, gi'en to every lad and every wench [boy or girl] as went, far and near,—a penny a-piece ; and them as carrit a choilt [carried a child] had tuppence." Usually at country funerals, after the interment, the relations first, and next their attendants, threw into the grave sprigs of bay, rosemary, or other odoriferous evergreens, which had been previously distributed amongst them. In some cases, a messenger went round the neighbourhood, " bidding " parties to the funeral, and at each house where he gave the invitation, he left a sprig of rosemary, &c. After the rites at the grave, the company adjourned to a neighbouring public-house, where they

---

* Rev. John Booker, Prestwich, in *Notes and Queries,* v. 543.
† *Richmondshire,* ii. 298.

were severally presented with a cake and ale, which was called an *arval*. This word seems to have greatly puzzled Dr. Whitaker. It is the Sueo-Gothic *arföl*, which is a compound of *arf*, inheritance, and *öl*, ale,—expressive of a feast given by the heir, at the funeral, on succeeding to the estate. The feast and its name were imparted to us by the Danes, whose *arfwöl* is described by Olaus Wormius as a solemn banquet, celebrated by kings and nobles, in honour of deceased relations, whom they are succeeding.

DALTON-IN-FURNESS.

The most singular mode of conducting funerals prevails at this place. A full meal of bread and cheese and ale is provided at the funeral house ; and, after the corpse is interred the parish clerk proclaims, at the grave-side, that the company must repair to some appointed public-house. Arrived there, they sit down by fours together, and each four is served with two quarts of ale.* One half of this is paid for by the conductor of the funeral, and the other half by the company. While they are drinking the ale, the waiter goes round with cakes, serving out one to each guest, which he is expected to carry home.†

OLD FUNERAL CUSTOMS AT WARTON.

A singular practice, which was growing obsolete in the time of Lucas (says Dr. Whitaker) once prevailed in the parish of Warton ; which was, that most householders were furnished with a kind of family pall, or finely wrought

---

* In many instances, in social feasts, four persons were regarded as a " mess."
    † The Rev. Mr. Hodgson's *Description of Westmorland.*

coverlet, to be laid over the bier when the corpse was carried to church. Amongst other funeral customs at Warton, were the great feasting and drinking ; the funeral dole, distributed to the poor; the casting of odoriferous herbs into the grave ; and the cake and *arval*-ale, already described, pp. 270, 271, *suprâ.**

FUNERAL CUSTOMS IN THE FYLDE.

When the last offices of respect to a departed friend or neighbour were to be rendered, a whole district, called " their side " of the country, was " bidden " or invited to assist in carrying the remains to their narrow home. At a stated hour the crowd assembled, not to mourn with widowed wife or weeping children, but to consume ale and tobacco, and to talk over their farms or trade till all was in readiness to depart for the completion of the obse-quies. A particular order was observed. From the door of his former home, and into, and out of, the church, the corpse was carried on the shoulders of four of his relatives —his nearest kinsman, the chief mourner, walking in front with the clergyman. At the close of the ceremony, after the sprigs of box or rosemary had been deposited on the coffin, each person also adding a sprinkling of dust, the rough voice of the parish clerk was heard grating harshly in that solemn moment, inviting the " bidden " to show further their respect to the deceased by partaking of a dinner provided at the village inn. How the day termi-nated may be supposed, and indeed was a matter of sad notoriety. Indeed, it was not very unusual to see those who were to convey the dead to the sepulchre, tottering from intoxication under their sad burden. The best

* Baines's *History of Lancashire.*

features of these old-time funerals were that doles in money were distributed to the aged and the very young; the poor were fed, and sometimes warm cloaks or other useful articles of attire were given, to be worn in memory of the departed.* Fifty-five years ago, says Mr. Thornber, writing in 1837, the more respectable portion of the inhabitants of Poulton were buried by candle-light—a custom long observed by some of the oldest families in the town. It was regarded as a sacred duty to expose a lighted candle in the window of every house as the corpse passed through the streets towards the church for inter-ment; and he was poor indeed who did not pay this tribute of respect to the dead. So late as 1813 this church was strewed with rushes.

MODE OF BURIAL OF A WIDOW WHO HAD TAKEN RELIGIOUS VOWS.

A daughter of William Balderstone, of Balderstone, in her widowhood, makes a will of which the following is the commencement:—" Seventh day of January, 1497. I, Dame Jane Pilkington, widow, make and ordain this my last will and testament : First, I bequeath my bodye to be buried in ye Nunnes Quire of Monketon, in my habit, holding my hand upon my breast, with my ring upon my finger, having taken in my resolves the mantel and the ring," &c.

FUNERAL CUSTOMS IN EAST LANCASHIRE.

In *Nicholas Assheton's Journal,* he mentions that the corpse of a Mrs. Starkie was carried to church by four

---

* Rev. W. Thornber's *History of Blackpool.*
† Dr. Whitaker's *Whalley,* addenda.

T

relatives; there was a sermon, and afterwards dinner, forty messes being provided for. On this, Dr. Whitaker remarks:—"An ancient usage. The nearest relations always took up the corpse at the door; and once more, if the distance was considerable, at the church gates. By forty messes, I suppose are to be understood so many dishes of meat. ' The editor (the Rev. Canon Raines) adds:—"This custom, which appears to be quite patriarchal, is still prevalent in some of the country parishes in South Lancashire. The custom of preaching funeral sermons on the day of the burial is now exploded, although so recently as 1776 the vicar of one of the largest parishes in Lancashire (Rev. John White, B.A., of Blackburn), objected to the building of a church in his parish unless he had 'some compensation made for the funeral sermons to be preached in it.'* I should rather understand the forty messes to be dinners provided for forty persons, although funerals in Lancashire at this period were conducted on a scale of prodigality scarcely to be conceived." [*The House and Farm Accounts of the Shuttleworths* give examples of three burial customs—that of a dole to the poor; at one place 40s. 7d., at another 57s. 4d., at a third 47s. 8d. (?) a penny to each person; that of payment to the clergyman for a funeral sermon, in one case 5s.; and that of providing dinners for the mourners, chiefly for those from a distance, in one case twenty-four messes of meat cost 58s. 8d.; in another instance seventy dined at 6d. the mess or meal, seventy-six and sixty-five at 5d.; in all 211 persons attending one funeral.—EDS.]

BIDDING TO FUNERALS.

Previously to the formation of cemeteries, and the employment of omnibus-hearses, it was customary to invite

* *Lancashire MSS.—Letters.*

large numbers to attend funerals. Guests were invited by
dozens ; and as each entered the house where the deceased
lay, he was met at the door by a female attendant habited
in black, and wearing a white apron, who offered him
spiced liquor from a silver tankard. In the house each person was presented with a bun and a slice of currant bread.
When the time for closing up the coffin arrived, each took
his last look at the corpse and presented a shilling, or more,
to the nearest relative of the deceased; who always sat at
the head of the coffin for this purpose. In the neighbourhoods of Little Hulton, Peel Yate, Walkden Moor, &c.,
it was till of late years the custom for two persons to be
nominated as " bidders " of guests to a funeral. These
went to the various houses of the persons to be invited,
and presented to each a sprig of rosemary; which the
guest wore or carried in the hand at the funeral. This
inviting or " bidding " was usually called " lating " or
" lathing ;" from the A.-S. verb *Lathian,* to invite, bid, or
send for.

———◆———

SITUATION AND DIRECTION OF GRAVES.

As churches are built to stand about East and West, the
greatest spaces in the churchyard are the North and South
sides of the church. Throughout Lancashire and the
North of England there is a universal superstition that the
south side of the church is the holiest or most consecrated
ground, and it may be observed that that side of the
graveyard is generally crowded with grave-stones, or green
hillocks of turf, while the north side has but few. This
is an old superstition, which held that the north side of the
church was really unhallowed ground, fit only to be the
last resting place of still-born infants and suicides. Then
almost all graves are ranged east and west ; and in a rare

tract of the Marprelate series, called "*Martin's Month's
Mind*" (1589) it is stated that "he would not be laid east
and west (for he ever went against the hair), but north
and south : I think because 'Ab aquilone omne malum'
(from the north comes all evil), and the south wind ever
brings corruption with it." The celebrated antiquary
Thomas Hearne, left orders for his grave to be made
straight by a compass, due east and west. Sir Thomas
Browne* observes that "the Persians were buried lying
north and south ; the Megarians and Phœnicians placed
their heads to the east ; the Athenians, some think, towards
the west, which Christians still retain ; and Bede will have
it to be the posture of our Saviour." One "Article of
Inquiry" in a visitation of the Bishop of Ely in 1662,
was—"When graves are digged, are they made six feet
deep (at the least), and east and west ?"

CUSTOMS OF MANORS.

This subject would require extensive notice, if the materials requisite for its elucidation were more numerous
and accessible. All prescriptive customs of manors have
existed beyond what is termed "legal memory"—*i. e.*,
from the reign of Richard I. (1189-1199). Many others,
relating to the military and other free tenures of the chief
tenants of manors, and to the socage and inferior or ser-
vile tenures, with the boons of the cottagers, &c., and the
various services attached to these different tenures, would
make a very curious piece of history of customs and
usages; but these are usually recorded only in private
grants, charters, and other deeds, or in copy-rolls and

* In his *Urn Burial.*

other records of manors, not generally accessible. The
following are some examples :—

THE HONOUR OF KNIGHTHOOD.

In the early ages of our history, the honour of knighthood, with the military services to which it was incident
under the feudal system, was often forced upon the subject. In the year 1278, a writ to the Sheriff of Lancashire
commanded him to distrain upon all persons seised of
land of the value of £20 yearly, whether held of the
King *in capite*, or of any other lords who ought to be
knights and were not; and all such were ordered forthwith to take out their patent of knighthood. Fourteen
years after this, a writ was issued, wherein the qualification
was raised to double the amount; and a writ, dated 6th
February, 1292, was issued to the Sheriff of Lancashire
(with others), proclaiming that all persons holding lands
in fee, or of inheritance, of the value of £40 per annum,
must take the order of knighthood before Christmas in
that year. The crown might relax or vary these services :
hence a writ to the Sheriff of Lancashire recites " that the
commonalty of England, having performed good services
against the Welsh, the king excuses persons not holding
lands of the value of £100 yearly from taking the order
of knighthood;" but all holding above that amount, and
not taking the order before the Nativity of the Virgin
(Sept. 8), were to be distrained upon. Subsequently,
injunctions were addressed to the Sheriff, commanding
him to make extents of the lands of those refusing to
take the order of knighthood, and to hold them for the
king until further orders. Another writ to the Sheriff of
Lancashire, of 6th April, 1305, directs him to proclaim that
all who should become knights, and are not, must repair

to London before the following Whit Sunday to receivei
that distinction, if properly qualified.*

MARITAGIUM.

On the marriage of the Princess Alianora (sister of
Edward III.) with the Earl of Guelders, an order was issued
to the abbot of Furness, and to the priors of Burscough,
Up-Holland, and Hornby, as well as to the abbot of
Whalley, and to the priors of Cartmell and Coningshead,
requesting them to levy the subsidy on their respective
houses, towards the *Maritagium,* an impost of early times,
which ceased with the feudal system.† This order the
priests were slow to obey, in consequence of which another letter was issued by the king from Pontefract,
reminding them of their neglect, and ordering them to
communicate their intention to the proper authority. No
further documents appear on the subject ; and it may be
presumed that this second application produced the desired
effect.*

PECULIAR SERVICES AND TENURES.

The following are entries in the "Testa de Nevill," a
book supposed to have been compiled towards the close of
the reign of Edward II. or the beginning of that of Edward
III., and consequently to exhibit the services and tenures
existing about the beginning of the 12th century:—Thomas
and Alicia de Gersingham, by keeping the king's [John's]
hawks in Lonsdale, till they became strong, when they
were to be committed to the Sheriff of Lancashire.   Luke

* Baines's *Lancashire.*
† Claus., 7 Edward III., 1333, p. 1, m. 23.

Pierpoint, by keeping an aëry; Adam de Hemelesdale, by constabulary at Crosby. Quenilda de Kirkdale, by conducting royal treasure. Richard Fitz Ralph, by constabulary at Singleton. John de Oxeclive, by being carpenter at Lancaster Castle. Adam Fitz Gilmighel, by being the king's carpenter. Roger the carpenter, by being carpenter in Lancaster Castle. Ralph Barun or Babrun, by being mason in Lancaster Castle. Walter, son of Walter Smith, by forging iron instruments. Roger Gernet, by being chief forester. William Gernet, by the service of meeting the king on the borders of the city, with his horse and white rod, and conducting him into and out of the city. William and Benedict de Gersingham, by the sergeantry of keeping the king's aëries of hawks. Gilbert Fitz Orm, by paying yearly 3*d.* or some spurs to Benedict Gernet, the heir of Roger de Heton, in thanage. Roger de Leycester, by paying 8*s.* and two arrows yearly. A great number of persons in thanage: others in drengage. John de Thoroldesholme, by larderery; Roger de Skerton, by provostry. Roger Fitz John, by making irons for the king's ploughs. Others, by gardenry, and by masonry, or the service of finding pot-herbs and leeks for Lancaster castle, smith's work, and carpentry; the burgesses of Lancaster, by free-burgage and by royal charter. Peter de Mundevill, by service of one brachet [a sort of hound] of one colour. The prior of Wingal, by he knows not what service. Lady Hillaria Trussebut, by no service, and she knows not by what warrant. Henry de Waleton, by being head sergeant or bailiff of the Hundred of Derbyshire [*i.e.* West Derby]. Galfridus Balistarius [Geoffrey Balistur] by presenting two cross-bows to the king. William Fitz William, by presenting one brachet, one *velosa* [? a piece of velvet] and two *lintheamina* [pieces of linen cloth]. Roger Fitz

Vivian holds the sergeantry of Heysham, by blowing the horn before the king at his entrance into and exit from the city of Lancaster. Thomas Gernet, in Heysham, by sounding the horn on meeting the king on his arrival in those parts. William Gresle, by presenting a bow without string, a quiver, 12 arrows, and a *buxon* [? possibly a quiver or arrow-case]. William Fitz Waukelin, by presenting one soar-hawk. Hervi Gorge, by presenting one plough, one *linthola* [piece of linen cloth], one *velosa* [piece of velvet], and one *auricular* [? a veil for the confessional]. Roger and Hugh de Auberville, by keeping one hawk. Several religious houses held in pure and free and perpetual alms, or what the Normans styled "Frank-almoigne." A large number of persons held by donation, in considera- tion of yearly rents, and some of these were nominal, as "a pepper-corn, if demanded," "a clove," "a red rose on St. John the Baptist's Day" (24th June), "a pair of white gloves or a peny," a "Manchester knife," &c.

SMITHELLS.—The mesne manor of Smithells in Sharp- les, near Bolton, is dependent upon the superior manor of Sharples, the lord of which claims from the owner of Smithells a pair of gilt spurs annually; and, by a very singular and inconvenient custom, the unlimited use of the cellars at Smithells Hall for a week in every year.*

It does not appear, however, that the lord of Smithells was bound to the quantity or to the quality of the liquors with which his cellars were at that time to be stored. This feudal claim seems now nearly abandoned, as it has not been enforced within the present century.†

* Dr. Whitaker's *Whalley.*
† Baines's *History of Lancashire.*

MANOR OF COCKERHAM.—REGULATIONS FOR THE SALE OF ALE.

The customs' dues of this manor appear to have been originally ordained by Brother William Geryn, cellarer of the Abbey of Cokersand, in 1326, and were confirmed by John the Abbot in 1st Richard III. (1483-4). The confirmation is in the English of the period; and among other curious ordinances, contains the following regulation as to the price, &c., of ale (the spelling is modernised) :—

' There shall no brewer let no tenant for to have ale for their silver out of their house, and such [may] have four gallons within their house, so that they bring a vessel with 'them. Ye shall not sell a gallon of ale above a halfpenny when ye may buy a quarter of good oats for 2d. Ye shall give ale-founders [manorial officers also called ale-tasters] a founding-gallon, or else a taste of each vessel, and your charge, on pain [penalty] of grievous amerciaments."*

MANORIAL CUSTOMS IN FURNESS.

Kirkby Ireleth.—In this manor the widow is entitled during her widowhood to the moiety of the estate whereof her husband died seised; but forfeits her right thereto upon re-marriage or breach of chastity. Every tenant, upon being admitted to a tenement, pays to the lord of the manor 20 years' quit-rent for a fine. Every entire tenement was formerly obliged to keep one horse and harness, for the king's service, on the borders or elsewhere. These were called "summer [? sumpter] nags," of which 30 were kept in Kirkby. The tenant was also to furnish a boon plough and a boon-harrow, that is, a day's ploughing

* Baines's *History of Lancashire.*

and harrowing; and no one is to let his land for any time exceeding 7 years, without licence. Tenements in this manor are forfeited to the lord by treason or felony. A tenant convicted of wilful perjury forfeits to the lord 20 years' rent, and for petty larceny, 10 years' rent.

PENNINGTON.—Pennington is the smallest parish in the county, and contains fewer streams than any other parish in North Lonsdale. Some feudal customs, obsolete in most places, are still observed in the manor of Pennington. A tenant on admission pays a fine of 16 years' quit-rent. On the death of the lord and on every change of the lord by descent, the tenant pays a further fine of 6 years' quit-rent; and a running-fine, town-term, or *gressom*, is payable every 7th year. The heir, where there is a widow, pays a heriot. Every tenant must plant two trees of the same kind for every one that he fells. Formerly every tenant was obliged to carry a horse-load once a year to Manchester and half a horse-load to Lancaster. In 1318 a dispute between the Pennington family and the Abbot of Furness, as to boon services, was thus decided:—
"That the manor of Pennington was held by the service of 30s., and of finding yearly, for one day in autumn, a man and woman, sufficient to mow at the Grange of Lindale, for every house with a court-yard except Sir William de Pennington's capital messuage; the convent to find the daily refreshment of each mower while employed, according to ancient custom; and Sir William granting that all the tenants of the manor, who had or might have ploughs, should plough half an acre of the Abbot's Grange at Lindale."*

MUCHLAND.—Immediately after the Conquest Aldingham was granted to Michael Flandrensis or le Fleming, and

† Baines's *Lancashire.*

his land was called Michael's land, to distinguish it from
that of the abbey of Furness; spelled often Mychel-land and
Mychelande, till it got corrupted into Muchland. In the
manor of Muchland, the tenant on being admitted to his
tenement pays to the lord of the manor two years' rent
over and above the usual annual rent. Every tenant paying 40s. rent was formerly obliged to find a horse and harness for the King's service, on the borders or elsewhere.
Every tenant who paid 20s. a year rent, was to furnish a
man harnessed for the King's service. Every old tenant
paid a *gressom* of one year's rent on the death of the lord,
and every new tenant pays two years' rent to the next
heir. The widow has one-third of the tenement during
her chaste widowhood. If a tenement is not presented
within a year and a day after the death of the tenant, or if
it be sold, set, or let without paying the fine, or *gressom,* for
a year and a day, then the lord, if there be not good distress upon the grounds, may seize such tenement into his
hands as a forfeiture, &c.

LOWICK.—Here the customs are much the same as in
Kirkby Ireleth, except as to forfeitures. The running
gressom, or town term, is a year's rent every seventh year,
paid to the lord. There are four house-lookers annually
appointed for reviewing and assigning timber for necessary repairs.

NEVIL HALL.—The admittance fine is two years' rent,
over and above the accustomed yearly rent. The heriot,
on the change of lord, is half a year's rent. The running
gressom, or town-term, is half a year's rent every seventh
year. Every tenant paying 20s. rent was formerly to
keep a horse harnessed in readiness for the King's service.
The widow in this manor, if the first wife, to have half the
tenement ; but if she be a latter wife, then only one-third
the tenement. A tenant may, whenever he pleases, give

his tenement to any of his sons; and in default of sons to any of his daughters, as he thinks fit. A tenant may let, or mortgage, any tenement or part of it for a year, without a licence; and may sell his own tenant-right, or any part of it, with licence from the lord. The rents mentioned above are old and immutable rents.*

MUCH-URSWICK.—These customs include a fine of 20*d.* to the lord of the manor on every change of tenancy, or on the death of the lord; except one large house, which paying 4*s.* rent, paid a fine of five times the lord's rent, or 5*d.* on the death of the lord, or a change of tenancy. The tenant's widow had half the estate during chaste widowhood. The tenants were obliged to carry a single horseload, anciently fish, once a year to Mowbreck Hall, near Kirkham; but this service was commuted for a small rent called carriage rent. Tenements in this manor, on treason or felony by the tenant are forfeited to the lord. A tenant convicted of wilful perjury, forfeits to the lord twenty years' rent, and for petty larceny, ten years' rent.†

THE ROYAL MANOR OF WARTON.—These customs are similar in many respects to those of the duchy manors in Furness. In the reign of Elizabeth a commission of survey, and a jury of twenty-four, from the neighbouring manors, made a return of the customs, which were confirmed by the Court of Exchequer. These manorial byelaws are applicable to customary tenants, and relate to the subjects of heirships, performance of suit and service, the powers of the steward, the enrolling of tenants, the payment of rents, amounts of fines, &c. A fine of two years' rent is to be imposed on changes of tenantry; all tenants

---

* West's *History of Furness.*
† Baines's *History of Lancashire.*

paying above 20s. rent were required to maintain a horse
and man with armour, tenants paying under 20s. being
commanded to serve in person : these services to be strictly
and fully executed in cases of need. Each tenant is
directed to repair his own homestead. In case of the
death of a married tenant, one-half of the tenement is
assigned to the widow, to be held during her chaste widowhood, and the other half to the heir or heirs. The crime
of fornication to be punished with forfeiture. Tenants
not to set, let, or mortgage for above three years without
licence; not to encroach on the common without permis-
sion. The manor court to have jurisdiction in cases of
tithe and tenant right; the tenants to be at liberty to take
ash wood. The tenants are not to be abated in their rents
for any loss they may suffer in their several proportions of
turbary, marsh and common. These manorial regulations
are now but seldom enforced, and the Court Baron of
Warton assembles only on rare occasions, not uncommonly
after intervals of years.*

FEUDAL PRIVILEGES OF THE HONOUR AND MANOR
OF HORNBY.—These ancient privileges comprised free
warren, subject to a fine of 10l. on encroachments on the
King's forests; right of market and fair at Arkholme and
at Hornby; court of view of frank-pledge; sheriff's turn;
free court of all pleas; assize of bread; soc, sac, tol, and
them; infangetheof and utfangetheof; hamsocn; leyr-
wite; murder; acquittance of shires and hundreds, lestage
[or lastage], aids of sheriffs and their bailiffs, and amerce-
ments; wardships, and works and enclosures of castles,
parks, and bridges; and of passage, frontage, stallage, toll,
paiage, and money given for murder; and right to pont-

* Baines's *History of Lancashire.*

age, stallage, hidage, and pickage. All these feudal customs were confirmed in the 12th Charles I. (1636) to Henry Parker, Lord Morley and Monteagle.*

A number of the above terms require explanation. " Money given for murder," implied the fines levied on a district in which a murder had been committed, and the criminal not discovered ; " the privilege of murder " was the power to levy such fines ; thus the town or hundred which suffered an Englishman, who had killed a Dane there to escape, was to be amerced sixty-six marks [44*l.*] to the King. *Hamsocn,* is the privilege or liberty of a man's own house, its violation is burglary. *Leyr* or *lecher wite,* is the privilege of punishing adultery and fornication. Passage is a toll for passing over water, as at a ford or ferry ; pontage is bridge toll ; stallage, a toll for stalls in a market ; paiage or pavage, is a paving toll. *Sac,* the right of a lord to hold pleas in his court, in causes of trespass among his tenants ; *soc,* the right to administer justice and execute laws ; *toll,* the right to levy tolls on tenants ; *them,* the right to hear, restrain, and judge bondmen and villeins, with their children, goods and chattels, &c. *Infangetheof,* the lord's privilege to judge any thief taken within his fee. *Outfangtheof,* the right of the lord to call men dwelling within his manor, and taken for felony outside his fee, to judgment in the lord's own court.

THE LORD'S YULE FEAST AT ASHTON.

Among the customs of the Manor of Ashton-under-Lyne, as described by the late Dr. Hibbert Ware, was the making of so-called " presents" by the tenants-at-will to

* Baines's *Lancashire.*

the lord of the manor, for the sake of partaking in the annual feast at the great hall. In the rental of Sir John de Assheton, made in November 1422, these presents are claimed as an obligatory service from the tenants-at-will, in the following terms :—" That they shall give their presents at Yole [Christmas] ; every present to such a value as is written and set in the rental; and the lord shall feed all his said tenants, and their wifes, upon Yole-day at the dinner, if they like for to come ; but the said tenants and their wifes, though it be for their ease not to come, they shall send neither man nor woman in their name,—but if [unless] they be their son or their daughter dwelling with them,—unto the dinner; for the lord is not bounden to feed them all, only the good man and the good wife." In some manor-houses of Lancashire, once dedicated to these annual scenes of festivity, may be observed an elevation of the floor [or *daïs*] at the extremity of the great hall, or, in the place of it, a gallery which stretches along one side of the room [many halls have both *daïs* and gallery] to accommodate the lord and his family, so that they might not be annoyed by the coarse rustic freedoms which the tenants would be too apt to take during the hours of their conviviality. In a hall, then, of this kind in the manor-house at Assheton, we may imagine the large Yule fire to be kindled; while in a gallery or raised floor Sir John of Assheton, his lady, and family, together with his kinsmen, Elland of Brighouse, and Sir John the Byron, are feasting apart, yet attentive to the frolics or old songs of the company below. It was on these occasions that peg-tankards were used, and horns that bore the names of the Saxons and Danes, whom the Normans had ousted out of their possessions. Of the description of ale that flowed merrily on these occasions we know little ; but there can be no doubt that it was like King Henry the

Eighth's ale, which contained neither hops nor brimstone.
We may suppose, then, that on annual festivals like these,
the wooden bowl or horn would pass freely through the
hands of Sir John of Assheton's tenants-at-will; among
whom were such personages as Hobbe Adamson, Hobbe
of the Leghes, William the arrow-smith, Roger the baxter,
Roger le smith, Jack the spencer, Jack the hind, Elyn
Wilkyn daughter, Elyn the rose, and the widows Mergot
of Staley, Peryn's wife, and Nan of the Windy Bank,—all
clad in their best hoods, and brown woollen jackets and
petticoats. The ancient musical instruments used in Lancashire were a kind of fiddle, not of the present form, and
a stringed instrument called the virginals. The provincial
songs of that period, few of which were less than half-an-
hour in length, rehearsed the deeds of Launcelot du Lake,
and his conquest of the giant Tarquin, at the castle of
Manchester; Ranulph of Chester, and his wars in the
Holy Land; or the warlike feats and amorous prowess
of the renowned Cheshire hero, Roger de Calverley. In
order to preserve, as much as possible, the degree of de-
corum that was necessary at such meetings, there was
firstly introduced a diminutive pair of stone stocks, of about
eighteen inches in length, for confining within them the
fingers of the unruly. This instrument was entrusted to
the general prefect of manorial festivities named the King
of Misrule, whose office it was to punish all who exceeded
his royal notions of decency. Accordingly such a character
appears among the list of Sir John of Assheton's tenants,
under the name of Hobbe the king. From these entertainments being supported by the contributions of the
tenants, they were derisively called *Drink-leans*. [*Læn*,
A.-S. a loan, a **gift**, a reward; *Læne*, adj., lean, slender,
fragile.]*

* *Illustration of the Customs of a Manor in the North of England.*

RIDING THE BLACK LAD AT ASHTON-UNDER-LYNE.

In the rental of Sir John Assheton, knight, of his Manor of Ashton-under-Lyne, A.D. 1422, it is stated that two of his sons, Rauf of Assheton, and Robyn of Assheton, by grants to them, " have the sour carr guld rode and stane rynges for the term of their lives." This donation (says Dr. Hibbert-Ware) evidently alludes to the privilege of *Guld-riding*, a custom that in Scotland at least is of great antiquity, having been intended to prevent lands from being over-run with the weeds, which, from their yellow colour, were named *gools* or *gulds*, *i.e.* the corn-marigold, or *Chrysanthemum Segetum* of Linn. Boethius (lib. 10) mentions a law of king Kenneth (probably rather of Alexander II.) to prevent the growth of *manaleta* or *guld*, and to impose a fine of oxen on proof of its infraction. The Rev. J. P. Bannerman, in a statistical account of the parish of Cargill, in Perthshire, states that with a view of extirpating this weed, " after allowing a reasonable time for procuring clean seed from other grounds, an act of the Baron Court was passed, enforcing an old Act of Parliament to the same effect, imposing a fine of 3*s*. 4*d*., or a wether sheep, on the tenants for every stock of *gool* that should be found growing in their corn at a particular day; and certain persons styled *gool-riders* were appointed to ride through the fields, search for *gool*, and carry the law into execution when they discovered it. Though the fine of a wether sheep is now commuted and reduced to a penny, the practice of *gool-riding* is still kept up, and the fine rigidly exacted." To this origin Dr. Hibbert-Ware attributes the custom peculiar to Ashton-under-Lyne of " Riding the Black Lad." He states that in the days of Sir John of Assheton (A.D. 1422) a large portion of low wet land in the vicinity of Assheton was named the Sour

U

Carr (carr being synonymous with the Scotch word *carse,* and the well-known term *sour* implying an impoverished state of the carr). It had been over-run with corn-marigolds or carr-gulds, which were so destructive to the corn that the lord of the manor enforced some rigorous measures for their extirpation, similar to the carr-guld riding in Perthshire. Ralph of Assheton, Sir John's son by a second marriage, and Robin, his brother, were on a certain day in the spring [Easter-Monday] invested with the power of riding over the lands of the carr, named the *Carr Guld Rode,* of levying fines for all *carr-gulds* that were found among the corn, and, until the penalties were paid, of punishing transgressors by putting them into the [finger] *stocks* or *stone rings,* or by incarceration. Ralph Assheton, by his alliance with a rich heiress, became the lord of the neighbouring manor of Middleton, and soon afterwards received the honour of knighthood; being at the same time entrusted with the office of Vice-Constable of the kingdom ; and it is added, of Lieutenant of the Tower. Invested with such authorities, he committed violent excesses in this part of the kingdom. Retaining for life the privilege granted him in Ashton of Guld-riding, he, on a certain day in spring, made his appearance in the manor, clad in black armour (whence his name of the Black Lad or Black Boy) mounted on a charger, and attended with a numerous train of his own followers, in order to levy the penalty arising from the neglect of clearing the land from carr-gulds. The interference of so powerful a knight belonging to another township could not but be regarded by the tenants of Assheton as the tyrannical intrusion of a stranger; and as Sir Ralph, sanctioned by the political power given him by Henry VI., exercised his privilege with the utmost severity, the name of the Black Lad is still regarded with sentiments of horror. Tradition has, indeed, perpetuated the prayer that was fervently ejaculated for a deliverance from his tyranny :—

> Sweet Jesu ! for thy mercy's sake,
> And for thy bitter passion,
> Save us from the axe of the Tower,
> And from Sir Ralph of Ashton.

Upon the death of the Black Knight, Sir John's heir and successor abolished the usage for ever, reserving for the estate a small sum of money for the purpose of perpetuating, in an annual ceremony, the dreaded annual visits of the Black Boy. This is still kept up. An effigy is made of a man in armour; and since Sir Ralph was the son of a second marriage (which, for this reason, had been esteemed by the heir of Sir John as an unfortunate match) the image is deridingly emblazoned with some emblem of the occupation of the first couple that are linked together in the course of the year. [Mr. Edwin Butterworth says with the initials of their names.] The Black Boy is then fixed on horseback, and, after being led in procession round the town, is dismounted, made to supply the place of a shooting-butt, and, all firearms being in requisition for the occasion, he is put to an ignominious death. [The origin of Riding the Black Lad, here suggested, is exceedingly ingenious; but it seems questionable whether any real data for it are given in the single passage cited from the rental of 1422. "The Sour Carr Guld Rode and the Stane Ringes" taken as they stand, may mean the Guld-ruyding, or ridding, as a piece of land cleared of stumps, &c., was called ; *ex. gr.* Hunt-royd, Orme-rod, Blake-rod, &c. The Stone Rings may be a piece of land so-called. There is no mention of the power to levy penalties, nor even of any official riding, but only the *rode*,—not road, as it has been interpreted, but ridded land, perhaps cleared from gulds and weeds, no less than from stubs, stumps, and stones.—Eds.]*

Mr. Roby, from the above materials, has written a tale of Sir Ralph's cruel seizure of a widow's only cow, as the heriot due to him as lord of the manor, on the death of her husband. Her half-witted son is said to have told Sir Ralph that on his death his master the devil would claim a heriot, and that Sir Ralph himself would be given up. On this Sir Ralph took fright, and sent back the heriot cow to the poor widow. Another tradition exists as to the origin of the custom of "Riding the Black Lad," which Mr. Roby thinks may have been fabricated merely to throw off the odium attached to the name of Sir Ralph. In the reign of Edward III. one Thomas Assheton fought under Queen Philippa in the battle of Neville's Cross. Riding through the ranks of the enemy, he bore away the royal standard from the Scotch king's tent, who himself was afterwards taken prisoner. King Edward, on his return from France, conferred on Thomas the honour of knighthood, with the title of " Sir Thomas Assheton of Assheton-under-Lyne." To commemorate this singular display of valour, Sir Thomas instituted the custom of " Riding the Black Knight or Lad" at Assheton, on Easter-Monday; leaving 10s. yearly to support it, together with his own suit of black velvet, and a coat of mail. Which of these accounts of the origin of the custom is correct, there is now no evidence to determine.

BOON SHEARING.

In the manor of Ashton-under-Lyne, every tenant-at-will was thus commanded :—" He that plough has, shall

* Dr. Hibbert-Ware's *Illustration of the Customs of a Manor in the North of England.*

plough two days.   He that half plough has, shall plough
a day, whenever the lord be liever [more willing], in wheet-
seeding, or in lenton seeding ; and every tenant harrow a
day with their harrow, in seeding time, when they bin
charged.   And they should cart, every tenant ten cartful
of turve from Doneam Moss to Assheton, and shere four
days in harvest, and cart a day corn."   This service, so
profitable to the lord, was familiarly called boon-work.
Hence an old adage still retained in the North of England, when a man is supposed to be working for nothing,
that " he has been served like a boon-shearer."*

THE PRINCIPAL OR HERIOT.

One of the services of Sir John Assheton's tenants-at-
will, in the manor of Ashton-under-Lyne, in the fifteenth
century, as appears by his rental of 1422, was that " they
should pay a principal at their death, to wit, the best beast
they have."   This was evidently a heriot.   As of a military vassal, or tenant by knight-service, his horse was the
heriot due to his lord at death ; so the custom became
extended to that class of dependents who were retained in
the lord's employ to perform the busier services of the
manor.   As their property consisted of cattle, or of implements of husbandry, the heriot due to the lord was the
best beast, cow, or horse, of which the tenant might die
possessed.   This condition being fulfilled, every further
claim upon the goods of the deceased was remitted.   At
times this expressive relic of ancient military subjection
was found exceedingly galling. In the manor of Assheton
there are many traditional stories still remaining on the

* Dr. Hibbert-Ware's *Illustration of the Customs of a Manor in the
North of England.*

subject of such principals or heriots. A tenant's boy, on
the death of his father, was driving an only cow to the
manor-house of the adjoining demesnes of Dukinfield.
He was met by the lord of the place, with whose person
and rank he was unacquainted, who questioned him whither he was taking his beast. "I am driving it as far as
Dukinfield for the heriot," replied the boy. "My father
is dead—we are many children—and we have no cow but
this. Don't you think the devil will take Sir Robert for
a heriot, when he dies?" The lad was fortunately addressing a humane landlord. "Take the cow back to thy
mother; I know Sir Robert,—I am going to Dukinfield
myself, and will make up the matter with him." *

——◆◆——

DENTON RENT-BOONS.

The lands of the Denton estates of the Hollands were
held in 1780 by seventeen tenants, subject to a rent of
294*l.* 6*s.* 8*d.* The entire property was held by lease of
lives, and this rental was exclusive of fines paid on the
renewal of leases. By the terms of their respective leases
the tenants were also pledged to the payment of certain
rent-boons, consisting of a dog and a cock, or (at the
landlord's option) of their equivalent in money—for
the dog 10*s.*, for the cock 1*s.*; the landlord thus providing
for his amusement in hunting and cock-fighting in a
manner least onerous to himself.†

* *Illustration of the Customs of a Manor in the North of England,*
by Dr. Hibbert-Ware.
† Rev. J. Booker's *Chapel of Denton.*

——◆◆——

A SAXON CONSTABLEWICK.

Until within these few years a relic of Saxon polity more ancient than the Domesday Survey existed in the Constablewick of Garstang, which continued to our own days, the *freo borh, friborg,* or Saxon manor, in a very perfect state. The free-burgh consisted of 11 townships, surrounding the original lordship to which all but one were subject. The reason for establishing this institution is stated in a Saxon law. The *Wita,* or counsellors, having considered the impunity with which trespasses against neighbours were committed, appointed over every ten friborgs, justiciaries whom they denominated *tien heofod* or " head of ten." These (says Dr. Keuerden) handled smaller causes between townsmen and neighbours, and according to the degree of the trespass, awarded satisfaction ; made agreements respecting pastures, meadows and corn-lands, and reconciled differences among neighbours. The constablewick of Garstang comprised the township of Garstang and ten other townships, all of which are styled hamlets in the books of the court, and were divided into three portions. Two constables were annually elected for this district, and were alternately taken from each third portion of the constablewick. The jury were nominated in a similar manner. The jury were accustomed to adjourn from the court to an eminence called Constable hillock, adjoining the river Wyre, where they made choice of the constables by inscribing their names upon slips of wood. These officers were empowered to collect the county-rates, and serve for all the hamlets. The court was held annually, by direction of a steward of the Duke of Hamilton, the superior lord of the wick, till 1816, when it fell into neglect, and its powers are now exercised in such of the townships only as are the property of the Duke. The adjournment of the court to the hillock is obviously the remnant of a custom far more ancient than the institution of the friborg itself.*

TAILLIAGE OR TALLAGE.

This was a kind of occasional property tax, levied by order of the monarch in emergencies, and throughout the kingdom. In the charter granted by Randle, Earl of Chester, to the burgesses of Stafford, about A.D. 1231, is a clause reserving to him and his heirs reasonable tallage, when the King makes or takes tallage of his burgesses throughout England. A precisely similar clause is found in Thomas Greslet's charter to his burgesses of Mamecestre in 1301. In the 11th Henry III. (1226-27) a still earlier talliage was made in Lancashire, which enables us to measure the relative importance of the principal towns in the county early in the thirteenth century. The impost was assessed by Master Alexander de Dorsete and Simon de Hal; and the payments were for the towns of Lancaster thirteen marks (£8 13s. 4d.); Liverpool, eleven marks, 7s. 8d. (£7 14s. 4d.); West Derby, seven marks, 7s. 8d. (£5 1s.); Preston, fifteen marks, 6d. (£10 0s. 6d.). The tenants in thanage paid ten marks (£6 13s. 4d.) to have respite, that they might not be talliaged. Baines deems it remarkable that Manchester, Stafford, and Wigan were not included; but in these old manors it was the lord of the manor who had the right to levy talliage within his manor. In 1332 a tallage of one-fifteenth was levied by Edward III., to enable him to carry on the war against Scotland.*

* Baines's *Lancashire.*

ROCHDALE TITHE, EASTER-DUES, MORTUARIES, ETC.

The following is a literal copy of a small hand-bill in possession of the writer, which appears to have been printed for distribution among the farmers and the parishioners generally, with the purpose of supplying information as to the various payments to be made to the vicar, or at all events to the parish church :—

An EXTRACT out of the *Parliament Survey,*

Taken the 10th of *January* 1620.

THE Parish of *Rochdale* is divided into four Divisions, viz. *Hundersfield, Spotland, Castleton,* and *Butterworth.* There is also belonging to the Rectory of *Rochdale,* the Parish Chapel of *Saddleworth,* in the County of *York;* and certain Parcels of Glebe Lands, lying in *Saddleworth.*

*** There is no Tythe Hay paid within the Parish, but a Penny a Year every one payeth that holdeth any Lands within the Parish.

No Tythe paid for Eggs, Apples, Hemp, or Flax.

The Manner of receiving the *Easter-Role* and Mortuarys are thus—each Horse payeth a Penny; for every married Man or Widow at the Offering, a Penny; every Plough a Penny; every Swarm of Bees a Penny; every Cow one Penny; and every Colt, and every Calf, one Halfpenny.

For Mortuarys—Every one buried in the Chancel payeth 6s. 8d. every one that dieth worth twenty Nobles, in moveable Goods, over and above his Debts, payeth 3s. 4d. if worth 30l. payeth 6s. 8d. if worth 40l. or upwards, 10s.—Stat. 21. Hen. 8. Chap. 6.

N.B. That House or Smoke, and Garden, hath been substituted in the Room of Horse and Plough.

*

In Closes where there are more than ten Stacks of Corn (or even tens) in one Close, *the odd Stacks shall not be tythed;* the Land-Owner setting up the Corn in Stacks, may be a good Consideration for the same; because of Common Right the Tytheman is to take the Corn Tythe in the Sheaf, but when the same is stacked, as is customary in many places, the Tytheman may not break any odd Stack, for he cannot tythe both by the Stack and Sheaf. And this was the Opinion of Serjeants *Poole* and *Kenyon,* and of Lawyer *Wilson.*

No Complaint concerning any small Tythes, &c. shall be determined by Justices of Peace, unless the Complaint be made within two Years after the same Tythes, &c. become due. Stat. 7. and 8. William 3. Chap. 6.

FARM AND AGRICULTURAL CELEBRATIONS IN THE FYLDE.

In the olden times almost every great agricultural operation had its peculiar festivities; now almost everywhere obsolete. The harvest home, its procession and feast, still linger the last of these rural celebrations, but shorn of much of its old ceremonial and jollity. " Shutting of marling" had also its gala-day. Then a "lord" and a "lady" presided at the feast; having been previously drawn out of the marl-pit by a strong team of horses, gaily decorated with ribbons, mounted by their drivers, who were trimmed out in their best. The procession paraded through the village lanes and streets, some of its members shaking tin boxes, and soliciting contributions from the bystanders. The money collected was expended in good cheer at the feast. Again, " Cob-seeding" was a time when mirth and good-nature prevailed. Like the " bee" of our American cousins, it was an occasion when all helped every one else in turn,—collecting, threshing, winnowing the crop on the field ; " housing" the seed ready prepared for the market; and when all the work of the day was finished, partaking of a substantial supper, and closing the evening with many a merry dance on the barn's clay floor.*

DALTON IN FURNESS.

Among the ancient customs of Dalton, is the practice of hiring reapers on Sundays in time of harvest. Endeavours have been made to abolish it; but by the statute of 27 Henry VI. cap. 5, for suppressing Sabbath-breaking, four Sundays in harvest time are excepted from the prohibition against holding markets and fairs on holydays, and the people of Dalton have construed it to the hiring of such servants. Till of late years there was at Dalton an annual festival called "The Dalton Hunt," in which the gentlemen of the district partook of the sports of the field by day, and joined the ladies in the ball-room at night. A suite of rooms was erected in the town, and handsomely fitted-up for this annual jubilee, which existed as early as the year 1703, as appears from the columns of the *London Gazette*, in which it is styled "the Dalton Route," and the pen of an elegant contributor to the *Tatler* has imparted to it additional celebrity. To the regret of the beaux and belles of the neighbourhood the "route" was discontinued in 1789, and has never since been revived. †

* Rev. W. Thornber's *History of Blackpool.*
† Baines's *Lancashire.*

LETTING SHEEP FARMS IN BOWLAND.

One custom, in letting the great sheep-farms in the higher parts of Bowland, deserves to be mentioned, as I do not know that it prevails anywhere else. It is this: That the flock, often consisting of 2000 sheep, or more, is the property of the lord, and delivered to the tenant by a schedule, subject to the condition of delivering up an equal number of the same quality at the expiration of the term. Thus the tenant is merely usufructuary of his own stock. The practice was familiar to the Roman law, and seems to have arisen from the difficulty of procuring tenants who were able to stock farms of such extent.*

MEDIÆVAL LATIN LAW TERMS.

The old charters and deeds of Manchester, Warrington, and other Lancashire towns, contain various words now obsolete, and amongst others the words *namare* and *namium,* which it is not easy to render accurately. The first may be translated to seize in pledge, to arrest, to distrain; the second is a pledge, or a distress, what is seized by distraint. In connexion with the substantive *namium,* the following anecdote of the great Sir Thomas More may be told, as illustrative of the obscurity of some of these ancient law terms. It is said that Sir Thomas, when travelling, arrived at Padua just as a boasting Professor had placarded the walls of that University with a challenge to all the world to dispute with him on any subject or in any art, and that Sir Thomas accepted the challenge, and proposed for his subject this question :—

" AN AVERIA CARUCÆ CAPTA IN VETITO NAMIO SINT IRREPLEGIBILIA ?''

* Dr. Whitaker's *Whalley.*

which, it is almost needless to add, proved such a stumbling-block to the challenger, who did not know even the very terms of the question, that he surrendered at discretion, and acknowledged himself vanquished.*

Perhaps the best way to English the puzzling question, would be to render it thus:—"Whether plough-cattle, taken in illegal distress, are irrepleviable?" But several of the words are susceptible of two meanings. Thus *averia* means goods, as well as cattle; *caruca*, a cart, as well as a plough; *namium*, a pledge, as well as a distress. It is not to be wondered at that the continental Professor found himself unable even to comprehend the terms of this perplexing question.

———◆———

CUSTOMS [DUES] AT WARRINGTON.

Amongst the Tower records are three royal charters bearing date respectively 3 Edward II., 15 Edward II., and 12 Edward III. (1309-10, 1321-2, 1338), and granting, for the purpose of effecting repairs in the bridges and pavements, certain temporary customs on articles brought into Warrington for sale. In the two first of these charters, a custom of one farthing is imposed on every 100 faggots and every 1000 turves; and of one halfpenny on every cart-load of wood or wind-blown timber. The last of the charters imposes a custom of one penny on every 1000 faggots, one farthing on every 10,000 turves, one penny on every ship-load of turves, and one halfpenny weekly on every cart-load of wood and coals [*carbonum*,? charcoal]. Amongst other articles, a custom was imposed on salt, on bacon, on cheese (probably from Cheshire), on butter, on lampreys, on salmon, on pelts of sheep, goats, stags, hinds,

* Mr. Beamont's *Warrington in the Thirteenth Century.*

deer, does, hares, rabbits, foxes, cats, and squirrels; on cloths in the entire piece; on grice work (*i.e.*, fur of the skins of blue weasels); on Cordovan leather, on oil in flasks (*lagenas olei*); on hemp, on linen webs; on Aylesbury webs and linen; on canvas, Irish cloths, Galways and worsteds; on silks, diapered with gold (*de Samite*) and tissue; on silks within gold; on sendal [or *cendal*, a kind of silk]; on cloth of baudekin [silk cloth, interwoven with threads of gold]; on gads of maple, and on Aberdeen gads; on every tun of wine (*et cinerum*—the ashes of burnt wine lees); on honey; on wool in sacks; on tin, brass, copper, iron, and lead; on alum, copperas, argil, and verdigris; on onions and garlic; and on stock-fish, salt mullet, herrings, and sea-fish, amongst a number of other articles.*

* Mr. W. Beamont, in *Warrington in* 1465.

INDEX.